BE PREPARED!

A COMPREHENSIVE SURVIVAL GUIDE
FOR INDIVIDUALS AND FAMILIES

ERIK LAWRENCE

BE PREPARED!
A Comprehensive Survival Guide for Individuals and Families
By Erik Lawrence

Published in the United States of America by Erik Lawrence

Printed in the United States of America

ISBN: 979-8-9862702-2-7

eBook ISBN: 979-8-9862702-3-4

ATTENTION U.S. MILITARY UNITS, U.S. GOVERNMENT AGENCIES AND PROFESSIONAL ORGANIZATIONS: Quantity discounts are available. Specialized versions or book excerpts can also be created to fit specific needs. For information, please contact Erik Lawrence via email at erik@vig-sec.com.

Although the author and publisher have made every effort to ensure the accuracy and completeness of information contained in this book, we assume no responsibility for the use or misuse of information, as well as errors, inaccuracies, omissions, or any inconsistency, contained herein. Portions of this manual are excerpts from outside sources but have been validated and modified as necessary.

Keep in mind that no amount of preparation can guarantee safety in every situation. Always be aware of your surroundings and trust your instincts.

DISCLAIMER

This book provides information on vehicle systems, off-road driving, and survival situations. It is intended to provide guidance and education to readers who wish to learn about these topics. However, it is important to note that the use of vehicles and participation in off-road driving and survival situations can be hazardous, and readers are advised to take all necessary precautions when engaging in these activities.

The author, Erik Lawrence, is a former Green Beret with years of experience in operating and instructing off-road driving in austere parts of the world. However, the information provided in this book is based on the author's personal experience and expertise, and is not intended to serve as a substitute for professional advice. Readers should seek the guidance of qualified professionals before engaging in any off-road driving, survival, or other related activities.

Readers are advised that the use of vehicles and participation in off-road driving and survival situations can result in injury, death, or property damage. The author and publisher are not responsible for any injuries, damages, or losses that may occur as a result of the use of this book or the information provided therein. By using this book, readers acknowledge and accept the risks associated with off-road driving and survival situations, and hold harmless the author and publisher from any liability or damages that may result from their use of this information.

Readers should take all necessary precautions to ensure their own safety when participating in off-road driving and survival situations. This may include obtaining proper training, using appropriate safety equipment, following all laws and regulations, and being aware of potential hazards and risks associated with the activities. The author and publisher are not responsible for any injuries, damages, or losses that may result from the failure of readers to take proper precautions.

In summary, the information provided in this book is intended to be educational and informative. However, readers are advised to take all necessary precautions and seek professional advice before engaging in any off-road driving or survival activities. The author and publisher are not responsible for any injuries, damages, or losses that may occur as a result of the use of this book or the information provided therein. By using this book, readers acknowledge and accept the risks associated with off-road driving and survival situations, and hold harmless the author and publisher from any liability or damages that may result from their use of this information.

~ CONTENTS ~

MOTIVATION

As a former Green Beret, I have seen firsthand the importance of being prepared for emergencies and disasters. During my time in the military, I was deployed to various parts of the world and encountered a wide range of challenging situations, from natural disasters to conflict zones. In these environments, I learned the importance of being self-sufficient, resilient, and able to adapt to changing circumstances.

These experiences inspired me to write this book on self-sustained preparedness. I believe that the principles of self-sustained preparedness are just as important for individuals and families in everyday life as they are for military personnel in the field. In times of crisis, having the skills, resources, and community support to meet your basic needs can be the difference between survival and hardship.

I also believe that self-sustained preparedness is not just about being able to survive in a disaster, but also about creating a more resilient and sustainable future. By taking steps to increase energy efficiency, grow food, and participate in local preparedness efforts, individuals and families can reduce their dependence on external sources, increase their resilience, and build a stronger and more sustainable community.

In writing this book, my goal is to share my experiences and insights on self-sustained preparedness with others, and to help individuals and families prepare for emergencies and disasters. I believe that by being proactive about preparedness and building a self-sufficient and resilient community, individuals and families can be better equipped to respond to emergencies and disasters and create a more sustainable future.

I believe that self-sustained preparedness is an important issue that is often overlooked, and I hope that this book will help to raise awareness and encourage individuals and families to take a proactive approach to preparedness. Whether you are a seasoned prepper or just starting to think about preparedness, I hope that this book will provide valuable information and inspiration to help you build a more resilient and self-sufficient future.

ERIK

April 2023

INTRODUCTION

In today's fast-paced and unpredictable world, it has become increasingly important for individuals and families to be self-sufficient and prepared for any eventualities. The recently declared ended COVID-19 pandemic brought to light the importance of having a contingency plan in place and the need to be self-sustained. During its nearly three-year run, the pandemic caused widespread disruption, leading to shortages of food, medicine and other essential supplies. It also highlighted the vulnerabilities of our modern day systems and the importance of being prepared for any future disruptions.

The concept of self-sustained preparedness refers to the ability of individuals and families to provide for their own needs without relying on external sources. This includes having a secure source of food, water, energy and financial stability, as well as being prepared for emergencies and disasters. Self-sustained preparedness is not just about survival. It also is about living a fulfilling life independent of external factors.

The purpose of this book is to provide a comprehensive guide for independent-minded individuals and families who want to become self-sustained and prepared for any eventualities. The book is designed to help readers understand the key components of self-sustained preparedness and provide practical guidance on how to implement these components in their own lives.

PART ONE of this book, "Everyday Preparedness and Security," provides valuable guidelines for individuals and, especially, families to adopt strategies to keep themselves safe. Its 10 chapters include tips on creating security plans for families, for their homes and for schools and colleges. It also advises on security while traveling and gives critical information for extreme emergencies such as kidnapping; chemical, biological or nuclear attacks, and bombs and bomb threats. Last, PART ONE gives tips on detecting surveillance and on the basics of first aid.

PART TWO of the book likewise contains 10 chapters, each of which covers a different aspect of self-sustained preparedness. The first chapter provides a definition of independent-minded individuals and families and the importance of self-sustained preparedness. The second chapter delves into the key components of self-sustained preparedness, including food and water security, energy independence, financial preparedness, and health and medical preparedness.

The third and fourth chapters delve deeper into the topic of self-sustained preparedness, explaining the concept and outlining its key concepts. The fifth and sixth chapters focus on building a self-sustained home, including designing such a home and implementing sustainable practices such as composting, recycling, and gardening.

The seventh and eighth chapters provide more guidance on preparing for emergencies and disasters, including developing a disaster plan, building an emergency kit, and evacuation planning.

The ninth chapter explains the importance of building a community of self-sustained individuals. Networking with like-minded individuals can involve sharing resources and knowledge, and participating in local preparedness efforts. The final chapter summarizes key points and offers final thoughts on the importance of self-sustained preparedness.

PART THREE's nine chapters are about building a vehicle system for survival or unexpected events are rooted in a conservative approach to preparedness. Conservative principles value self-reliance, personal responsibility, and individual freedom, and recognize that government agencies and other organizations may not always be able to provide the resources and support necessary to respond to emergencies and other unexpected events.

PART THREE's primary goal is to provide individuals and families with the knowledge and tools they need to be self-reliant in the face of unexpected events. This includes providing information on how to choose the right vehicle, what emergency supplies to stock, and how to make modifications and customizations to ensure that the vehicle is capable of off-road travel or other specialized functions.

Moreover, PART THREE aims to empower individuals and families to take responsibility for their own safety and security, rather than relying solely on government agencies or other organizations. This reflects a conservative approach to preparedness, which values individual freedom and personal responsibility.

Another goal is to provide individuals and families with a comprehensive understanding of the risks and challenges they may face in an emergency or unexpected event. This includes understanding the different types of natural disasters and other emergencies that may occur, as well as the economic and social challenges that may arise in times of crisis.

By presenting this information, this section can help individuals and families to anticipate and prepare for potential risks, and to develop a plan of action that is tailored to their specific needs and resources. This reflects a conservative approach to preparedness, which emphasizes the importance of careful planning and preparation in order to mitigate potential risks and ensure personal safety and security.

A third goal is to provide individuals and families with the skills and knowledge necessary to respond to emergencies and other unexpected events in a safe and effective manner. This includes providing information on basic vehicle maintenance, emergency communication and navigation, and water and food storage and preparation.

By publishing this information, the author hopes he can help individuals and families to take action in times of crisis, rather than being overwhelmed by fear, confusion, or uncertainty. This reflects a conservative approach to preparedness, which values self-reliance and the ability to take action in the face of adversity.

A fourth goal is to encourage a culture of preparedness among individuals, families, and communities. By providing information on the importance of being prepared, and by offering practical guidance on how to build a vehicle system for preparedness, PART THREE can help to raise awareness and inspire action by readers.

This reflects a conservative approach to preparedness, which recognizes that the responsibility for preparedness lies not just with individuals and families, but with communities as a whole. By working together to build resilient communities that are prepared for unexpected events, individuals and families can ensure that they have access to the resources and support they need to weather the storm.

Last, a key objective is to provide individuals and families with a sense of confidence and security in the face of the unknown. By providing practical guidance and information on how to build a vehicle system for preparedness, the resulting knowledge can help to alleviate fears and anxieties related to potential risks and challenges.

One values the importance of mental and emotional resilience in times of crisis. By providing individuals and families with the knowledge and tools they need to be self-reliant and prepared, the information can help to foster a sense of confidence and security that is essential for personal and community resilience.

Building a vehicle system for preparedness can provide individuals and families with the knowledge, tools, and skills they need to be self-reliant and prepared in the face of unexpected events. And be gaining practical guidance and information on how to build a vehicle system for preparedness, individuals and families can take responsibility for their own safety and security, and take action in the face of adversity. Furthermore, encouraging a culture of preparedness among individuals, families, and communities helps to ensure that we are better prepared for the unexpected, and can work together to build resilient communities that are capable of weathering the storm. Ultimately, the goals and objectives of a book on building a vehicle system for preparedness, which values individual freedom, personal responsibility, and the ability to take action in the face of adversity.

Last, **PART FOUR's** 14 chapters examine why a trailer/RV system is important for preparedness. In recent years, more and more people have started to prepare for unexpected events and emergencies, such as natural disasters, civil unrest, and economic instability. Many people have turned to trailer/RV systems to be proactively ready for any unexpected events that may arise. There are several reasons why a trailer/RV system is important for preparedness, and these reasons can be broken down into a few key categories.

First and foremost, a trailer/RV system can provide a safe and comfortable living space during an emergency or survival situation. While some people may be able to hunker down in their homes during a natural disaster or other emergency, others may not have that option. For example, if you live in an area prone to hurricanes, you may need to evacuate your home and seek shelter elsewhere. In this case, a trailer/RV can provide a safe and comfortable place to stay until it is safe to return home.

A trailer/RV can also provide a sense of mobility and flexibility during an emergency. For example, if you need to evacuate your home due to a natural disaster or other emergency, a trailer/RV can allow you to take your living space with you. You won't be limited to staying in a designated emergency shelter or hotel, and you'll have more control over your living situation.

In addition to providing a safe and comfortable living space, a trailer/RV system can also be an important tool for self-sufficiency. For example, many trailer/RV systems come equipped with water storage and filtration systems, as well as food storage and preparation options. This means that you can stay hydrated and fed during an emergency, even if basic services like water and electricity are disrupted.

Another benefit of a trailer/RV system is that it can be customized to suit your individual needs and preferences. For example, you may want to add solar panels to your trailer/RV to provide power, or install a composting toilet to reduce your environmental impact. These types of modifications can be difficult or impossible to make to a traditional home, but they are relatively easy to do with a trailer/RV system.

Finally, a trailer/RV system can provide a sense of security and peace of mind during times of uncertainty. Knowing that you have a safe and comfortable place to stay during an emergency, and that you have the tools and resources you need to be self-sufficient, can be a source of comfort in an otherwise stressful situation.

Overall, there are many reasons why a trailer/RV system is important for preparedness. Whether you are preparing for natural disasters, civil unrest, economic instability, or other unexpected events, a trailer/RV can provide a safe and comfortable living space, a sense of mobility and flexibility, self-sufficiency, customization, and peace of mind. By taking the time to build a trailer/RV system that meets your individual needs and preferences, you can be prepared for whatever the future may bring.

A Note about Personal Responsibility

Personal responsibility is the idea that individuals are accountable for their own actions and decisions, and that they have a duty to take care of themselves and their own well-being. In today's world, personal responsibility is more important than ever, as individuals face increasing uncertainty and unexpected events that can threaten their safety and security.

At its core, personal responsibility is about taking ownership of one's own life and being proactive about one's own well-being. This means taking steps to ensure one's own safety and security, such as being prepared for emergencies and unexpected events, and taking care of one's physical and mental health. It also means being accountable for one's own decisions and actions, and taking responsibility for any mistakes or missteps along the way.

Personal responsibility is a vital component of self-sufficiency and resilience, which are essential qualities for surviving and thriving in today's world. By taking personal responsibility for one's own life and well-being, individuals can build the skills and resources necessary to adapt to changing circumstances and overcome challenges.

However, personal responsibility is not just about taking care of oneself. It is also about taking care of others and contributing to the well-being of society as a whole.

This means being an active and engaged member of one's community, volunteering and helping others, and working to make the world a better place.

Unfortunately, in today's society, personal responsibility is often viewed as a burden or a chore, rather than as a privilege and a duty. Many people rely on others to take care of them, and look to government or other institutions to provide for their needs. This mindset can be dangerous, as it can lead to a lack of self-sufficiency and resilience, and a sense of entitlement that can be difficult to overcome.

Ultimately, personal responsibility is about taking control of one's own life and destiny, and working to make the world a better place for oneself and others. By embracing personal responsibility and taking proactive steps to prepare for unexpected events, individuals can build the skills and resources necessary to survive and thrive in today's world.

PART ONE:
EVERYDAY PREPAREDNESS AND SECURITY

1. A General Security Checklist

Common-sense tips to protect yourself and your loved ones.

• Instruct your family and associates not to provide strangers with information about you or your family.

• Trust your instincts; if the situation doesn't seem right, get away from the situation as quickly as possible.

• Stay alert to your surroundings; walk with confidence and purpose, try not to travel alone, especially at night or in areas unfamiliar to you.

• Do not give unnecessary personal details to information collectors and restrict personal data when using the Internet. Shred all documents with personal data, particularly account or ID numbers.

• Be alert to strangers on your property for no apparent reason. Report all suspicious persons loitering near your residence or office; attempt to provide a complete description of the person and/or vehicle to police or security.

• Vary your daily routines to avoid creating habitual patterns. If possible, vary your travel times and routes to and from work or regular destinations.
• Refuse to meet with strangers outside of your workplace.

• Always advise associates or family members of your destination when leaving the office or home and your anticipated time of arrival.

• Do not open doors to strangers, particularly when you are alone; teach your children this!

• Memorize the key phone numbers you might need quickly: office, home, police, security, etc. Place selected numbers on your phone's speed-dial list – but not the numbers of your loved ones.

• Use the "Lock/Security" features on cell phones, PDAs, laptops, etc.

• Always be cautious about giving out information regarding family travel plans or security measures and procedures.

• If you are overseas, learn and practice a few key phrases in the native language, such as "I need a policeman, doctor, ambulance..." Learn the cultural sensitivities of the area and abide by them as much as possible.

• Seek quality security training to fill in the gaps you have and hone the security skills you do possess.

2. A Residential Security Plan

• Install a security system: This can include cameras, motion sensors, and alarms. This will help deter potential intruders and allow you to monitor your home remotely.

• Lock all doors and windows: Make sure all doors and windows are locked when you are not at home and when you are sleeping. This includes sliding glass doors, which can be easily lifted off their tracks.

• Trim hedges and bushes: Keep hedges and bushes around your home trimmed so that potential intruders cannot hide behind them.

• Use exterior lighting: Install exterior lighting around your home, including motion sensor lights. This will make it difficult for potential intruders to sneak around your property.

• Secure your garage: Make sure your garage and the door to your home from the garage are locked and that any vehicles inside are also locked.

• Get to know your neighbors: Develop a relationship with your neighbors and keep an eye out for each other's properties.

• Educate yourself about local crime: Stay informed about local crime and take extra precautions if crime rates in your area are high.

• Have an emergency plan: Have a plan in place for what to do in case of a break-in, fire, or other emergency. Make sure everyone in your household knows the plan and how to contact emergency services.

Note: This is a general Residential security plan, and you might need to customize it according to your specific needs and location. Also, consult with professional security service providers for a more detailed and advanced plan.

Residential Security Tips

• Secure all doors and windows with deadbolts and/or security bars.

• Install a security alarm system and ensure that it is properly maintained and activated when necessary.

• Use surveillance cameras to monitor the property, both inside and outside.

• Keep the property well-lit at night, with motion-sensor lights installed in strategic locations.

• Keep bushes and trees trimmed to eliminate potential hiding spots for intruders.

• Keep valuables, such as jewelry and electronics, out of sight and in a secure location.

• Use privacy window film or curtains to prevent outsiders from seeing into the property.

• Keep a record of all important documents, such as passports and birth certificates, in a safe place.
• Have a communication plan in case of emergency and make sure everyone in the household is familiar with it.

• Make sure you have appropriate insurance in case of loss or damage.

• Keep emergency contact numbers nearby and instruct everyone in the household on how to contact emergency services.

• Have a fire escape plan in case of emergency and make sure everyone in the household is familiar with it.

• Regularly check and update your security systems, including alarm systems, surveillance cameras, and software to ensure they are up to date and working properly.

• Be aware of the latest security threats and keep informed of any recent incidents in your area.

• Have a plan in place for responding to a security breach, such as a break-in or natural disaster.

• Consider hiring security personnel or security companies to provide additional protection for your property.

• Be mindful of online security, such as creating strong passwords, keeping software updated and being careful of phishing emails.

• Finally, always be vigilant and trust your instincts. If something seems out of place or suspicious, report it to the authorities immediately.

3. A Family Security Plan

Establish a family emergency plan: Have a plan in place for what to do in case of emergencies such as natural disasters, fires, or home invasions. Make sure all family members know the plan and how to contact emergency services.

• Have a designated meeting place: In case of an emergency, choose a designated meeting place outside of your home where everyone can meet.
• Practice emergency drills with your family, such as a fire drill or home invasion drill, so everyone knows what to do in case of an emergency.

• Review safety tips with your family, such as how to properly use a fire extinguisher or first aid kit.

• Secure your home: Make sure all doors and windows are locked, and consider installing a security system, cameras, and alarm systems.

• Encourage open communication with your family and discuss any concerns or issues they may have.

• Be aware of strangers: Teach your children to be aware of strangers and not to open the door to anyone they don't know.

• Keep emergency numbers, such as the police and fire department, handy and make sure everyone in the family knows them.

• Use social media wisely: Remind your family members to be cautious when sharing personal information on social media, and to limit the amount of personal information they share online.

• Educate yourself about local crime: Stay informed about local crime and take extra precautions if crime rates in your area are high.

Note: This is a general Family security plan, and you might need to customize it according to your specific needs and location. Also, consult with professional security service providers to have a more detailed and advanced security plan.

Tips for Securing the Family at Home

• Lock all doors and windows: Make sure all doors and windows are locked when you are not at home and when you are sleeping. This includes sliding glass doors, which can be easily lifted off their tracks.

• Install a security system: Consider installing a security system that includes cameras, motion sensors, and alarms. This will help deter potential intruders and allow you to monitor your home remotely.

• Use exterior lighting: Install exterior lighting around your home, including motion sensor lights. This will make it difficult for potential intruders to sneak around your property.

• Secure your garage: Make sure your garage is locked and that any vehicles inside are also locked.

• Keep valuables out of sight, such as jewelry, cash, and important documents, to prevent them from being targeted by potential intruders.

• Keep emergency numbers, such as the police and fire department, handy and make sure everyone in the family knows them.

- Be aware of strangers: Teach your children to be aware of strangers and not to open the door to anyone they don't know.
- Use social media wisely: Remind your family members to be cautious when sharing personal information on social media, and to limit the amount of personal information they share online.

- Educate yourself about local crime: Stay informed about local crime and take extra precautions if crime rates in your area are high.

- Have an emergency plan: Have a plan in place for what to do in case of a break-in, fire, or other emergency. Make sure everyone in your household knows the plan and how to contact emergency services.

Note: This is a general list, and you may need to customize it according to your specific needs and location. Also, consult with professional security service providers to have a more detailed and advanced security plan.

Cellphone Security

Cellphone security refers to the measures taken to protect cellular phones and the personal information of individuals who use them from unauthorized access, misuse, or damage. Here are some tips for securing your cellular phone:

- Use a strong passcode: Use a passcode or PIN to protect your cellular phone, and make sure that it is not easily guessed or shared with others.

• Keep software updated: Keep the software on your cellular phone up to date to ensure that it is protected against known vulnerabilities and security threats.

• Limit access: Limit the number of people who have access to your cellular phone, and make sure that only authorized individuals can make changes to settings or configurations.

• Use encryption: Use encryption to protect sensitive information transmitted over the cellular phone, such as credit card numbers or personal information.

• Be aware of phishing scams: Be aware of phishing scams, where scammers try to trick you into giving them personal information over the phone. Always be skeptical of unsolicited phone calls and never give out personal information unless you are certain of the caller's identity.

• Call blocking/screening: Use call blocking or screening features to block unwanted calls and protect yourself from telemarketing and robocalls.

• Secure your VoIP (Voice Over Internet Protocol): If you are using VoIP, make sure that your network is secure, and use a VPN (Virtual Private Network) to encrypt your communications.

• Dispose of old cellular phone properly: When disposing of old cellular phone, make sure to wipe all personal information from the device and recycle it properly.

• Be cautious with public telephone: Be cautious when using public telephones, as they may have been tampered with or have hidden cameras or other security risks.

By following these tips, you can help protect your cellular phone and personal information from unauthorized access and misuse.

Special Precautions for Children

• Teach children about personal safety, such as how to recognize and avoid strangers and how to handle emergency situations.

• Use parental controls on televisions, computers, and mobile devices to restrict access to inappropriate content and limit the amount of time children spend online.

• Talk to children about online safety, including the importance of keeping personal information private, not talking to strangers online, and not sharing personal information or pictures.

• Teach children about "stranger danger" and how to recognize and avoid potentially dangerous situations.

• Establish ground rules for internet use and make sure that children understand the importance of following them.

• Monitor children's internet activity, including the websites they visit and the people they talk to online.

• Use GPS tracking devices, such as a smartwatch, to know the location of your child in case of emergency.

• Have a code word or phrase that children can use to let you know if they are in danger or if they need help.

• Teach children about emergency numbers, such as 911, and make sure they know how to call for help.

• Be a good role model for your children and teach them the importance of safety and security by following safety and security measures yourself.

Note: This is a general list, and you may need to customize it according to your specific needs and location. Also, consult with experts and professionals in the field of child safety to have a more detailed and advanced security plan.

Special Precautions for Children at Childcare Providers and Facilities

• Research childcare providers carefully and look for those that have a good reputation and a history of providing safe and secure care for children.

• Check for accreditation: Look for childcare providers that are accredited by professional organizations, such as the National Association for the Education of Young Children (NAEYC) or the National Child Care Association (NCCA).

• Check for licenses and inspections: Make sure that the childcare provider is licensed and that they have passed all necessary inspections.

• Check for background checks: Ask the childcare provider if they conduct background checks on all staff members and if they have policies in place to prevent child abuse.

• Check for emergency plans: Find out if the childcare provider has emergency plans in place and if they have regular fire drills and evacuation procedures.

• Check for security measures: Check to see if the childcare provider has security measures in place, such as security cameras, locked doors, and alarm systems.

• Check for open communication: Find out if the childcare provider has open communication with parents and if they provide regular updates on their child's care and development.

• Check for staff qualifications: Look for childcare providers that have qualified, trained, and experienced staff members.

• Check for staff to child ratio: Check to see if the childcare provider has a good ratio of staff members to children and if they have enough staff members to provide proper care and supervision.

• Regularly visit the facility: Regularly visit the childcare provider's facility and observe the care and supervision your child is receiving.

Note: This is a general list, and you may need to customize it according to your specific needs and location. Also, consult with experts and professionals in the field of childcare and safety to have a more detailed and advanced security plan.

Mail or Packages Security

Mail and package security refers to the measures taken to protect mail and packages from theft, damage, or tampering. Here are some tips for securing your mail and packages:

• Use a locked mailbox or a post office box to protect your mail from theft.

• Use package lockbox: If you are expecting a valuable package, consider using a package lockbox or a smart locker that allows you to receive and pick up your package securely.

• Track your packages using the tracking number provided by the carrier and be aware of the expected delivery date.

• Use signature confirmation for valuable or sensitive packages to ensure that they are only delivered to the intended recipient.

• Request for package hold at the post office or carrier service if you are not going to be home during the expected delivery time.

• Be aware of mail theft, particularly around the holidays when mailboxes are frequently targeted by thieves.

• Be cautious of unexpected mail or packages, as they may contain dangerous or harmful materials.

• Watch out for package scams, where scammers pretend to be delivery companies and ask for personal information or payment in exchange for a package.

• Have your mail held at the post office if you're going to be away for an extended period of time.

• Secure your mail and packages inside your home, keep them in a safe place and do not leave them out in the open where they can be easily stolen.

By following these tips, you can help protect your mail and packages from theft, damage, or tampering.

Security Considerations When Away from Home

• Keep your home looking lived in: Make your home look lived in when you're away by using timers for lights and appliances, having someone mow your lawn or shovel your driveway, and stopping mail and newspaper deliveries.

• Secure all entry points: Make sure all doors and windows are locked and secure before leaving your home. Consider installing deadbolts and window locks for added security.

• Use smart home security devices, such as cameras, alarms, and motion sensors, to monitor your home remotely and be alerted of any suspicious activity.

• Inform a trusted neighbor or friend of your plans to be away and ask them to keep an eye on your property.

• Keep valuables, such as jewelry and cash, out of sight and in a safe place to prevent them from being targeted by potential thieves.

43

• Don't advertise your plans on social media or other public platforms, as it can alert potential thieves to your absence.

• Make arrangements for your pets to be taken care of while you are away, such as hiring a pet sitter or taking them to a boarding facility.

• Unplug appliances and electronics to reduce the risk of fire and power surges.

• Secure your vehicle: Make sure your vehicle is locked and parked in a safe location, and don't leave valuables or personal information inside.

• Be aware of your surroundings and take note of any suspicious activity when you're away from home.

Note: This is a general list, and you may need to customize it according to your specific needs and location. Also, consult with experts and professionals in the field of security to have a more detailed and advanced security plan.

Preventing Account Fraud

Account fraud refers to the unauthorized use of someone's personal information to access their financial accounts or steal their money. Here are some tips for preventing account fraud:

• Use strong passwords and never use the same password for multiple accounts. Use a mix of letters, numbers, and special characters.

• Be cautious of phishing scams, where scammers try to trick you into giving them your personal information through fake emails or websites. Do not click on any links or enter personal information unless you are certain of the sender's identity.

• Monitor your accounts regularly and check for any suspicious activity, such as unauthorized transactions or changes to your personal information.

• Keep your personal information private and don't share it with anyone unless you are certain of their identity.

• Use two-factor authentication, where available, to add an extra layer of security to your accounts.

• Be cautious of unsolicited phone calls or emails, particularly those that ask for personal information.

• Use anti-virus and anti-malware software to protect your computer and mobile devices from malware and viruses that can steal your personal information.
• Be cautious when using public Wi-Fi, as they may be unsecured and can be used by hackers to steal personal information.

• Shred sensitive documents, such as credit card statements, before discarding them to prevent them from falling into the wrong hands.

• Report any suspicious activity or unauthorized transactions to your bank or financial institution immediately. By following these tips, you can help prevent account fraud and protect your personal information from being stolen.

Preventing Identity Fraud

Identity fraud refers to the unauthorized use of someone's personal information, such as their name, Social Security number, or credit card information, to open accounts, make purchases, or obtain loans in their name. Here are some tips for preventing identity fraud:

- Keep your personal information private and don't share it with anyone unless you are certain of their identity.

- Use strong passwords and never use the same password for multiple accounts. Use a mix of letters, numbers, and special characters.

- Monitor your credit reports regularly and check for any suspicious activity, such as unauthorized accounts or changes to your personal information.

- Be cautious of phishing scams where scammers may try to trick you into giving them your personal information through fake emails or websites. Do not click on any links or enter personal information unless you are certain of the sender's identity.

- Use two-factor authentication, where available, to add an extra layer of security to your accounts.

- Be cautious of unsolicited phone calls or emails, particularly those that ask for personal information.

- Use anti-virus and anti-malware software to protect your computer and mobile devices from malware and viruses that can steal your personal information.

- Be cautious when using public Wi-Fi, as they may be unsecured and can be used by hackers to steal personal information.

- Shred sensitive documents, such as credit card statements, before discarding them to prevent them from falling into the wrong hands.

- Report any suspicious activity or unauthorized use of your personal information to the relevant authorities and financial institutions immediately.

By following these tips, you can help prevent identity fraud and protect your personal information from being stolen.

4. College/Boarding School Security

Utilize Locks/Locking Devices/Security Systems

The best campus safety tip for college students like you is to always lock up doors and windows when you are away. You'd be surprised how many break-ins are just the criminal opening the door or window. It's estimated that a shocking fact is that almost 40% college students don't lock their dorm doors when they leave. If locking your doors is not enough to protect your valuables; you can purchase other locking devices such as a small safe or lock box for your laptop to ensure your computer security. Or if your roommates and you have electrical devices and personal belongings worth thousands of dollars in your dorm, you may consider installing a portable battery powered security camera to ensure the dorm security after obtaining the consent of your school.

Take Advantage of Campus Safety Apps

Many campuses utilize campus safety apps. Check with the campus safety office to verify which mobile app is utilized for your campus. You can use these apps to report minor incidents to campus police through texting forms or push the emergency button if you feel unsafe on campus, notifying campus police dispatch of your GPS location.

Know the Campus Security Programs Provided by Schools

Take full advantage of the campus security resources is a handy campus safety tip, especially for the college freshmen. Most schools provide a wide range of campus security programs (See the 2018 *Safest College Campuses in America*), such as campus escort services, the Blue light emergency phone stations, safety maps with suggested secure routes, etc. The best way to learn about your campus security programs is resorting to your campus security officers. Should you ever find yourself in trouble, it will be much easier if you know this information.

Don't Let the Electronics Steal
Your Attention to Your Surroundings

Most college students are often immersed in their smart phones or listening to music on headphones while walking on campus, not knowing what is going on around them. This, in fact, could be a dangerous signal – the determined robbers may have noticed your absence of mind and regard you as the next target. The moment you find yourself becoming unaware of the surroundings, it is the time for you to turn the music down, put your phone away and stay vigilant to what's happening.

Be Familiar with the Campus Environment

This is one of the most useful campus safety tips for college incoming freshmen and international students, who might need some time to become accustomed to the new surroundings. If such is also the case with you, spend some time with your friends walking around the campus to get familiar with campus landmarks and locate the emergency system areas, so that you can easily navigate your way around.

Avoid Walking Alone at Night

On average, sexual assaults are more likely to occur at night. One important campus safety tip for female college students is to avoid walking alone at night. You can go with a friend late at night and walk on the designated pathways and well-lit areas. If there is no companion, you can download a campus safe app and hold your thumb down on the safe button in case of any emergencies.

Be Careful Before Getting into a Car

For college students owning cars, according to the National Crime Victimization Survey (NCVS), approximately 38,000 carjackings occur each year in the US and a weapon was used in 74% of carjacking occurrences. So, before you open the car door, look into the backseat to see if there is an uninvited guest. When it is dark at night, you can use a flashlight to illuminate under the car and the backseat. Also, be wary of people asking for directions, handing out flyers, etc. If someone makes you feel uneasy, get in your car quickly and drive away.

Carry Defense Items with You

Having a defense item at hand is one of the most practical personal safety tips for college students. Pepper spray, a taser, a whistle or other non-lethal weapons are all useful campus security items you can put in your bag when you are out. Never underestimate the function of these small items. They may make a life-saving difference in harmful situations. For example, in case you are stalked by someone, you can use a whistle to call for help and seize the opportunity to run away.

Don't Accept Substances from Strangers

Drug abuse is a conspicuous campus security issue on college campuses these days. One factor responsible for the high rates of drug abuse among college students is that you are surrounded by other people experimenting with recreational and performance-enhancing drugs. You should be aware that the powders, pills, and liquids can be absolutely anything, in any concentration. Do not accept any substances from casual acquaintances or strangers, otherwise you may end up addicted before you realize it.

Protect Your Privacy on Social Media

While social media apps are convenient tools to share updates with friends and family, they also allow strangers to have easy access to your profiles and know your whereabouts and plans. It is important to protect your privacy and location when you post something online. Disable location services for social media apps and keep your posts concerning your personal information private to avoid this information falling into the wrong hands.

Tell Your Friends Your Whereabouts

Before you go to some place on your own, tell your friends or family where you are going and your expected return time. If you don't appear by a certain time, they can try and reach you to verify that you are safe. This on-campus safety tip for colleges can be of great help especially when you are in a risky situation.

Follow Your Intuition (Trust Your Gut)

Sometimes your intuition can be more than accurate. When you notice someone exhibiting suspicious behavior in the dorm, don't be afraid to report it to the dorm security guard. This safety tip for living on campus could eliminate many potential incidents. And when you feel uncomfortable in certain place, leave right away, and go to an area with lights and people. Don't hesitate to call the police for help if something seems abnormal.

5. Security While Traveling or Living Overseas

Security while traveling or living overseas is an important consideration, as you may be at a higher risk of crime, terrorism, and other security threats. Here are some tips for staying safe while traveling or living overseas:

• Research the destination, including any potential security risks, such as crime, terrorism, or political unrest, and take appropriate precautions.

• Keep a low profile and avoid drawing attention to yourself, particularly when it comes to your wealth or valuables.

- Be aware of your surroundings and take note of any suspicious activity or individuals.

- Avoid dangerous areas and areas known for crime or terrorism.

- Use common sense and avoid taking unnecessary risks, such as wandering alone in unfamiliar areas at night.

- Keep a copy of important documents, such as your passport, in a safe place and carry a photocopy with you at all times.

- Stay in touch with friends and family and let them know your plans and whereabouts.

- Be cautious with personal information, particularly when it comes to your passport and credit card information and avoid sharing it with strangers.

- Learn basic emergency phrases in the local language, including Register with the embassy: Register with the embassy or consulate of your home country in the country you are visiting or living in. This will allow them to contact you in case of emergency, and they can also provide you with information on local security risks.

- Have a plan in case of emergency and know the location of the nearest hospital, police station, and embassy.

- Be aware of local laws and customs, as breaking them can result in legal trouble or even imprisonment.

• Avoid political demonstrations and other large gatherings, as they can turn violent quickly.

• Invest in travel insurance, including coverage for medical emergencies and evacuation, in case of an emergency.

• Keep electronic devices, such as phones and laptops, secure and avoid using public Wi-Fi to access sensitive information.

By following these tips, you can help protect yourself and stay safe while traveling or living overseas. However, it's important to keep in mind that no amount of preparation can guarantee safety in every situation. Stay aware of your surroundings and trust your instincts.

Ground Transportation Security

Ground transportation security refers to the measures taken to protect individuals and their belongings while using various forms of ground transportation, such as buses, trains, taxis, and ride-sharing services. Here are some tips for ensuring ground transportation security:

• Use reputable transportation providers, such as licensed taxi companies and ride-sharing services with good ratings and reviews.

• Check the vehicle: Before getting into a taxi or ride-sharing car, check the license plate and driver identification to make sure they match the information provided by the service.

• Be aware of your surroundings and take note of any suspicious activity or individuals.

· Keep valuables, such as wallets and jewelry, out of sight to prevent them from being targeted by potential thieves.

• Use seat belts: Always use seat belts when riding in a vehicle for added protection in case of an accident.
• Avoid using public transportation during late hours, as it can be more dangerous and less frequented than during the day.

• Use the safety features of the transportation, such as emergency buttons or alarms, in case of an emergency.

• Have a plan in case of emergency, such as knowing the location of the nearest hospital and police station.

• Keep your phone charged and accessible at all times in case of an emergency.

• Be aware of the route the transportation is taking and if it seems suspicious or deviates from the usual route, speak up or leave the vehicle.

By following these tips, you can help ensure your safety while using ground transportation and reduce the risk of becoming a victim of crime or other security threats.

Vehicle Usage Overseas with a Security Consideration

Using a vehicle overseas can be a convenient way to explore a new area, but it also comes with security considerations. Here are some tips for ensuring vehicle security while traveling or living overseas:

• Research the destination, including any potential security risks, such as crime, terrorism, or political unrest, and take appropriate precautions.

• Rent from reputable companies and verify that they have proper insurance and safety measures in place.

• Inspect the vehicle before accepting it, and make sure it is in good working condition and equipped with the necessary safety features.

• Use a GPS device to navigate unfamiliar roads and to avoid dangerous areas.

• Keep valuables, such as wallets and jewelry, out of sight to prevent them from being targeted by potential thieves.

• Keep the doors locked and windows closed, especially when parked or stopped in traffic.

• Avoid parking in isolated areas and opt for well-lit and populated areas instead.

• Have a plan in case of emergency, such as knowing the location of the nearest hospital and police station.

- Be aware of local laws and customs, as breaking them can result in legal trouble or even imprisonment.

- Use a steering wheel lock to deter potential thieves from stealing the vehicle.

By following these tips, you can help ensure your safety and the security of your vehicle while using it overseas. It's important to be aware of the potential risks and take necessary precautions to avoid them.

Parking Security

Parking security refers to the measures taken to protect vehicles and their contents while parked in various locations. Here are some tips for ensuring parking security:

- Park in well-lit areas, especially at night, to deter potential thieves.

- Use a steering wheel lock to deter potential thieves from stealing the vehicle.

- Use parking garages or lots, which often have security cameras and attendants on duty, instead of parking on the street.

- Keep valuables, such as wallets and jewelry, out of sight to prevent them from being targeted by potential thieves.

- Keep windows closed and doors locked, even when parked for a short period of time.

- Be aware of your surroundings and take note of any suspicious activity or individuals.

- Use anti-theft devices, such as alarms or steering wheel locks, to deter potential thieves.

- Use car tracking devices to locate your vehicle if it is stolen.

- Park in attended lots, where the parking attendant can keep an eye on the vehicle.

- Take note of parking signs and obey the parking regulations, to avoid getting a ticket or having your vehicle towed.

By following these tips, you can help ensure the security of your vehicle while it is parked. It's important to be aware of potential risks and take necessary precautions to protect your vehicle and its contents.

Overseas Security Travel Tips

Traveling overseas can be an exciting experience, but it also comes with security considerations. Here are some tips for ensuring your safety while traveling overseas:

- Research the destination, including any potential security risks, such as crime, terrorism, or political unrest, and take appropriate precautions.

- Keep a low profile and avoid drawing attention to yourself, particularly when it comes to your wealth or valuables.

- Be aware of your surroundings and take note of any suspicious activity or individuals.

- Avoid dangerous areas and areas known for crime or terrorism.

- Use common sense and avoid taking unnecessary risks, such as wandering alone in unfamiliar areas at night.

- Keep a copy of important documents, such as your passport, in a safe place and carry a photocopy with you at all times.

- Stay in touch with friends and family and let them know your plans and whereabouts.

- Be cautious with personal information, particularly when it comes to your passport and credit card information and avoid sharing it with strangers.

- Learn basic emergency phrases in the local language, including how to ask for help and how to call for emergency services.

- Register with the embassy or consulate of your home country in the country you are visiting, this will allow them to contact you in case of emergency and they can also provide you with information on local security risks.

- Have a plan in case of emergency and know the location of the nearest hospital, police station, and embassy.

• Be aware of local laws and customs, as breaking them can result in legal trouble or even imprisonment.

• Avoid political demonstrations and other large gatherings, as they can turn violent quickly.

• Invest in travel insurance, including coverage for medical emergencies and evacuation, in case of an emergency.

By following these tips, you can help ensure your safety while traveling overseas. Remember to stay aware of your surroundings!

Overseas Security Driving Tips

Driving overseas can be a convenient way to explore a new area, but it also comes with security considerations. Here are some tips for ensuring vehicle and personal security while driving overseas:

• Research the destination, including any potential security risks, such as crime, terrorism, or political unrest, and take appropriate precautions.

• Rent from reputable companies and verify that they have proper insurance and safety measures in place.

• Inspect the vehicle before accepting it, and make sure it is in good working condition and equipped with the necessary safety features.

• Use a GPS device to navigate unfamiliar roads and to avoid dangerous areas.

• Keep valuables, such as wallets and jewelry, out of sight to prevent them from being targeted by potential thieves.

• Keep the doors locked and windows closed, especially when parked or stopped in traffic.

• Avoid parking in isolated areas and opt for well-lit and populated areas instead.

• Have a plan in case of emergency, such as knowing the location of the nearest hospital and police station.

• Be aware of local laws and customs, such as driving on the opposite side of the road, speed limits and other driving rules.

• Avoid night driving, as it can be more dangerous and less frequented than during the day.

• Keep your phone charged and accessible at all times in case of an emergency.

By following these tips, you can help ensure your safety and the security of your vehicle while driving overseas. Remember to obey the local traffic laws, stay alert and aware of your surroundings, and plan your route in advance. If you encounter any trouble or feel unsafe, do not hesitate to seek help from the local authorities.

Security Considerations for Labor Disputes

Labor disputes can include strikes, protests, and other forms of worker action that can disrupt business operations and potentially lead to violent or dangerous situations. Here are some security considerations for labor dispute situations:

- Develop a plan for how to handle a labor dispute, including who will be responsible for coordinating security efforts, how to communicate with employees, and how to respond to any potential violence or disruptions.

- Monitor the situation closely and stay informed about any potential labor disputes or strikes that may affect your business.

- Communicate with employees and provide them with information on how to stay safe during a labor dispute.

- Secure the perimeter of your business, including entrances, exits, and loading docks, to prevent unauthorized access or vandalism.

- Identify potential hotspots where conflicts may occur, such as picket lines or protest areas, and take extra precautions to secure these areas.

- Train employees on how to handle confrontations and how to de-escalate tense situations.

- Prepare for the worst-case scenario, including the possibility of violence or civil unrest, and have a plan in place for how to respond to these situations.

• Have a good relationship with the union: It's important to have a good relationship with the union, this can help prevent disputes and keep communication open in case of one.

• Keep emergency numbers handy: Keep emergency numbers, such as the police and fire department, handy in case of emergency.

• Work with local authorities, such as the police and emergency services, to ensure that they are aware of the situation and can provide support if needed.

• Be prepared to shut down operations temporarily, if necessary, to ensure the safety of employees and customers.

• Have a risk assessment done, to identify the potential risks, prior to the labor dispute, this will help your company to be prepared.

• Be fair and flexible when dealing with the labor dispute, this will help to resolve the situation faster and prevent it from escalating.

• Provide support for employees who may be impacted by the labor dispute, such as counseling or financial assistance.

By taking these security considerations into account, businesses can better prepare for and manage labor disputes, and help to ensure the safety of employees, customers, and property. It's important to have a plan in place and to be prepared for any potential disruptions or violence that may occur.

Security Considerations for Commercial Vehicles

Commercial vehicles, such as delivery trucks and semi-trucks, play a critical role in many businesses, but they also come with unique security considerations. Here are some tips for ensuring commercial vehicle security:

• Implement security protocols such as requiring drivers to lock all doors and windows when the vehicle is parked, and to keep a daily log of the vehicle's movements.

• Use GPS tracking devices to monitor the vehicle's movements and location in real-time, which can be helpful in case of theft or unauthorized use.

• Use security cameras: Install security cameras on the commercial vehicles to deter theft and monitor driver behavior.

• Conduct background checks on all commercial drivers to ensure that they have a clean driving record and no criminal history.

• Train drivers on security protocols and best practices, including how to handle confrontations and how to prevent theft.

• Have a protocol for keys, including who has access to them and how they are stored and tracked.

• Set up geofencing for commercial vehicles, this will alert you when the vehicle goes outside of the designated area.

- Regular maintenance on commercial vehicles will help ensure their good working condition and proper function in case of an emergency.

- Secure the cargo, this will help prevent theft and damage to the goods being transported.

By following these tips, businesses can help ensure the security of their commercial vehicles and the goods they transport. It's important to have a plan in place and to be prepared for potential security threats.

Security Considerations for Air Travel

Air travel is one of the most common forms of transportation, but it also comes with unique security considerations. Here are some tips for ensuring air travel security:

- Research the airline and the country you're traveling to, including any potential security risks, and take appropriate precautions.

- Check in early and give yourself plenty of time to navigate through security and board your flight.

- Arrive at the airport in advance, especially during peak travel times, to avoid last-minute stress and long lines.

- Keep carry-on items to a minimum, as many items are not allowed on flights and can slow down the security screening process.

- Follow TSA guidelines for carry-on items and liquids and be prepared to remove items from your bag for inspection.

• Be aware of your surroundings at all times and take note of any suspicious activity or individuals.

• Do not leave your belongings unattended, as they may be considered a security threat.

• Follow instructions from airport security personnel, as they are there to ensure the safety of all passengers.

• Report any suspicious activity to airport security or other appropriate authorities immediately.

• Keep your passport and boarding pass on hand at all times and make sure they are valid and not expired.

By following these tips, you can help ensure your safety and the security of your belongings while traveling by air. Remember to stay alert and aware of your surroundings and to follow the instructions of airport security personnel at all times.

Security Considerations for your Personal Information

Protecting your personal information is crucial in today's digital age, as it can be vulnerable to theft and misuse. Here are some tips for ensuring the security of your personal information:

• Use strong passwords for all of your accounts and avoid using the same password for multiple accounts.

• Use two-factor authentication, such as a code sent to your phone or an app, to add an extra layer of security to your accounts.

• Keep your computer and devices updated with the latest security patches and software.

• Use a firewall to protect your computer and devices from unauthorized access.

• Be careful with emails, especially ones that ask for personal information or contain links or attachments.

• Keep personal information such as your address, phone number, and social security number private.

• Use a VPN to encrypt your internet connection and protect your personal information when using public Wi-Fi.

• Use anti-virus and anti-malware software to protect your computer and devices from malware and viruses.

• Be cautious with social media and be aware of the information that you share and who you share it with.

• Monitor your credit reports regularly, to check for any suspicious activity or unauthorized access to your personal information.

By following these tips, you can help ensure the security of your personal information and reduce the risk of identity theft and fraud. Remember to also be vigilant and keep an eye out for any suspicious activity in your accounts, credit reports, and other personal information. If you suspect that your personal information has been compromised, act quickly and contact the necessary authorities and institutions to take the appropriate measures to protect your identity.

Security Considerations for Your Luggage

Luggage security refers to the measures taken to protect your personal belongings and valuables while traveling. Here are some tips for ensuring luggage security:

- Use durable and lockable luggage and use TSA-approved locks to keep your belongings secure.

- Keep valuables in carry-on luggage: Keep valuables, such as passports, cash, and jewelry, in your carry-on luggage, rather than checked luggage, to reduce the risk of theft.

- Pack smartly and avoid leaving empty spaces in your luggage that can be filled with contraband.

- Keep an inventory of your belongings and their location in your luggage, so that you can quickly identify any missing items.

- Label your luggage with your name, address, and contact information, so that it can be returned to you if it gets lost.

- Be aware of your surroundings at all times, especially when you are in crowded or unfamiliar places, to reduce the risk of theft or tampering.

- Don't advertise your travel plans on social media, especially when you are traveling to a destination known for theft.

• Use luggage tracking devices (Apple AirTag) to keep track of your luggage in case it gets lost.

• Keep the checked baggage ticket for verification of claim or if the luggage is lost.

• Be mindful of the airport staff, and keep your luggage in sight at all times, to reduce the risk of theft.

• Keep important documents and essentials with you, such as your passport, ID, and any medication you need, in your carry-on luggage, so that they're always accessible.

By following these tips, you can help ensure the security of your luggage and personal belongings while traveling. Remember to always be aware of your surroundings, and to take the necessary precautions to protect your valuables.

Security Considerations for Your Clothing

Security considerations for clothing can include things like hidden pockets to conceal valuables, reinforced seams to prevent tearing, and reflective materials to increase visibility while walking or biking at night. Some clothing is also specifically designed to protect against the elements, such as cold weather gear or waterproof materials. Additionally, it is important to consider the cultural and social context in which clothing is worn, as certain items may be viewed as inappropriate or unsafe in certain locations.

Security Considerations at an Airport

Security considerations at an airport include measures to prevent acts of terrorism, smuggling, and other illegal activities. For examples:

Passenger screening

A major consideration in airport security. These measures typically include metal detectors, X-ray machines, and pat-downs. Some airports also use advanced technologies such as full body scanners and biometric identification systems to screen passengers.

Baggage screening

Another important aspect of airport security. Luggage and personal items are scanned for potential threats, and any suspicious items are further inspected.

Airport perimeter security

Also crucial. It includes measures such as surveillance cameras, access control systems, and patrols by airport security personnel.

Airport personnel

Likewise an important consideration in airport security. They are trained to identify suspicious behavior and respond appropriately to potential threats.

All these measures are taken to ensure the safety of passengers and airport personnel and to prevent illegal activities and terrorist attacks.

Security Considerations While Dining

Security considerations while dining include measures to protect against physical harm, theft, and food contamination.

Personal safety

This can be a concern when dining in certain areas or at certain times of day. It is important to be aware of one's surroundings and to choose a well-lit, populated area to dine in. Avoiding isolated or poorly lit areas can also help to reduce the risk of crime.

Theft

Another concern while dining, particularly when dining in crowded or tourist-heavy areas. It is important to keep personal belongings close and to be aware of pickpocketing and other forms of theft.

Food contamination

Also a security consideration when dining. It is important to ensure that food is properly stored and prepared to reduce the risk of foodborne illness. Dining at reputable establishments and avoiding street vendors or other questionable food sources can help to reduce the risk of food contamination.

Additionally, it is important to be aware of cultural and social context when dining in different parts of the world, as certain customs or taboos may be considered offensive or unsafe.

Security considerations for vices

Security considerations for vices include measures to protect against physical harm, addiction, and legal consequences.

Drugs and alcohol

Common vices that can have serious health consequences, including addiction and overdose. To reduce the risk of harm, it is important to use these substances in moderation and to avoid using them in combination with other substances.

Gambling

Another vice that can have negative consequences, including addiction and financial problems. To reduce the risk of harm, it is important to set and stick to a budget and to avoid chasing losses.

Smoking

Likewise a vice that can have negative health consequences, including lung cancer and heart disease. To reduce the risk of harm, it is important to quit smoking or to use harm-reduction measures such as switching to e-cigarettes.

All of these vices are illegal in many countries and regions, and engaging in them can result in legal consequences. Therefore, it is important to be aware of the laws and regulations regarding these vices in your area and to engage in them responsibly and legally.

It also is important to be mindful of the risks associated with vices, and to take steps to minimize harm and prevent addiction. Seeking professional help or support can be beneficial if you are struggling with addiction or negative consequences as a result of engaging in vices.

6. Kidnapping/Hostage
for Ransom Survival

Surviving a kidnapping or hostage situation for ransom involves a combination of physical and psychological strategies. The most important thing to remember is to stay calm and not to resist the kidnappers.

Physical strategies include being aware of your surroundings and taking note of any potential escape routes. It is also important to maintain good physical health by eating, drinking, and getting enough sleep.

To increase the chances of survival during a kidnapping or hostage situation, it's important to establish a good relationship with the kidnappers. This may include showing respect and cooperation and being willing to communicate and negotiate with them.

To prepare for such a situation, it can be helpful to learn basic self-defense techniques, to be in good physical shape, and to have a plan for how to react if kidnapped or taken hostage.

If you are kidnapped and/or held for ransom, it's also important to stay aware of your rights as a victim and to know that many countries have specialized agencies to handle such cases.

It's also important to note that in some cases, the kidnappers may be state-sponsored or have political motivations, it's important to be aware of the context in which the incident is happening.

In general, the best way to survive a kidnapping or hostage situation is to stay calm, be aware of your surroundings, establish a good relationship with the kidnappers, and to have a plan in place in case of such an event.

Tips to ensure surviving a hostage situation

• *Stay calm:* It's important to keep a clear head and not to panic. This will help you make better decisions and increase your chances of survival.

• *Don't resist:* It's important to comply with the kidnappers' demands and not to resist. Resisting may increase the risk of violence.

• *Be aware of your surroundings:* Take note of potential escape routes and any objects that could be used as weapons.

• *Establish a connection:* Try to establish a connection with the kidnappers. Showing respect and cooperation can help to decrease the level of violence and increase the chances of release.

• *Communicate:* If possible, try to communicate with the kidnappers and negotiate. This can help to build trust and increase the chances of release.

• *Prepare yourself:* It's important to be in good physical shape and to know basic self-defense techniques in case of an opportunity to escape.

• *Keep a low profile:* Try to blend in with the other hostages and to avoid drawing attention to yourself.

• *Stay informed:* Stay informed of the situation and any developments that may affect your safety.

• *Remember your rights:* Know your rights as a victim and the resources available to you.

- **Have a plan:** Have a plan in place in case of a hostage situation and share it with your loved ones.

It is important to remember that every situation is unique and that these tips may not apply in every case. The most important thing is to stay calm and to assess the situation, so you can make the best decisions for your survival.

Actions at an Attempted Kidnapping

If you are faced with an attempted kidnapping, it's important to take immediate action to increase the chances of escape and to alert others of the situation. Here are some tips on what to do:

- **Yell and make noise:** Draw attention to yourself by yelling, screaming, or making loud noise. This can deter the kidnapper and alert others to the situation.

- **Run:** If possible, run away from the kidnapper as quickly as possible. Look for a safe place to hide or seek help.

- **Fight back:** If running is not an option, fight back with whatever you have at hand. Use pepper spray, a personal alarm, or any nearby objects to defend yourself.

- **Remember details:** Try to remember as many details about the kidnapper as possible, such as their appearance, clothes, and mode of transportation. This information can be helpful for the authorities.

- **Get to safety:** Once you are safe, contact the authorities immediately and provide them with the details of the attempted kidnapping.

- *Seek help:* Reach out to a counselor or therapist to help process the trauma of an attempted kidnapping.

- *Consider self-defense classes:* Consider taking self-defense classes to be better prepared for such situations in the future.

It is important to remember that every situation is unique and that the most important thing is to stay calm, assess the situation and act quickly to increase your chances of escape.

Action at a physical attack

If you are faced with a physical attack, it's important to take immediate action to increase the chances of defending yourself and getting away safely. Here are some tips on what to do:

- *Stay alert:* Be aware of your surroundings and be prepared for a potential attack.

- *Use your voice:* Yell, scream, or make loud noise to draw attention to yourself and deter the attacker.

- *Run:* If possible, run away from the attacker as quickly as possible. Look for a safe place to hide or seek help.

- *Use self-defense techniques:* If running is not an option, use self-defense techniques to defend yourself. This can include strikes to vulnerable areas such as the eyes, throat, and groin.

- *Use objects as weapons:* Use any nearby objects as weapons to defend yourself such as a bag, a phone, a pen or even a hot drink.

- **Get to safety:** Once you are safe, contact the authorities immediately and provide them with the details of the attack.

- **Seek help:** Reach out to a counselor or therapist to help process the trauma of a physical attack.

- **Consider self-defense classes:** Consider taking self-defense classes to be better prepared for such situations in the future.

It is important to remember that every situation is unique and that the most important thing is to stay calm, assess the situation and act quickly to increase your chances of defend yourself and escape safely.

Preparing the Family for Possible Kidnapping

Preparing a family for the possibility of kidnapping involves taking steps to reduce the risk of kidnapping, as well as creating a plan for what to do in the event of a kidnapping.

- **Increase awareness:** Educate family members about the risks of kidnapping and the warning signs of a potential kidnapping. Teach them how to be aware of their surroundings and how to recognize potential threats.

- **Establish a security plan:** Develop a security plan that includes steps to reduce the risk of kidnapping, such as limiting the sharing of personal information online, avoiding isolated or unfamiliar areas, and varying daily routines.

• **Create a communication plan:** Establish a plan for how family members will communicate with each other during a crisis, and make sure everyone knows how to contact each other and the authorities.

• **Provide emergency contact information:** Keep emergency contact information, including phone numbers and addresses, in a safe and easily accessible place.

• **Train family members:** Train family members in self-defense techniques and basic survival skills, including how to escape from a kidnapper, how to find help, and how to stay calm under pressure.

• **Discuss and practice the plan:** Discuss the plan with all family members and practice the different scenarios, it will help them to be more prepared in case of a real-life situation.

• **Have a kidnap and ransom insurance:** Consider having a kidnap and ransom insurance to cover expenses that may arise in case of a kidnapping.

It is important to remember that while it's impossible to completely eliminate the risk of kidnapping, taking steps to prepare and educate your family can greatly increase the chances of survival in case of a kidnapping.

Dealing with Hostage-Takers

Dealing with hostage-takers can be a complex and dangerous situation that requires a calm and measured approach. Here are some tips on how to handle a hostage situation:

- **Stay calm:** It's important to keep a clear head and not to panic. This will help you make better decisions and increase your chances of survival.

- **Don't resist:** It's important to comply with the kidnappers' demands and not to resist. Resisting may increase the risk of violence.

- **Communicate:** If possible, try to communicate with the kidnappers and negotiate. This can help to build trust and increase the chances of release.

- **Show respect:** Show respect to the kidnappers and try to understand their motivations. This can help to decrease the level of violence and increase the chances of release.

- **Be aware of your surroundings:** Take note of potential escape routes and any objects that could be used as weapons.

- **Establish a connection:** Try to establish a connection with the kidnappers and with the other hostages. Showing respect and cooperation can help to decrease the level of violence and increase the chances of release.

- **Follow the kidnappers' instructions:** Follow the kidnappers' instructions and avoid doing anything that may provoke them or escalate the situation.

- **Be patient:** Hostage situations can take a long time to resolve, so it's important to stay patient and to have faith that the authorities will work to resolve the situation safely.

• **Seek help:** Reach out to a counselor or therapist to help process the trauma of being held hostage.

It is important to remember that every situation is unique and that the most important thing is to stay calm, assess the situation and act in a way that increases the chances of survival.

Staying in control in a hostage situation

Staying in control during a hostage situation can be challenging, but there are steps that can be taken to maintain a sense of control and to increase the chances of survival.

• **Stay calm:** It's important to keep a clear head and not to panic. This will help you make better decisions and increase your chances of survival.

• **Focus on your breathing:** Take deep breaths and focus on maintaining a steady breathing pattern. This can help to reduce anxiety and to keep you calm.

• **Use visualization techniques:** Use visualization techniques to imagine yourself in a safe and peaceful place. This can help to reduce stress and to keep you focused.

• **Keep a positive attitude:** Try to maintain a positive attitude and to focus on the potential for a positive outcome. This can help to increase your chances of survival.

• **Communicate with other hostages:** Establish a connection with other hostages and work together to stay calm and to find a way to escape.

• **Stay informed:** Stay informed about the situation and any developments that may affect your safety.

• **Follow the kidnappers' instructions:** Follow the kidnappers' instructions and avoid doing anything that may provoke them or escalate the situation.

• **Be patient:** Hostage situations can take a long time to resolve, so it's important to stay patient and to have faith that the authorities will work to resolve the situation safely.

• **Seek help:** Reach out to a counselor or therapist to help process the trauma of being held hostage.

It is important to remember that every situation is unique and that the most important thing is to stay calm, assess the situation and act in a way that increases the chances of survival.

Keeping occupied in a hostage situation

Being held hostage can be a traumatic and stressful experience, and it's important to find ways to stay occupied and to keep your mind occupied to help pass the time and to reduce stress.

• **Try to focus on the present moment and not to dwell on the past or the future:** This can help to reduce stress and anxiety.

• **Find small things to occupy yourself with:** Look around you and find small things to occupy yourself with, such as counting objects, or organizing your personal belongings.

• *Try to stay physically active:* If possible, try to stay physically active by doing exercises such as stretching, or yoga.

• *Use your imagination:* Try to use your imagination to create mental images or to play mental games such as chess or Sudoku.

• *Read or listen to something:* If you have something to read or listen to, such as a book or music, it can help to pass the time and to take your mind off the situation.

• *Communicate with other hostages:* Establish a connection with other hostages and work together to find ways to stay occupied and to keep your spirits up.

• *Try to focus on positive thoughts:* Try to focus on positive thoughts and memories and try to imagine a positive outcome to the situation.

• *Seek help:* Reach out to a counselor or therapist to help process the trauma of being held hostage, and to find ways to cope with the stress of the situation.
It is important to remember that every situation is unique and that the most important thing is to stay calm, assess the situation and act in a way that increases the chances of survival.

Tips if Interrogated as a Hostage

• Stay calm and cooperate with the kidnappers.

• Try to establish a rapport and form a connection with them.

• Avoid making sudden movements or attempting to escape, as this may provoke the kidnappers.

• Listen carefully to their demands and try to comply with them as much as possible.

• If you are questioned, provide only basic personal information, and avoid discussing sensitive topics such as politics or religion.

• Take note of any identifying details about your kidnappers and the location where you are being held.

• Keep mental and physical health by staying positive and doing exercise.

• If possible, communicate with your family and friends to let them know you're alive and well.

• Be aware that most kidnappings end peacefully so don't lose hope.

• It's important to remember that every situation is different, and the best course of action may vary. It's always best to consult with professionals such as law enforcement or a crisis management team if you find yourself in a similar situation.

Actions to take during a hostage rescue

• Follow the instructions of law enforcement or rescue team members. They are trained to handle these situations and will have a plan in place to safely rescue hostages.

• Stay calm and remain quiet. This will reduce the risk

of alerting the kidnappers or hostages to the rescue team's presence.

• Try to stay in one place and make yourself visible to the rescuers. This will make it easier for them to locate and secure you.

• If possible, use a flashlight or other light source to signal your location to rescuers.

• Remain still and do not make any sudden movements. This will reduce the risk of being mistaken for a kidnapper by the rescuers.

• If you are able to, try to provide information about the layout of the building and the location of the kidnappers and hostages to the rescuers.

• If you are able to escape, do so and move quickly and quietly to a safe location.

• Once rescued, follow any additional instructions given by the rescuers and be prepared to provide a statement to the authorities.

It is important to understand that the priority of the rescue team is the safety of the hostages, so the actions you take should support that goal. Remember that the situation is unpredictable and it's always best to follow the instructions of the trained professionals who are handling the rescue.

Alternatives for Violent or Suicide Attacks

When dealing with extremist groups who do not plan to release you but use you as fodder to make a statement, you might be forced to make some difficult decisions. Only you will be able to determine when the situation has become desperate, forcing you to take action. Following are some points to ponder, facing the worst possible outcome.

- Your nationality and religion could make you a target.

- Being properly trained in identifying the captors and their intentions will assist you in your decision to fight.

- There might be trained air marshals or undercover personnel nearby preparing intervene, in which case your actions might not help.

- Most important: You must be mentally prepared to fight to the death; when you begin, there is no turning back.

- You must be ruthless in your attack; you are now fighting for your life; take no quarters.

- Your actions could save others or doom others.
- Self-sacrifice might be better than passive submission.

Everyone recalls the incredible heroism and self-sacrifice displayed by the passengers of United Airlines Flight 93 on September 11, 2001, when they rushed the cockpit door and forced their al-Qaeda hijackers to plunge the aircraft into a meadow near Shanksville, Pennsylvania.

7. Chemical, Biological, Nuclear and Radiological Attacks

Chemical attack

Terrorists will sometimes use a mechanical device, aerosol dispersant or projectile to deliver a toxic substance with chemical effects to kill or incapacitate a target area. Examples of the substances include choking agents, blister agents, blood agents and nerve agents.

Indicators of possible chemical weapons use

- nausea, disorientation, difficulty breathing, convulsions
- definite casualty patterns.
- unusual numbers of dead or dying animals
- lack of insects
- unexplained casualties
- multiple victims
- serious illnesses
- unusual liquids, spray, or vapor
- visible droplets or oily film
- unexplained odor
- low-lying clouds or fog unrelated to weather
- suspicious devices or packages
- unusual metal debris
- abandoned spray devices
- unexplained munitions

The type and amount of agent, concentration and environmental factors will greatly affect the result of a chemical attack.

If you suspect a chemical attack or release

• Do not touch anything or anyone without protective clothing.

• If you have contacted a chemical, clean yourself immediately.

• Seek in place protection, like uncontaminated buildings and/or vehicles.

• Cover yourself as best as you can (use field expedient items that are available, e.g., trash bags, table clothes, etc.).

• Stay upwind and upgrade from any suspected site.

• If contaminated, follow the instructions of the first responders so you do not cross-contaminate other areas and persons.

Basic decontamination of chemical agents

• Carefully blot the agent off; do not spread and use clean articles.

• Strip off contaminated clothing.

• Flush the area affected with large amounts of water, but do not let it run onto uncontaminated parts of your body.

Biological attack

Devices to deliver living organisms or materials derived from them used to kill or incapacitate a target area include contamination via small vials or larger containers, munitions, aerosols or even insect vectors. Biological weapons might include bacteria, viruses, toxins, and fungi.

Indicators of possible biological weapon use

- sick or dying animals, people or fish
- unusual illnesses for a region or area
- definite patterns inconsistent with natural diseases
- spraying or suspicious devices or packages
- unusual swarms of insects

Most biological agents have a delayed effect, so if identified quickly they usually can be treated. Remember, biological agents are naturally occurring and have been around a long time. Understand that some biological agents, such as anthrax, do not cause contagious diseases. Others, such as the smallpox virus, can be transmitted from person to person.

In the event of a biological attack, public health officials might not immediately be able to provide information on what you should do. It could take time to determine exactly what the biological agent and resulting illnesses are, how the illness should be treated and who might have been exposed. You should watch TV, listen to the radio, or check the Internet for official news including the following:

- Are you in the group or area authorities believe might have been exposed?

- What are the signs and symptoms of the disease?

- Are medications or vaccines being distributed?

- If counteracting agents are being distributed, where are the distribution points? Who should get them and how should they be administered?

- Where should you seek emergency medical care if you become sick?

During a declared biological emergency

- If a family member becomes sick, it is important to be suspicious.

- Do not assume, however, that you should go to a hospital emergency room, or that a particular illness is the result of biological attack. Symptoms of many common illnesses can overlap.

- Use common sense, practice good hygiene and cleanliness to avoid spreading germs, and seek medical advice.

- Consider if you are in the group or area authorities believe to be in danger.

- If your symptoms match those described and you are in the group considered at risk, immediately seek emergency medical attention.

If you are potentially exposed

• Follow instructions of doctors and other public health officials.

• If the disease is contagious, expect to receive medical evaluation and treatment. You could be advised to stay away from others or even quarantined.

• For non-contagious diseases, expect to receive medical evaluation and treatment.

If you become aware of an unusual and suspicious substance nearby

• Quickly get away.

• Protect yourself. Cover your mouth and nose with layers of fabric that can filter the air but still allow breathing. Examples include two or three layers of cotton such as a tee-shirt, handkerchief or towel. Otherwise, several layers of tissue or paper towels will help.

• Wash any affected areas with plenty of soap and water.

• Contact authorities.

• Watch TV, listen to the radio, or check the Internet for official news and information, including what the signs and symptoms of the disease are, if medications or vaccinations are being distributed and where you should seek medical attention if you become sick.

• If you do become sick, by all means seek immediate medical attention.

Basic decontamination of biological agents

• Wet down areas where the agent is suspected to prevent it from re-suspending in the air and spreading.

• Wash anything suspected of being contaminated with a commercial bleach solution.

Nuclear attack

Fission devices (military-produced bombs) are aimed at inflicting the most massive and long-lasting physical destruction to the largest area possible. Though nuclear weapons have been used only twice in warfare, at least three hostile, or potentially hostile, nations (Russia, China and North Korea) harbor these weapons of mass destruction in their arsenals. Because of the doctrine called mutually assured destruction (meaning any aggressive action against the United States or ally would immediately bring the prospect of similar or superior retaliation)—the possibility of an overt act by a hostile nation in the form of a nuclear attack remains slight.

Terror groups such as ISIS, al-Qaeda, or Hezbollah, however, harbor no such inhibitions. The potential for a terrorist threat of nuclear attack remains slight but real.

Indicators of possible nuclear weapon use

• blindingly bright flash followed by enormous blast sound
• powerful and destructive shock wave
·• intense heat
• giant, mushroom-shaped cloud erupting skyward from blast.

- immediate radiation burns
- acute radiation poisoning

Your distance from ground zero (the initial point of the explosion) and the yield of the weapon will determine how the blast and ensuing radiation affect you. If the detonation occurs within a relatively short distance, say, less than a few miles, then your chances of survival are slim at best. Setting the worst prospect aside, you might retain a few options.

Three ways to survive a nuclear blast and minimize radiation exposure

- *Shielding:* The heavier and denser the materials between you and the source of the explosion, the better. This is why local officials will advise you to remain indoors if an attack occurs. In some cases, the walls in your home or workplace will be sufficient shielding to protect you for a short period of time.

- *Distance:* The more distance between you and the source of the radiation, the weaker the blast effects and the less radiation you will receive. In the most serious situations, local officials might call for an evacuation ahead of time, thereby increasing the distance between you and ground zero.

- *Time:* Limiting the time spent near a source of radiation reduces the amount of exposure you will receive. In short, if you survive the initial blast and are able to travel, move as quickly and as far away from the site as you are able.

Accidental radiation release or 'dirty bomb' attack

State and local governments, with support from the federal government and utilities, have developed plans to deal with an accidental radiation release with a radius of 10 miles from nuclear powerplants, as well as an area called an Ingestion Planning Zone within a radius of 50 miles from the plant.

Residents within the 10-mile emergency-planning zone are regularly given emergency information materials (via brochures, the phone book, calendars, utility bills, etc.). The materials contain instructions for evacuation and sheltering, special arrangements for the handicapped, contacts for additional information, etc. Residents should be familiar with these emergency information materials.

Radiological emergency plans also call for a prompt Alert and Notification System. If needed, this system will be activated quickly to inform the public of any potential threat from natural or man-made events. The system uses either sirens, tone alert radios, route alerting (known as the "Paul Revere" method), or a combination to notify the public to tune their radios or televisions to the Emergency Alert System (EAS).

Little or none of these procedures might apply to a so-called dirty-bomb attack, which uses conventional explosives to spread radioactive material over a populated area. Nevertheless, some of the procedures developed to deal with accidental radiation releases can also apply.

If an emergency occurs, you should be aware of the primary means of exposure to harmful radiation as well as basic decontamination procedures that you can initiate.

Be aware of routes of radiation exposure

- inhalation of radiated particles
- ingestion of radiated particles or foods
- skin absorption

Basic decontamination procedures

• Wet down areas where the agent is suspected to prevent it from re-suspending in the air and spreading.

• Remove items and clothing that have been radiated from your vicinity—e.g., place them in garbage bags and toss them outside.

• Wash anything suspected of being contaminated with a commercial bleach solution.

8. Bombs

Bombs can be constructed to look like almost anything and can be placed or delivered in any number of ways. The probability of finding a bomb that looks like the stereotypical bomb is almost nonexistent. The only common denominator that exists among bombs is that they are designed or intended to explode.

Most bombs are homemade and are limited in their design only by the imagination of, and resources available to, the bomber.

Remember, when searching for a bomb, suspect anything that looks unusual—but never approach a suspicious object—let trained bomb technicians determine what is or is not a bomb.

Bomb threats

Bomb threats are delivered in a variety of ways. The majority are called in directly by the would-be bomber, though occasionally the calls are made through a third party. Sometimes, a threat is communicated in writing or via recording.

The most common reasons for making a bomb threat

• The caller wants to minimize personal injury or property damage. In such cases, the caller is probably the person who placed the device or someone who has become aware of such information.

• The caller wants to create an atmosphere of anxiety and panic, which will in turn result in a disruption of the normal activities at the targeted facility.

Whatever the reason for the threat, there must be a response to it, because innocent life must be protected. With proper planning, however, the dangers to life, limb and property can be reduced.

Responding to bomb threats

If the threat is by telephone

In the case of bomb threats via telephone, the caller is can be the best source of information about the bomb.

• Keep the caller on the line as long as possible. Ask him or her to repeat the message. If possible, record every word.

• If the caller does not indicate the location of the bomb or the time of detonation, continue asking for this information—it's possible you will elicit the information.

• Remind the caller that the building is occupied, and the detonation of a bomb could kill or seriously injure many innocent people, and therefore if the bomber is tracked down the prosecution could result in the death penalty or a life sentence.

• Pay particular attention to background noises, such as motors running, music playing or any other sound that might give a clue to the caller's location or identity.

• Listen closely to see if you can determine the caller's gender, voice quality, emotional state, accent or possible speech pattern or impediment.

• Immediately after the caller hangs up, report the threat to the person designated by management to receive such information.

It is always desirable that more than one person listen in on the call. To do this, your organization should develop a covert signaling system, perhaps a coded buzzer to a second reception point. A calm response to the caller could result in obtaining additional information. This is especially true if the caller seems to wish to avoid injuries or deaths. If told that the building is occupied or cannot be evacuated in time, the bomber might even be willing to give more specific information on the bomb's location, components, or method of initiation.

Report the information immediately to the police department, fire department, ATF, FBI, and other appropriate agencies. Then remain available because law-enforcement personnel will want to interview you.

If the threat is written

• Save all materials, including any envelope or container.

• Once the message is recognized as a bomb threat, avoid further handling of the materials.

• Turn over the materials as soon as possible to law enforcement. They will attempt to retain evidence such as fingerprints, handwriting or typewriting, paper and postal marks—all will prove essential in tracing the threat and identifying the writer.

While written messages are usually associated with generalized threats and extortion attempts, a written warning of a specific device should never be ignored.

Bomb-threat checklist*
* Partially sourced from DHS/CISA Office for Bombing Protection checklist

Questions to ask the caller

• When is bomb going to explode?
• Where is it right now?
• What does it look like?
• What kind of bomb is it?
• What will cause it to explode?
• Did you place the bomb?
• Why?

- What is your name?
- What is your address?

Very important

- Can you call back in 15 minutes?
- How can I contact you if I need more information or have trouble meeting your demands?

Basic information to relay to law enforcement

- exact wording of the threat
- sex of caller
- race of caller
- approximate age of caller
- length of call
- number at which call is received
- time and date of call

Was the caller's voice...

- calm?
- nasal?
- angry?
- stuttering?
- excited?
- lisping?
- slow?
- rapid?
- ragged?
- loud?
- soft?
- raspy?

- deep?
- laughing?
- clearing throat often?
- breathing deeply?
- crying?
- normal?
- cracking?
- distinct?
- disguised?
- accented?
- slurred?
- familiar?

If the voice was familiar, whom did it sound like? Was the threat language...

- well-spoken?
- incoherent?
- evidently from an educated person?
- recorded?
- foul?
- irrational?
- pre-written and being read by the caller?

If there were background noises, were they from...

- street sounds?
- human voices?
- animal sounds?
- crockery?
- a PA system?
- music?
- static?
- household sounds?

- a long-distance call?
- a telephone booth?
- automobiles or other motorized vehicles?
- factory machinery?
- office machinery?
- other?

Questions to ask if a hostage is involved

- Who is this?
- Where are you calling from?
- Is this a prank?
- How do I know this is not a prank?
- May I speak to the hostage?
- Is the hostage all right?
- What do you want?

Mail bomb recognition points

If you suspect that a package might contain a bomb, you will want to take note of important details when notifying authorities.

- foreign postmark
- restrictive markings, such as "Confidential" or "Personal"
- excessive postage
- handwritten or poorly typed address
- incorrect titles
- titles but no names
- misspelled names or common words
- oily stains or discoloration

- no return address
- excessive weight
- rigidity
- lopsided or uneven packaging
- protruding wires or aluminum foil
- excessive securing material, (masking tape or string)
- other visual inconsistencies

Hardened security measures

Most commercial structures and individual residences already contain some security measures, whether planned or unplanned. Locks on windows and doors, for example, or outside lighting are designed and installed to contribute toward the security of a facility and the protection of its occupants.

In considering measures to increase security for your building or office against violent attack or bomb threats, you should contact your local police department for guidance. No single security plan is adaptable to all situations. Nevertheless, the following recommendations can contribute to reducing your vulnerability.

The exterior configuration of a building or facility is very important

Unfortunately, in most instances architects have given little or no consideration to security, particularly in the case of thwarting or discouraging a bomb attack. By a few, relatively simple additions, however, such as fencing and lighting, and by controlling access, a building's vulnerability to a bomb attack can be reduced significantly.

Bombs being delivered by car or left in a car are a grave reality

• Parking should be restricted, if possible, to 300 feet away from the building or buildings in a complex.

• If restricted parking is not feasible, properly identified employee vehicles should be parked closest to the facility, with visitor vehicles parked at a distance.

• Heavy shrubs and vines should be kept close to the ground to reduce their potential to conceal criminals or bombs.

• Window boxes and planters are perfect receptacles for bombs. Unless there is an absolute requirement for such ornamentation, they are better removed. If they must remain, a security patrol should be employed to check them regularly.

A highly visible security patrol can be a significant deterrent.

• Even if security comprises only one day guard and one night guard, that person should be utilized outside the building.

• If an interior guard is required, consider installing closed-circuit television cameras that cover the exterior perimeters.

• Have an adequate alarm system installed by a reputable company that can service and properly maintain the equipment.

• Post signs indicating that such a system is in place.

• Install entrance and exit doors with hinges and hinge pins on the inside to prevent removal.

• Solid wood or sheet metal-faced doors provide extra integrity that a hollow core wooden door cannot provide.

• A properly fitting steel doorframe can be equally important.

The ideal security situation is a building with no windows

• If windows are required, bars, grates, heavy mesh screens or steel shutters offer good protection from otherwise unwanted entry.

• It is important that the openings in the protective coverings are not too large. Otherwise, a bomb can be introduced into the building while the bomber remains outside.

• Floor vents, transoms and skylights should also be covered.

• Note that fire safety considerations preclude the use of certain window coverings. Municipal ordinances should be researched, and safety considered before any of these renovations are undertaken.

Access controls are likewise critical in preventing security breaches

• Establish controls for positively identifying personnel who are authorized access to critical areas and for denying access to unauthorized personnel.

• These controls should extend to the inspection of all packages and materials being taken into critical areas.

• Security and maintenance personnel should be alert for people who act in a suspicious manner, as well as objects, items, or parcels which look out of place or suspicious.

• Surveillance should be established to include potential hiding places (e.g., stairwells, rest rooms, and any vacant office space) for unwanted individuals.

• Doors or access ways to such areas as boiler rooms, mailrooms, computer areas, switchboards, and elevator control rooms should remain locked when not in use.

• It is important to establish a procedure for the accountability of keys. If keys cannot be accounted for, locks should be changed.

Good housekeeping is also vital for building security

• Trash or dumpster areas should remain free of debris. A bomb or device can easily be concealed in the trash.

• Combustible materials should be properly disposed of, or secured if further use is anticipated.

Install detection devices at all entrances and closed-circuit television in those areas previously identified as likely places where a bomb may be placed. This, coupled with the posting of signs indicating such measures are in place, is a good deterrent.

If there is an explosion

• Take shelter against your desk or a sturdy table.
• Exit the building immediately.
• Do not use elevators.
• Check for fire and other hazards.
• Take your emergency supply kit if time allows.

If there is a fire

• Exit the building immediately.

• If there is smoke, crawl under the smoke to the nearest exit and use a cloth, if possible, to cover your nose and mouth.

• Use the back of your hand to feel the upper, lower, and middle parts of closed doors.

• If the door is not hot, brace yourself against it and open slowly.

• If the door is hot, do not open it. Look for another way out.

• Do not use elevators.

• If your clothes catch fire, use the stop-drop-and-roll maneuver to put out the flames.

• Do not run.

If you are at home, go to your previously designated outside meeting place

• Account for your family members and carefully supervise small children.

• GET OUT and STAY OUT. Never go back into a burning building.

• Call 911 or your local emergency number.

9. Surveillance Detection

Whether you are a hard-working citizen or Federal Agent basic surveillance detection is a tried-and-true life skill to prevent you from becoming the victim of an avoidable attack/crime.

These techniques are designed to be learned and practices daily and once learned and properly applied do not interfere with normal activities. Do not be time and place predictable is the most salient point for surveillance detection. Also, most people look but do not see so become comfortable in providing accurate descriptions. A far higher number of crimes are committed after the conduct of basic and often amateur surveillance to assess the chance of success of an attack on the victim.

Basic Surveillance Detection

What to watch for around vehicles

- Repeated sightings (different time and locations)
- Correlating activities (start/stop/same route)
- Parked in key locations to surveil
- Target/victim fixation
- Photographing/videotaping activities

Watch for suspicious demeanor in strangers in your area/travels

- Do not ignore groups you feel are no threat like females, elderly, children, taxi drivers, shop operators, delivery persons, waitresses, maintenance, beggars, handicapped and mentally unstable individuals.

- Individuals attempting to fit in but do not.

- Look for individuals that are projecting an image that they are doing something other than what they are really doing.

Verbal indicators – attempting to influence with the following

- "Honestly"
- "Truthfully"

- "Believe me"
- "To be perfectly frank"
- "I swear"
- Inability to answer or reluctant
- Answers a question with a question
- Shaky voice
- Responds with unrelated information (rehearsed answers)
- Suspicious demeanor
- Determined look "death stare" victim fixation
- Blushing or turning pale
- Obvious shaking
- Averting eyes or refusing to make eye contact
- Covering of the eyes
- Rubbing their nose, grooming mustache or hair, yawning, licking their lips excessively
- Tugging at clothes, playing with fingernails or jewelry
- Rubbing their hands together, wiping their palms, hiding their hands

Construct preplanned route to your normal visits that allow for you to detect and identify if you are being surveilled by criminal or terrorist individuals or groups.

- Fixed points, i.e., street corners, stores, shops, that are secure, provide a wide range of vision and are accessed 24 hours a day. Allows you to look around while having a reason to be there.

- Have a colleague be at this fixed point prior to you, while you are there, and then follow you in the event you feel you are being followed.

• While on a route plan for locations that channel-ize anyone that would be following you, so you know when to look and not constantly look. Road crossings, foot bridges, malls and one-way streets are examples of this.

Observation and description

Describing individuals (A thru I)

- Age/Sex
- Build
- Complexion
- Dress
- Elevation
- Face
- Gait
- Hair
- Interesting features

Describing vehicles

- Color
- Make (manufacturer)
- Style/Model
- Year of manufacture
- License Number and issuing location
- Other unique items of interest

Describing locations

- Proper name
- Road/Street address
- Color
- Materials constructed from

Describing activities (SALUTE)

- **S**ize (of activity)
- **A**ctivity (What is happening?)
- **Lo**cation (Where?)
- **U**niform (clothing description)
- **T**ime (When?)
- **E**quipment (What did they have with them?)

10. First Aid Basics

This section is not meant to teach you these techniques but refresh you. If you know you need medical refresher training, seek professional instruction.

Immediate Survey

- Check consciousness: "Are you Okay?" If not, call 911 immediately.
- Look, listen, and feel (5 seconds).
- Open airway (tilt head, lift chin).
- Look, listen, and feel again (5 seconds).
- If no rise and fall of the chest, give two slow breaths for 1.5 seconds each.
- Check for pulse.
- Check for bleeding.

Choking victim

• When you encounter a choking adult—one who is still conscious—he or she will show you the sign of hands to the throat.

• Identify yourself. Tell the person that you know the Heimlich maneuver. Ask the person, "Can you cough? Can you speak?"

• If the victim can cough or speak, do not perform the Heimlich maneuver or pat them on the back. Encourage them to cough instead.

When you need to begin the Heimlich maneuver

• Start with the proper stance and hand placement. Locate the top of the pelvis (approximately at the belly button); put one foot between the victim's feet and slide one hand around the person's waist with your thumb pointing toward the belly button.

• Put the other hand on top of the first, then pull up and back-toward you—as many times as it takes to get the object out or until the person becomes limp.

• These will be violent thrusts, as many times as it takes.

Unconscious victim with airway obstruction

• Tilt the head back/lift the chin.

- Squeeze the victim's nostrils.

- Blow into the victim's mouth, two breaths for 1.5 seconds each.

- If no rise in the chest, reposition with head tilt/chin lift.

- Blow two more breaths for 1.5 seconds each.

- If no rise in the chest, perform 5 abdominal thrusts.

- Perform a finger sweep of the mouth to remove any protrusion (in an infant only if an obstruction can be seen).
- Repeat the head tilt/chin lift.

- Two more breaths for 1.5 seconds each.

- If still no rise in the chest, repeat steps.

- When you get rise in the chest from the breath, go to "Look, Listen and Feel."

- If you have a pulse and no breathing, continue to perform rescue breathing.

- If no breath or pulse, perform CPR.

Rescue breathing

If the person has a pulse but is not breathing, you must perform rescue breathing. For an adult, give one rescue breath every 5 seconds. If the victim does take a breath on their own, recount the 5 seconds. If there is still no breath, then repeat the one breath per 5 seconds.

When you feel a pulse and the person is breathing on his or her own, put them in the recovery position□rotating the victim onto their side until help arrives. This helps keep the airway clear of any further obstructions.

CPR

Adult CPR is performed on anyone over age 8. The basics here will apply□with minor modifications□to children and infants as well.

Approach any emergency situation by first looking at the big picture: Is there anything that could harm you? Make sure the scene is safe before you enter into it.

- Is the person on a street? Watch out for automobiles.
- Is the person in a swimming pool? Do you know how to swim?
- Is electricity involved?
- Are there any strange smells?

Once you've determined that the scene is safe, approach the victim. If there is no movement or apparent consciousness, shake the victim and shout.

Important! If there is any chance that the victim might have a spinal injury, **do not** shake him or her. Do shout and gently tap the victim on the shoulder. If you know the person's name, say it: "Bill, Bill, can you hear me?" If the victim is an adult and there is no response, call 911 or your local emergency number immediately.

ABC's of CPR

Once you've called for help, go back to the victim and begin your ABC's:

- A is airway.
- B is breathing.
- C is circulation.

Open the airway, tilting the head and lifting the chin. Pushing down on the head and lifting up on the chin removes the tongue from the back of the throat.

The tongue is the most common airway obstruction in an unconscious person. If the victim is going to breathe on his or her own, it should happen as soon as you clear the airway. If you do not hear, see, or feel any breathing, you must give two breaths.

Give everyone two breaths initially

- Pinch the person's nose and put your lips over the other person's lips and blow until you see the chest rise. If you have a protective device, use it.

• Watch out of the corner of your eye to be sure you blow just enough to see the chest rise.

**Assess the response by looking
to see if the chest rises and falls**

• Put your face close to the victim's so that you can hear and
• feel them breathing.
• If you do not hear or feel any breathing, give the victim two breaths.

As soon as you complete two breaths, move to C

• Check the pulse at the carotid artery in the neck, which is easily found by locating the Adam's Apple and sliding your fingers just to the side.

• Feel around in this area. If there is no thumping under your fingers in a 3-second time span, begin chest compressions.

• Start by finding the proper placement for your hands. Locate the base of the sternum, the spot where all the ribs come together in the center of the chest.

• Place two fingers on that point. Put the heel of the other hand beside those two fingers. Interlace your fingers, lock your elbows, and compress the victim's chest, using your body weight, to the necessary depth of 2 inches deep.

• Or remember: two hands, 2 inches.

- Count aloud as you compress 15 times and follow by giving the victim two breaths.

- All of this completes one cycle.

Repeat for a total of 4 cycles - about 1 minute in elapsed time. Then check again for a pulse in the neck and watch for signs that the person is breathing.

Special cases

- If the victim has dentures, leave them in. Dentures can help create a seal around the victim's lips.

- If your mouth won't fit over the victim's, simply put your hand over his mouth and blow into his nose.

Blow just enough air to see the chest rise. Over-inflation of the lungs can force air into the subject's stomach, causing him or her to vomit. This creates an airway obstruction. If this occurs, turn the victim toward you, sweep out the vomit, and continue your rescue efforts.

A Well-Equipped First-Aid Kit

- sterile adhesive bandages-assorted sizes
- four-to-six 2-inch sterile gauze pads
- four-to-six 4-inch sterile gauze pads
- hypoallergenic adhesive tape
- three triangular bandages
- three rolls of 2-inch sterile roller bandages
- three rolls of 3-inch sterile roller bandages
- scissors

- tweezers
- sewing needle
- moistened towelettes
- dust particulate masks
- hydrogen peroxide or commercial antiseptic
- thermometer
- two tongue blades
- petroleum jelly or other lubricant
- assorted sizes of safety pins
- cleansing agent and/or soap
- two pairs of Latex gloves
- sunscreen
- aspirin or non-aspirin pain reliever
- anti-diarrheal medication
- antacid (for stomach upset)
- syrup of ipecac (to induce vomiting)
- laxative
- activated charcoal

PART TWO: PERSONAL PREPAREDNESS

11. Definition of Independent-Minded Individuals and Families

Independent-minded individuals and families are individuals who value self-sufficiency and independence in all aspects of their lives. These individuals are proactive in their approach to life and are not afraid to take control of their own destiny. They believe in being prepared for any eventualities and being able to provide for their own needs without relying on external sources.

Independent-minded individuals and families are driven by a desire for self-reliance and the ability to live a fulfilling life that is not dependent on external factors. They are motivated by a desire to take control of their own lives and to be in a position to provide for their own needs, regardless of the circumstances.

Self-sufficiency is a key component of independent-minded individuals and families. They strive to be self-sufficient in all areas of their lives, including food and water security, energy independence, financial stability, and health and medical preparedness. These individuals believe that being self-sufficient is the key to living a fulfilling life and being prepared for any eventualities.

Food and Water Security

Food and water security are critical components of self-sufficiency. Independent-minded individuals and families strive to have a secure source of food and water that is not dependent on external sources. This includes having a garden or farm where they can grow their own food, having a water collection and storage system, and being prepared to store food for emergencies.

Energy Independence

Energy independence is another important aspect of self-sufficiency. Independent-minded individuals and families strive to have a secure source of energy that is not dependent on external sources. This includes investing in renewable energy sources such as solar and wind power, and implementing energy-efficient practices in their homes and lifestyles.

Financial Preparedness

Financial preparedness is a critical component of self-sufficiency. Independent-minded individuals and families strive to be financially stable and to have a secure source of income that is not dependent on external sources. This includes investing in their own education and career development, as well as having a savings plan and emergency fund in place.

Health and Medical Preparedness

Health and medical preparedness are critical components of self-sufficiency. Independent-minded individuals and families strive to be prepared for any health emergencies and to have a secure source of medical care that is not dependent on external sources. This includes having a well-stocked first aid kit, investing in their own health and wellness, and being prepared to provide for their own medical needs in case of a disaster or emergency.

Bottom Line
Independent-minded individuals and families are individuals who value self-sufficiency and independence in all aspects of their lives. They are proactive in their approach

to life and are not afraid to take control of their own destiny. They believe in being prepared for any eventualities and being able to provide for their own needs without relying on external sources. This includes having a secure source of food and water, energy, financial stability, and medical care. Being an independent-minded individual or family is about taking control of your own life and being prepared for any eventualities.

12. Importance of Self-Sustained Preparedness

Self-sustained preparedness refers to the ability of individuals and families to provide for their own needs and be prepared for any eventualities. In today's fast-paced and unpredictable world, self-sustained preparedness has become increasingly important for individuals and families who want to take control of their own lives and be prepared for any eventualities.

Protects Against Disruptions

One of the key reasons why self-sustained preparedness is so important is that it protects against disruptions. In today's world, disruptions can come in many forms, including natural disasters, economic downturns, and pandemics. By being self-sustained and prepared for any eventualities, individuals and families can minimize the impact of these disruptions and be better equipped to provide for their own needs.

For example, in the event of a natural disaster, self-sustained individuals and families are better prepared to provide for their own needs, as they have a secure source of food and water, energy, financial stability, and medical care. Similarly, in the event of a financial crisis, self-sustained individuals and families are better prepared to weather the storm, as they have a secure source of income and a savings plan in place.

Increases Personal Freedom

Another reason why self-sustained preparedness is so important is that it increases personal freedom. When individuals and families are self-sufficient and prepared for any eventualities, they are not dependent on external sources for their basic needs. This gives them a sense of control and freedom in their lives, as they are able to provide for themselves and their families.

For example, self-sustained individuals and families may have a garden or farm where they grow their own food, or a water collection and storage system, which provides them with a secure source of food and water. Similarly, they may have a renewable energy source, such as solar or wind power, which provides them with energy independence.

Promotes Personal Growth

Self-sustained preparedness also promotes personal growth. By taking control of their own lives and being prepared for any eventualities, individuals and families can develop new skills and knowledge, which can help to increase their personal and professional growth.

For example, individuals and families who are self-sustained may learn new skills such as gardening, composting, or emergency preparedness. These skills can help to increase their knowledge and understanding of self-sustained preparedness and can provide a sense of accomplishment and fulfillment.

Builds Stronger Communities

Self-sustained preparedness also helps to build stronger communities. When individuals and families are self-sufficient and prepared for any eventualities, they are more likely to participate in local preparedness efforts and to network with like-minded individuals.

For example, self-sustained individuals and families may participate in community gardening projects, composting initiatives, or local disaster preparedness efforts. This can help to build a sense of community and to bring people together around a common goal.

Increases Financial Stability

Self-sustained preparedness can also help to increase financial stability. By being self-sufficient and prepared for any eventualities, individuals and families can reduce their dependence on external sources, which can result in significant cost savings.

For example, self-sustained individuals and families may be able to reduce their energy bills by using renewable energy sources or reduce their food expenses by growing their own food. Similarly, they may be able to reduce their medical expenses by investing in their own health and wellness and being prepared for any medical emergencies.

Bottom Line
The importance of self-sustained preparedness cannot be overstated. It protects against disruptions, increases personal freedom, promotes personal growth, builds stronger communities, and increases financial stability. By being

self-sustained and prepared for any eventualities, individuals and families can take control of their own lives and be better equipped to provide for their own needs, regardless of the circumstances.

13. Understanding Self-Sustained Preparedness

Self-sustained preparedness refers to the ability of individuals and families to provide for their own needs and be prepared for any eventualities. This includes having a secure source of food and water, energy, financial stability, and medical care, as well as being prepared for emergencies and disasters.

Key Components of Self-Sustained Preparedness

The key components of self-sustained preparedness include:

- Food and water security
- Energy independence
- Financial preparedness
- Health and medical preparedness

Food and water security refers to having a secure source of food and water that is not dependent on external sources. This includes having a garden or farm where individuals and families can grow their own food, having a water collection and storage system, and being prepared to store food for emergencies.

Energy independence refers to having a secure source of energy that is not dependent on external sources. This includes investing in renewable energy sources such as solar and wind power, and implementing energy-efficient practices in homes and lifestyles.

Financial preparedness refers to having a secure source of income that is not dependent on external sources. This includes investing in education and career development, having a savings plan and emergency fund in place, and being prepared for financial emergencies.

Health and medical preparedness refers to being prepared for any health emergencies and having a secure source of medical care that is not dependent on external sources. This includes having a well-stocked first aid kit, investing in health and wellness, and being prepared to provide for medical needs in case of a disaster or emergency.

Building a Self-Sustained Home

One of the key components of self-sustained preparedness is building a self-sustained home. A self-sustained home is designed to provide for the basic needs of individuals and families, including food and water security, energy independence, and health and medical preparedness.

Building a self-sustained home involves designing a home that is sustainable and energy-efficient, and implementing sustainable practices such as composting, recycling, and gardening. This can help to reduce the dependence on external sources and to provide for the basic needs of individuals and families.

Preparing for Emergencies and Disasters

Another important component of self-sustained preparedness is preparing for emergencies and disasters. This includes developing a disaster plan, building an emergency kit, and evacuation planning.

A disaster plan is a plan that outlines the steps individuals and families should take in the event of a disaster or emergency. This includes having a secure place to go, having a means of communication, and having a supply of food, water, and other essential supplies.

Disasters can happen at any time and can disrupt daily life, causing stress and uncertainty. Having a disaster plan in place can help individuals and families be prepared and reduce the impact of a disaster. Here is an outline of a disaster plan for individuals and families:

Identify Potential Hazards

The first step in creating a disaster plan is to identify potential hazards that could affect your area. This could include natural disasters such as hurricanes, earthquakes, or wildfires, or man-made disasters such as power outages or chemical spills.

Assemble an Emergency Kit

The next step is to assemble an emergency kit. This kit should include items such as food, water, first aid supplies, clothing, and important documents. It should also include items such as a flashlight, battery-operated radio, and a cell phone charger. The emergency kit should be easily accessible and stored in a safe place.

Choose an Emergency Meeting Place

Choose an emergency meeting place where family members can go to if they are separated during a disaster. This could be a nearby park, a friend's house, or a designated meeting place such as a school or community center.

Develop a Communication Plan

Develop a communication plan for staying in touch with family members during a disaster. This could include having a designated person to call, having a designated meeting place, or using a designated social media platform to communicate.

Create an Evacuation Plan

Create an evacuation plan for leaving your home if necessary. This plan should include a designated evacuation route, a designated evacuation destination, and a plan for transportation.

Prepare a Financial Plan

Prepare a financial plan for managing finances during a disaster. This could include having a savings account, having a plan for accessing funds in an emergency, and having insurance coverage for your home and belongings.

Review and Update Plan Regularly

It is important to review and update your disaster plan regularly. This could include updating contact information, emergency meeting places, and emergency kits.

Bottom Line
Having a disaster plan in place can help individuals and families be prepared for any eventualities. By following these steps, individuals and families can reduce the impact of a disaster and increase their chances of staying safe and secure during a crisis.

Having an emergency kit can help provide peace of mind and increase the chances of staying safe and secure during a crisis. By including these essential items in your emergency kit, individuals and families can be prepared for any eventualities and better equipped to provide for their own needs during a disaster.

Evacuation planning involves having a plan in place for evacuating in the event of a disaster or emergency. This includes having a means of transportation, having a secure place to go, and having a plan for reuniting with family members.

14. Key Components of Self-Sustained Preparedness

Self-sustained preparedness refers to the ability of individuals and families to provide for their own needs and be prepared for any eventualities. It is a proactive approach to life that empowers individuals and families to take control of their own lives and be prepared for any eventualities, regardless of the circumstances. The key components of self-sustained preparedness include food and water security, energy independence, financial preparedness, and health and medical preparedness.

Food and Water Security

Food and water security is a critical component of self-sustained preparedness. In the event of a disaster or emergency, access to food and water can be disrupted, making it essential to have a secure source of these necessities.

Food security can be achieved by having a garden or farm where individuals and families can grow their own food, or by having a well-stocked pantry and emergency food supplies. In addition, it is important to have a water collection and storage system, and to be prepared to store food for emergencies.

Water security is equally important, and individuals and families should have a secure source of water that is not dependent on external sources. This can be achieved by having a water collection and storage system, or by investing in a water filtration system.

Energy Independence

Energy independence is another critical component of self-sustained preparedness. In the event of a disaster or emergency, access to energy can be disrupted, making it essential to have a secure source of energy that is not dependent on external sources.

Energy independence can be achieved by investing in renewable energy sources such as solar or wind power, or by implementing energy-efficient practices in homes and lifestyles. This can help to reduce the dependence on external sources and to provide for the energy needs of individuals and families.

Financial Preparedness

Financial preparedness is an important component of self-sustained preparedness. In the event of a disaster or emergency, access to financial resources can be disrupted, making it essential to have a secure source of income that is not dependent on external sources.

Financial preparedness can be achieved by investing in education and career development, having a savings plan and emergency fund in place, and being prepared for financial emergencies. This can help to increase financial stability and reduce the dependence on external sources.

Health and Medical Preparedness

Health and medical preparedness is a critical component of self-sustained preparedness. In the event of a disaster or emergency, access to medical care can be disrupted, making it essential to have a secure source of medical care that is not dependent on external sources.

Health and medical preparedness can be achieved by having a well-stocked first aid kit, investing in health and wellness, and being prepared to provide for medical needs in case of a disaster or emergency. This can help to increase the overall health and well-being of individuals and families.

Bottom Line
The key components of self-sustained preparedness include food and water security, energy independence, financial preparedness, and health and medical preparedness. By taking control of these areas, individuals and families can be prepared for any eventualities and better equipped to provide for their own needs, regardless of the circumstances. By being self-sufficient and prepared, individuals and families can live a fulfilling and sustainable life that is not dependent on external factors.

15. Building a Self-Sustained Home

Building a self-sustained home is a critical component of self-sustained preparedness. A self-sustained home is designed to provide for the basic needs of individuals and families, including food and water security, energy independence, and health and medical preparedness.

Designing a Self-Sustained Home

Designing a sustainable home involves incorporating sustainable and energy-efficient practices into the design and construction of a home. This includes using environmentally friendly materials, such as bamboo flooring and recycled insulation, and implementing energy-efficient systems such as solar panels and energy-efficient appliances.

Energy Efficiency

Investing in renewable energy sources, such as solar and wind power, is another important component of building a self-sustained home. This can help reduce the dependence on external sources of energy and provide a secure source of energy in the event of a disaster or emergency.

Energy efficiency is an important component of self-sustained preparedness. It involves reducing the amount of energy used in a home or community, reducing dependence on external sources of energy, and improving energy independence.

Energy-Efficient Appliances and Lighting

Using energy-efficient appliances and lighting is an important component of energy efficiency. This includes using Energy Star-rated appliances, such as refrigerators and washing machines, and using LED lighting instead of traditional incandescent lighting.

Insulation and Weatherization

Insulating and weatherizing a home is another important component of energy efficiency. This includes adding insulation to walls, attics, and floors, and weatherizing windows and doors to reduce the amount of energy used for heating and cooling.

Renewable Energy Sources

Investing in renewable energy sources, such as solar and wind power, is an important component of energy efficiency. These sources of energy can provide a secure source of energy that is not dependent on external sources, and can reduce the amount of energy used from traditional sources.

Energy-Efficient Transportation

Using energy-efficient transportation, such as electric vehicles, is another component of energy efficiency. This can reduce the amount of energy used for transportation and reduce dependence on external sources of energy. Biking and walking are other forms of energy-efficient transportation. They are low-cost, healthy, and produce zero emissions. Biking and walking can be used for short trips, such as running errands or commuting, and can help reduce the amount of energy used for transportation. Energy efficiency is an important component of self-sustained preparedness. It involves reducing the amount of energy used in a home or community, reducing dependence on external sources of energy, and improving energy independence. By taking these steps, individuals and families can be better equipped to provide for their own energy needs and be prepared for any eventualities.

Water Collection and Storage

Building a water collection and storage system is an important component of building a self-sustained home. This includes having a system for collecting rainwater, such as a rain barrel or cistern, and a system for storing water, such as a water tank or well. This can help reduce the dependence on external sources of water and provide a secure source of water in the event of a disaster or emergency.

Food Production

Food production is an essential component of self-sustained preparedness. It involves growing and harvesting food in a sustainable and self-sufficient manner, providing a secure source of food that is not dependent on external sources.

Gardening and Farming

Gardening and farming are the primary methods of food production for self-sustained individuals and families. Gardening can involve growing a variety of fruits and vegetables in a backyard garden, while farming can involve growing crops on a larger scale. Both methods can provide a source of fresh produce and can help reduce the dependence on external sources of food.

Raising Livestock

Raising livestock, such as chickens, cows, and goats, is another method of food production for self-sustained individuals and families. Livestock can provide a source of meat, dairy, and eggs, and can also provide fertilizer for a garden.

Aquaponics and Hydroponics

Aquaponics and hydroponics are innovative methods of food production that involve growing plants in water, without soil. These methods can be used to grow a variety of fruits and vegetables, and can provide a source of food in areas where traditional gardening methods may not be feasible.

Food production is an essential component of self-sustained preparedness. It involves growing and harvesting food in a sustainable and self-sufficient manner, providing a secure source of food that is not dependent on external sources. By taking control of their food production, individuals and families can be prepared for any eventualities and better equipped to provide for their own needs.

Bottom Line

Building a self-sustained home involves incorporating sustainable and energy-efficient practices into the design and construction of a home, implementing sustainable practices, building a water collection and storage system, and investing in renewable energy sources. By taking these steps, individuals and families can provide for their own needs and be prepared for any eventualities, ensuring a fulfilling and sustainable future.

16. Implementing Sustainable Practices

Implementing sustainable practices in a home is an important component of building a self-sustained home. This includes composting, recycling, and gardening. Composting can help reduce waste and provide fertilizer for a garden, while recycling can help reduce the amount of waste sent to landfills. Gardening can provide a source of fresh produce and can also provide a source of exercise and relaxation.

Composting

Composting is a sustainable and environmentally friendly practice that is an important component of self-sustained preparedness. It involves breaking down organic waste, such as food scraps and yard waste, into a nutrient-rich soil amendment.

Benefits of Composting

Composting has many benefits, including reducing waste sent to landfills, providing a source of fertilizer for gardening and farming, and reducing the need for synthetic fertilizers. Composting can also improve soil health and structure, helping plants to grow stronger and healthier.

Composting Methods

There are several methods of composting, including traditional composting, vermicomposting, and bokashi composting. Traditional composting involves creating a compost pile and allowing organic waste to break down over time, while vermicomposting involves using worms to break down the organic waste. Bokashi composting is a method of composting food waste in an airtight container, using a special mix of microorganisms.

Composting at Home

Composting at home is easy and can be done in a backyard or on a balcony. A compost bin can be purchased or made from recycled materials, and organic waste can be added to the bin on a regular basis. The compost should be turned regularly to allow for proper aeration and to speed up the composting process.

In conclusion, composting is a sustainable and environmentally friendly practice that is an important component of self-sustained preparedness. It reduces waste sent to landfills, provides a source of fertilizer for gardening and farming, and reduces the need for synthetic fertilizers. By composting at home, individuals and families can reduce their waste and improve their environmental impact.

Recycling

Recycling is a critical component of self-sustained preparedness and a key part of reducing waste and conserving resources. It involves collecting and processing materials, such as paper, glass, plastic, and metal, that would otherwise be sent to a landfill.

Benefits of Recycling

Recycling has many benefits, including reducing the amount of waste sent to landfills, conserving natural resources, reducing greenhouse gas emissions, and saving energy. By recycling, individuals and families can reduce their environmental impact and help to create a sustainable future.

Types of Recyclable Materials

There are many types of recyclable materials, including paper, cardboard, glass, plastic, metal, and electronics. It is important to understand the types of materials that can be recycled and to properly sort and recycle these materials.

Recycling Programs

Recycling programs are available in many communities, and individuals and families can participate in these programs by properly sorting and recycling their waste. Some communities also offer curbside recycling pickup, making it easy and convenient to recycle.

Reducing Waste through Recycling

Reducing waste through recycling is an important component of self-sustained preparedness. This can be done by properly sorting recyclable materials, reducing the use of disposable items, and reusing items whenever possible.

Recycling is a critical component of self-sustained preparedness. It reduces waste sent to landfills, conserves natural resources, reduces greenhouse gas emissions, and saves energy. By properly sorting and recycling their waste, individuals and families can reduce their environmental impact and help to create a sustainable future.

Gardening and Agriculture

Gardening and agriculture are important components

of self-sustained preparedness. They provide a source of fresh produce, reduce dependence on external sources of food, and promote sustainable and environmentally friendly practices.

Types of Gardening

There are several types of gardening, including traditional gardening, container gardening, and vertical gardening. Traditional gardening involves growing crops in a backyard or community garden, while container gardening involves growing crops in pots or containers. Vertical gardening involves growing crops vertically, making it possible to grow crops in small spaces.

Agriculture

Agriculture involves growing crops on a larger scale, and can include traditional farming practices, such as growing crops in fields, or more innovative practices, such as hydroponics and aquaponics. Agriculture can provide a source of food for individuals and families, as well as a source of income.

Sustainable Agriculture

Sustainable agriculture is a type of agriculture that promotes environmentally friendly practices, such as using natural fertilizers and avoiding the use of harmful pesticides. Sustainable agriculture can help reduce the impact on the environment and provide a source of fresh, healthy produce.

Community Gardening and Agriculture

Community gardening and agriculture are important components of self-sustained preparedness. Community gardens and farms provide a source of fresh produce for individuals and families, and can also provide a source of community involvement and social interaction.

Bottom Line

Gardening and agriculture are important components of self-sustained preparedness. They provide a source of fresh produce, reduce dependence on external sources of food, and promote sustainable and environmentally friendly practices. By participating in gardening and agriculture, individuals and families can provide for their own food needs and be better equipped to prepare for any eventualities.

17. Preparing for Emergencies and Disasters

Preparing for emergencies and disasters is an important component of self-sustained preparedness. Disasters can strike at any time and can have significant impacts on individuals and families. Preparation can help reduce the impact of disasters and ensure that individuals and families are better equipped to respond and recover.

Developing a Disaster Plan

A disaster plan is another important component of preparedness. The plan should include information on evacuation routes, meeting places, and emergency contacts. The plan should be discussed and reviewed with all members of the household, including children.

Preparing for Specific Disasters

Preparing for specific disasters, such as hurricanes, earthquakes, and wildfires, is an important component of self-sustained preparedness. This may involve taking specific steps, such as securing loose items, creating an evacuation plan, and having a disaster supply kit on hand.

Community Preparedness

Community preparedness is also an important component of self-sustained preparedness. This may involve participating in community disaster drills, supporting local emergency responders, and working with neighbors to prepare for disasters.

Building an Emergency Kit

An emergency kit is a collection of essential items that individuals and families should have on hand in case of an emergency or disaster. Having an emergency kit can help provide peace of mind and increase the chances of staying safe and secure during a crisis. Here is an outline of items that should be included in an emergency kit:

Food and Water:
- Non-perishable food items such as granola bars, crackers, and canned goods
- A manual can opener
- At least 1 gallon of water per person, per day
- Water purification tablets or a water filtration system

First Aid Supplies:
- Band-aids, gauze, and adhesive tape
- Pain relievers such as ibuprofen and acetaminophen
- Antiseptic wipes or solution
- A first aid manual

Clothing and Bedding:
- A change of clothes for each person
- Warm blankets or sleeping bags
- Rain gear and waterproof shoes

Tools and Supplies:
- A flashlight with extra batteries
- A battery-operated radio
- A multi-tool or knife
- Duct tape and plastic sheeting
- A whistle and signal mirror

Personal Hygiene and Sanitation:
- Toilet paper
- Wet wipes or hand sanitizer
- Trash bags
- Personal hygiene items such as toothbrushes and toothpaste

Important Documents:
- Identification for each family member
- Insurance policies and important medical information
- Bank account and credit card information
- A list of emergency contact numbers

Miscellaneous:
- Cash in small denominations
- Matches or a lighter
- A map of the area
- A compass

It is important to regularly check and update the emergency kit to ensure that it contains the necessary supplies. The emergency kit should be easily accessible and stored in a safe place.

18. Evacuation Planning

Evacuation planning is a critical component of self-sustained preparedness and is an important part of preparing for emergencies and disasters. Evacuation planning involves preparing for the possibility of leaving your home due to a disaster, and ensuring that you have a safe and effective plan in place.

Identifying Evacuation Routes

Identifying evacuation routes is an important first step in evacuation planning. This may involve researching evacuation routes in your area and determining the best route to take in the event of an emergency. It is important to have multiple routes in case one route is blocked or unsafe.

Preparing an Evacuation Kit

Preparing an evacuation kit is another important step in evacuation planning. The kit should include items such as non-perishable food, water, a first aid kit, a flashlight, and a battery-powered radio. The kit should be easily accessible and stored in a safe place, such as a basement or closet.

Designating a Meeting Place

Designating a meeting place is an important component of evacuation planning. This may be a family member's home, a community center, or another designated location. The meeting place should be known by all members of the household and should be easy to locate.

Planning for Pets and Livestock

Planning for pets and livestock is an important component of evacuation planning. This may involve arranging for a safe place for pets and livestock to stay, or making arrangements to evacuate them with you.

Bottom Line
Evacuation planning is a critical component of self-sustained preparedness. By identifying evacuation routes, preparing an evacuation kit, designating a meeting place, and planning for pets and livestock, individuals and families can be better equipped to respond to emergencies and disasters and ensure their safety and well-being.

19. Building a Community of Self-Sustained Individuals

It is important to build a community of self-sustained individuals. This includes networking with like-minded individuals, sharing resources and knowledge, and participating in local preparedness efforts.

Building a community of self-sustained individuals can help to increase resilience and to provide support and resources in the event of a disaster or emergency. It can also help to build a sense of community and to bring people together around a common goal of self-sustained preparedness.

Understanding self-sustained preparedness involves understanding the key components of self-sustained preparedness, including food and water security, energy independence, financial preparedness, and health and medical preparedness. It also involves building a self-sustained home, preparing for emergencies and disasters, and building a community of self-sustained individuals. By taking these steps, individuals and families can take control of their own lives and be prepared for any eventualities, ensuring a fulfilling and sustainable future.

Benefits of Being Self-Sustained

Self-sustained individuals and families are those who are able to provide for their own needs and are not dependent on external sources. Being self-sustained has many benefits, both in terms of personal fulfillment and practical preparedness. In this section, we will explore the key benefits of being self-sustained.

Increased Resilience

One of the key benefits of being self-sustained is increased resilience. When individuals and families are self-sufficient, they are better prepared to withstand any disruptions or emergencies that may arise. This includes having a secure source of food and water, energy, financial stability, and medical care, which can help to mitigate the impact of any disruptions.

For example, in the event of a natural disaster, self-sustained individuals and families are better prepared to provide for their own needs and are less likely to be affected by shortages of food, water, or other essential supplies. Similarly, in the event of a financial crisis, self-sustained individuals and families are better prepared to weather the storm, as they have a secure source of income and a savings plan in place.

Increased Independence

Another benefit of being self-sustained is increased independence. When individuals and families are self-sufficient, they are not dependent on external sources for their basic needs. This gives them a sense of control and independence in their lives, as they are able to provide for themselves and their families.

For example, self-sustained individuals and families may have a garden or farm where they grow their own food, or a water collection and storage system, which provides them with a secure source of food and water. Similarly, they may have a renewable energy source, such as solar or wind power, which provides them with energy independence.

Increased Sense of Fulfillment

Being self-sustained can also lead to an increased sense of fulfillment. When individuals and families are self-sufficient, they are able to live a life that is not dependent on external factors. This can give them a sense of pride and satisfaction in their ability to provide for themselves and their families.

For example, self-sustained individuals and families may take pride in growing their own food, using renewable energy sources, or being prepared for emergencies. These activities can provide a sense of accomplishment and fulfillment, as they are able to take control of their own lives and provide for their own needs.

Increased Savings

Being self-sustained can also lead to increased savings. When individuals and families are self-sufficient, they are able to reduce their dependence on external sources, which can result in significant cost savings.

For example, self-sustained individuals and families may be able to reduce their energy bills by using renewable energy sources, or reduce their food expenses by growing their own food. Similarly, they may be able to reduce their medical expenses by investing in their own health and wellness and being prepared for any medical emergencies.

Increased Community Involvement

Being self-sustained can also lead to increased community involvement. When individuals and families are self-sufficient, they are often more likely to participate in local preparedness efforts and to network with like-minded individuals.

For example, self-sustained individuals and families may participate in community gardening projects, composting initiatives, or local disaster preparedness efforts. This can help to build a sense of community and to bring people together around a common goal.

Bottom Line
Being self-sustained has many benefits, including increased resilience, independence, fulfillment, savings, and community involvement. By being self-sufficient and prepared for any eventualities, individuals and families can live a fulfilling and sustainable life that is not dependent on external factors. They can provide for their own needs, including food and water security, energy independence, financial stability, and health and medical preparedness, which can help to mitigate the impact of any disruptions or emergencies.

In addition, being self-sustained can lead to increased savings, as individuals and families are able to reduce their dependence on external sources. This can result in significant cost savings in areas such as energy, food, and medical expenses.

Being self-sustained also can lead to increased community involvement, as individuals and families are more likely to participate in local preparedness efforts and to network with like-minded individuals. This can help to build a sense of community and bring people together around a common goal.

The benefits of being self-sustained are numerous and far-reaching, encompassing both personal fulfillment and practical preparedness. By taking control of their own lives and being prepared for any eventualities, individuals and families can live a fulfilling and sustainable life that is not dependent on external factors.

20. Building a Community of Self-Sustained Individuals

Building a community of self-sustained individuals is an important component of self-sustained preparedness. A community of self-sustained individuals can provide support, resources, and assistance in times of need, and can help to create a resilient and sustainable future.

Building Community Networks

Building community networks is an important step in building a community of self-sustained individuals. This may involve connecting with neighbors, joining community groups, and participating in community events. Building community networks can provide a sense of community, support, and connection.

Sharing Resources and Knowledge

Sharing resources and knowledge is another important component of building a community of self-sustained individuals. This may involve sharing resources, such as tools, seeds, and equipment, as well as sharing knowledge and skills, such as gardening, composting, and energy efficiency. Sharing resources and knowledge can help to build a more resilient and sustainable community.

Collaborating on Projects

Collaborating on projects is another important component of building a community of self-sustained individuals. This may involve working together on community gardens, renewable energy projects, or disaster preparedness initiatives. Collaborating on projects can help to build community spirit, create a sense of shared purpose, and achieve common goals.

Supporting Local Businesses

Supporting local businesses is another important component of building a community of self-sustained individuals. This may involve shopping at local stores, supporting local farmers, and participating in local markets. Supporting local businesses can help to create a sustainable local economy and reduce dependence on external sources.

In conclusion, building a community of self-sustained individuals is an important component of self-sustained preparedness. By building community networks, sharing resources and knowledge, collaborating on projects, and supporting local businesses, individuals and families can create a resilient and sustainable community that is better equipped to respond to emergencies and disasters.

Networking with Like-Minded Individuals

Networking with like-minded individuals is an important component of self-sustained preparedness. Connecting with others who share similar values and goals can provide support, resources, and inspiration, and can help to build a stronger and more resilient community.

Joining Community Organizations and Groups

Joining community organizations and groups is a great way to network with like-minded individuals. This may involve joining community gardens, renewable energy groups, or disaster preparedness organizations. Joining these organizations and groups can provide opportunities to connect with others who share similar interests and goals.

Participating in Local Events and Workshops

Participating in local events and workshops is another way to network with like-minded individuals. This may involve attending local fairs, festivals, and workshops on topics such as gardening, renewable energy, and disaster preparedness. Attending these events and workshops can provide opportunities to learn and connect with others who share similar interests.

Connecting Online

Connecting online is another way to network with like-minded individuals. This may involve joining online forums, social media groups, and discussion boards on topics such as self-sustained preparedness, renewable energy, and sustainable living. Connecting online can provide opportunities to connect with others from around the world and share resources and knowledge.

Building Local Networks

Building local networks is another important component of networking with like-minded individuals. This may involve connecting with neighbors, participating in local events and activities, and working with local organizations and businesses. Building local networks can provide opportunities to connect with others in the community and build a stronger and more resilient community.

Networking with like-minded individuals is an important component of self-sustained preparedness. By joining community organizations and groups, participating in local events and workshops, connecting online, and building local networks, individuals and families can connect with others who share similar interests and goals and build a stronger and more resilient community.

Sharing Resources and Knowledge

Sharing resources and knowledge is an important component of self-sustained preparedness and can help to build a stronger and more resilient community. Sharing resources and knowledge can provide opportunities for individuals and families to learn from one another, access resources that they may not have otherwise, and support one another in times of need.

Sharing Skills and Expertise

Sharing skills and expertise is an important component of sharing resources and knowledge. This may involve teaching others about gardening, renewable energy, or disaster preparedness, or learning from others about these topics. Sharing skills and expertise can provide opportunities to learn and grow, and can help to build a more knowledgeable and self-sufficient community.

Sharing Tools and Equipment

Sharing tools and equipment is another important component of sharing resources and knowledge. This may involve sharing tools, such as gardening tools, power tools, and hand tools, or equipment, such as generators, solar panels, and water storage systems. Sharing tools and equipment can help to reduce costs, conserve resources, and build a more resilient community.

Sharing Information and Resources

Sharing information and resources is another important component of sharing resources and knowledge. This may involve sharing resources, such as books, articles, and websites, or information about local resources, such as community gardens, farmers markets, and local businesses. Sharing information and resources can help to build a more informed and connected community.

Collaborating on Projects

Collaborating on projects is another important component of sharing resources and knowledge. This may involve working together on community gardens, renewable energy projects, or disaster preparedness initiatives. Collaborating on projects can provide opportunities to share resources, knowledge, and skills, and can help to build a stronger and more resilient community.

Sharing resources and knowledge is an important component of self-sustained preparedness. By sharing skills and expertise, tools and equipment, information and resources, and collaborating on projects, individuals and families can build a stronger and more resilient community and be better equipped to prepare for emergencies and disasters.

Participating in Local Preparedness Efforts

Participating in local preparedness efforts is an important component of self-sustained preparedness and can help to build a stronger and more resilient community. Local preparedness efforts can include community disaster drills, neighborhood watch programs, and community disaster response teams.

Community Disaster Drills

Community disaster drills are important components of local preparedness efforts. Disaster drills can help individuals and families practice evacuation procedures, test emergency response plans, and identify areas for improvement. Participating in community disaster drills can help to build community preparedness and ensure that individuals and families are better equipped to respond to emergencies and disasters.

Neighborhood Watch Programs

Neighborhood watch programs are another important component of local preparedness efforts. Neighborhood watch programs involve neighbors working together to identify and report suspicious activity and to ensure the safety of their community. Participating in neighborhood watch programs can help to build community safety and preparedness and ensure that individuals and families are better equipped to respond to emergencies and disasters.

Community Disaster Response Teams

Community disaster response teams are another important component of local preparedness efforts. Disaster response teams are trained to respond to emergencies and disasters, and can provide support and assistance to individuals and families in times of need. Participating in community disaster response teams can help to build community preparedness and ensure that individuals and families are better equipped to respond to emergencies and disasters.

Supporting Local Emergency Responders

Supporting local emergency responders is another important component of local preparedness efforts. This may involve volunteering, making donations, or participating in community events that support local emergency responders. Supporting local emergency responders can help to build community preparedness and ensure that individuals and families are better equipped to respond to emergencies and disasters.

Bottom Line

Participating in local preparedness efforts is an important component of self-sustained preparedness. By participating in community disaster drills, neighborhood watch programs, community disaster response teams, and supporting local emergency responders, individuals and families can build a stronger and more resilient community and be better equipped to prepare for emergencies and disasters.

PART TWO CONCLUSION

In conclusion, self-sustained preparedness is a comprehensive approach to preparing for emergencies and disasters that emphasizes self-sufficiency, resilience, and community involvement. Key components of self-sustained preparedness include building a self-sustained home, growing food, increasing energy efficiency, preparing for emergencies and disasters, building a community of self-sustained individuals, networking with like-minded individuals, sharing resources and knowledge, and participating in local preparedness efforts. By taking a proactive approach to self-sustained preparedness, individuals and families can increase their resilience, reduce their dependence on external sources, and be better equipped to respond to emergencies and disasters.

Recap of Key Points

- Self-sustained preparedness is a comprehensive approach to preparing for emergencies and disasters that emphasizes self-sufficiency, resilience, and community involvement.

- Building a self-sustained home, growing food, increasing energy efficiency, preparing for emergencies and disasters, and participating in local preparedness efforts are key components of self-sustained preparedness.

- Building a community of self-sustained individuals, networking with like-minded individuals, and sharing resources and knowledge can help to build a stronger and more resilient community.

- Preparing for emergencies and disasters involves having an emergency kit, a disaster plan, and taking steps to prepare for specific disasters.

- Evacuation planning is a critical component of self-sustained preparedness and involves preparing for the possibility of leaving your home due to a disaster.

- Participating in local preparedness efforts, such as community disaster drills, neighborhood watch programs, and community disaster response teams, can help to build community preparedness and ensure that individuals and families are better equipped to respond to emergencies and disasters.

- By taking a proactive approach to self-sustained preparedness, individuals and families can increase their resilience, reduce their dependence on external sources, and be better equipped to respond to emergencies and disasters.

Final Thoughts on the Importance of Self-Sustained Preparedness

As a former Green Beret, I can attest to the importance of self-sustained preparedness in times of crisis. In the field, we are often required to operate in austere environments with limited resources, and self-sustained preparedness is key to our success.

The principles of self-sustained preparedness are equally important for individuals and families in every-day life. In times of crisis, having the skills, resources, and community support to meet your basic needs can be the difference between survival and hardship.

Self-sustained preparedness is not just about being able to survive in a disaster, but also about creating a more resilient and sustainable future. By taking steps to increase energy efficiency, grow food, and participate in local preparedness efforts, individuals and families can reduce their dependence on external sources, increase their resilience, and build a stronger and more sustainable community.

In conclusion, the importance of self-sustained preparedness cannot be overstated. By taking a proactive approach to preparedness and building a self-sufficient and resilient community, individuals and families can be better equipped to respond to emergencies and disasters and create a more sustainable future.

PART THREE: VEHICLE PREPAREDNESS

21. The Importance of Being Prepared

The world is an unpredictable place. Natural disasters, economic recessions, pandemics, and other unexpected events can strike at any moment, leaving individuals and communities vulnerable and unprepared. In such circumstances, those who have taken the time and effort to prepare themselves and their families for the unexpected are often the ones who come out on top.

The importance of being prepared cannot be overstated. Preparation can take many forms, from having a well-stocked pantry to having a comprehensive emergency plan in place. Regardless of the specific type of preparation, the overarching principle is the same: by taking proactive steps to anticipate and mitigate potential risks, individuals and families can minimize the negative impact of unexpected events and maintain their safety and security.

One of the key benefits of being prepared is that it can help individuals and families weather economic hardships. Recessions and other economic downturns can cause significant financial strain for many people, often leading to job losses, reduced incomes, and increased expenses. By building up a financial cushion in advance of such events, individuals can be better positioned to weather the storm and avoid falling into poverty or financial ruin.

Similarly, being prepared can help individuals and families cope with natural disasters. Hurricanes, earthquakes, floods, and other natural disasters can cause significant damage to homes and property, and can also disrupt access to basic necessities like food and water. By having emergency supplies and a well-thought-out evacuation plan, individuals and families can increase their chances of staying safe and minimizing property damage in the event of a disaster.

Another benefit of being prepared is that it can help individuals and families cope with unexpected health crises. In the wake of the COVID-19 pandemic, many people have been forced to grapple with illness, hospitalization, and even death. By taking proactive steps to build up their physical and emotional resilience, individuals can increase their chances of recovering quickly from illness and maintaining their mental and emotional wellbeing in the face of stress and trauma.

Of course, being prepared is not just important for individuals and families. Businesses, organizations, and even entire countries can benefit from preparation as well. In the business world, companies that have contingency plans in place for unexpected events are often better positioned to weather economic downturns, adapt to changing market conditions, and respond to emergencies like data breaches or natural disasters. Similarly, governments that have robust emergency management systems in place are better positioned to respond to natural disasters, pandemics, and other crises, and can ensure that critical infrastructure like hospitals, water treatment facilities, and power plants continue to function even in the face of adversity.

Despite the clear benefits of being prepared, however, there are many people who remain skeptical of the value of proactive planning. Some argue that preparing for the worst is unnecessary or even counterproductive, as it can lead to paranoia or excessive anxiety. Others may feel that they simply don't have the time, resources, or energy to prepare for potential risks.

To some extent, these concerns are valid. It is true that preparing for the worst can sometimes be time-consuming, expensive, or emotionally draining. However, the risks of not being prepared are far greater. Without a plan in place, individuals and families are more vulnerable to economic hardship, natural disasters, and health crises. They may also be more likely to experience feelings of stress, anxiety, and helplessness in the face of adversity.

Furthermore, being prepared does not necessarily mean living in a state of constant fear or anxiety. In fact, many people who take proactive steps to prepare for the unexpected report feeling more confident, empowered, and in control of their lives. By knowing that they have taken steps to mitigate potential risks, they are better able to focus on the present moment and enjoy life to the fullest.

Ultimately, the importance of being prepared cannot be overstated. By taking proactive steps to anticipate and mitigate potential risks.

Why a Vehicle System Is a Crucial Component of Preparedness

In today's world, where natural disasters, economic downturns, and other unexpected events seem to be occurring with increasing frequency, being prepared is more important than ever. One key component of preparedness is having a reliable vehicle system in place that can help individuals and families navigate unexpected challenges and emergencies. In this book, we will explore the reasons why a vehicle system is a crucial component of preparedness.

The first reason why a vehicle system is crucial for preparedness is that it allows individuals and families to, quickly and safely, evacuate in the event of a natural disaster or other emergency. Hurricanes, earthquakes, and wildfires can strike with little warning, leaving people with only a short window of time to gather their belongings and evacuate. In such circumstances, having a reliable vehicle that is well-stocked with emergency supplies can mean the difference between life and death.

For example, in the wake of Hurricane Katrina in 2005, thousands of people were left stranded in New Orleans, unable to evacuate due to flooded roads and bridges. Many of these people lacked access to food, water, and medical supplies, and were forced to endure harrowing conditions for days or even weeks. By contrast, those who had a reliable vehicle system in place were able to evacuate quickly and safely, and were better positioned to weather the aftermath of the storm.

The second reason why a vehicle system is crucial for preparedness is that it allows individuals and families to access necessary resources in the event of an emergency. In the wake of a natural disaster or other emergency, access to food, water, and medical supplies may be limited or nonexistent. By having a well-stocked vehicle that includes emergency supplies like non-perishable food, water filtration systems, and first-aid kits, individuals and families can ensure that they have access to these critical resources when they need them most.

Moreover, a vehicle system can allow individuals and families to travel to areas that are better equipped to handle emergencies. For example, in the event of a major power outage, individuals and families may be able to travel to an area that has power and access to basic necessities like food and water. Similarly, in the event of a natural disaster, individuals and families may be able to travel to an area that has access to medical care and other resources that are critical to their survival.

The third reason why a vehicle system is crucial for preparedness is that it can serve as a means of protection and security in the event of a crisis. In times of crisis, law and order may break down, leaving individuals and families vulnerable to theft, violence, and other crimes. By having a reliable vehicle system in place, individuals and families can protect themselves and their belongings, and can quickly travel to areas that are safer and more secure.

For example, in the wake of Hurricane Katrina, many people who were stranded in New Orleans reported being subject to violence, looting, and other crimes. By contrast, those who had a reliable vehicle system in place were able to quickly evacuate and travel to areas that were more secure and protected.

A vehicle system can be a crucial component of economic preparedness, particularly for individuals and families who live in rural or remote areas. In the event of an economic downturn or other crisis, access to goods and services may be limited or nonexistent, particularly in areas that are far removed from urban centers. By having a reliable vehicle that is capable of off-road travel and that is well-stocked with emergency supplies, individuals and families can ensure that they have access to the goods and services they need, regardless of the state of the economy.

Bottom Line

A vehicle system is a crucial component of preparedness, particularly in today's world where natural disasters, economic downturns, and other unexpected events are becoming increasingly common. By having a reliable vehicle that is well-stocked with emergency supplies, individuals and families can quickly and safely evacuate in the event of a natural disaster or other emergency, access necessary resources when they are in short supply, and protect themselves and their belongings in times of crisis. Moreover, a vehicle system can be a means of economic preparedness, particularly for those who live in rural or remote areas.

It is important to note that relying solely on government agencies or first responders during an emergency can be risky. Such agencies may be overwhelmed or under-resourced, particularly in the aftermath of a natural disaster or other crisis. By contrast, having a reliable vehicle system in place can ensure that individuals and families are able to take action and respond to emergencies quickly and effectively, without having to rely on others for help.

Of course, building a reliable vehicle system for preparedness requires careful planning and attention to detail. Individuals and families must assess their needs and resources, choose the right vehicle for their needs, and stock it with the appropriate emergency supplies. Additionally, it may be necessary to invest in modifications or customizations to ensure that the vehicle is capable of off-road travel or other specialized functions.

To repeat, a vehicle system is a crucial component of preparedness, particularly in today's world where natural disasters, economic downturns, and other unexpected events are becoming more common. By having a well-stocked vehicle that is capable of off-road travel, individuals and families can quickly and safely evacuate in the event of an emergency, access necessary resources, and protect themselves and their belongings in times of crisis. Moreover, a reliable vehicle system can be a means of economic preparedness, particularly for those who live in rural or remote areas. With careful planning and attention to detail, individuals and families can build a vehicle system that helps them to be prepared for whatever the future may bring.

22. Assessing Your Needs and Resources

Identifying Scenarios

In today's world, where natural disasters, economic downturns, and other unexpected events are becoming increasingly common, being prepared is more important than ever. One key component of preparedness is identifying the scenarios you need to prepare for. By understanding the potential risks and challenges that you may face, you can take proactive steps to anticipate and mitigate those risks, and ensure that you are well-prepared for whatever the future may bring.

It is important to note that individuals and families bear a primary responsibility for preparing themselves for potential risks and challenges. While government agencies and other organizations may be able to provide some resources and support in times of crisis, it is ultimately up to individuals and families to take responsibility for their own safety and security, and to anticipate and prepare for potential risks and challenges.

The first step in identifying the scenarios you need to prepare for is to understand the different types of natural disasters and other emergencies that may occur in your area. This can include hurricanes, earthquakes, wildfires, floods, and other events that are common in your region. By understanding the potential risks associated with these events, you can take proactive steps to prepare your home and vehicle for potential damage or disruption.

For example, if you live in an area that is prone to hurricanes, you may need to prepare your home and vehicle for strong winds, heavy rains, and flooding. This may involve installing hurricane shutters, securing loose out-door items, and ensuring that your vehicle is equipped with emergency supplies like water, non-perishable food, and first-aid kits.

The second step in identifying the scenarios you need to prepare for is to understand the economic and social challenges that may arise in times of crisis. This can include job loss, food and water shortages, and disruptions in essential services like healthcare and transportation.

By understanding the potential economic and social challenges associated with different types of emergencies and unexpected events, you can take proactive steps to prepare your finances and resources. This may involve building up a financial cushion, stocking your home and vehicle with emergency supplies, and identifying sources of food and water in your area.

The third step in identifying the scenarios you need to prepare for is to understand the potential health risks associated with different types of emergencies and unexpected events. This can include exposure to hazardous materials, waterborne illnesses, and other health risks that may arise in the aftermath of a natural disaster or other crisis.

By understanding the potential health risks associated with different types of emergencies, you can take proactive steps to prepare your home and vehicle for potential exposure to hazardous materials, and to stock up on medical supplies and equipment that may be necessary in the event of an emergency.

The fourth step in identifying the scenarios you need to prepare for is to understand the potential risks associated with civil unrest or other social disturbances. This can include rioting, looting, and other forms of social unrest that may arise in the aftermath of a natural disaster or other crisis.

By understanding the potential risks associated with civil unrest or other social disturbances, you can take proactive steps to ensure your personal safety and security. This may involve preparing your home and vehicle with security measures like alarms and locks, and stocking up on non-lethal self-defense items like pepper spray or tasers.

Identifying the scenarios you need to prepare for is a crucial component of preparedness, particularly in today's world where natural disasters, economic downturns, and other unexpected events are becoming more common. By understanding the potential risks and challenges associated with different types of emergencies and unexpected events, individuals and families can take proactive steps to prepare their homes and vehicles, build up their resources, and ensure their personal safety and security. As a conservative it is important to note that individuals and families bear a primary responsibility for preparing themselves for potential risks and challenges, and should take proactive steps to ensure their own safety and security. While government agencies and other organizations may be able to provide some resources and support in times of crisis, it is ultimately up to individuals and families to take responsibility for their own preparedness.

By being proactive in identifying the scenarios you need to prepare for, you can be better equipped to weather unexpected events and minimize their impact on your life. This reflects a conservative approach to preparedness, which values self-reliance, personal responsibility, and the ability to take action in the face of adversity.

Moreover, identifying the scenarios you need to prepare for can help to foster a culture of preparedness among individuals, families, and communities. By raising awareness of potential risks and challenges, and by providing practical guidance on how to prepare for them, individuals and families can work together to build resilient communities that are capable of weathering the storm.

In the end, the conservative approach to identifying the scenarios you need to prepare for is about being proactive and taking responsibility for your own safety and security. By understanding the potential risks and challenges associated with different types of emergencies and unexpected events, and by taking practical steps to prepare for them, you can be better equipped to face whatever the future may bring.

Assessing Resources, Budget and Time Constraints

One key component of preparedness is assessing your resources, budget, and time constraints. By understanding the resources you have available, and the limitations you may face, you can take proactive steps to prepare for potential risks and challenges in a realistic and effective manner.

It is important to note that individuals and families bear a primary responsibility for preparing themselves for potential risks and challenges. While government agencies and other organizations may be able to provide some resources and support in times of crisis, it is ultimately up to individuals and families to take responsibility for their own safety and security, and to assess their resources, budget, and time constraints in order to effectively prepare for potential risks and challenges.

The first step in assessing your resources, budget, and time constraints is to take an inventory of the resources you have available. This may include financial resources, physical resources, and human resources. By understanding the resources you have available, you can begin to identify potential gaps and limitations that may need to be addressed in order to effectively prepare for potential risks and challenges.

For example, if you have limited financial resources, you may need to focus on building up your emergency supplies over time, rather than trying to purchase everything all at once. Similarly, if you have limited physical resources, such as a small living space, you may need to be creative in how you store your emergency supplies and equipment.

The second step in assessing your resources, budget, and time constraints is to set a budget for your preparedness efforts. By setting a budget, you can ensure that you are making the most effective use of your financial resources, and that you are able to prioritize the most important items and equipment.

For example, you may need to prioritize emergency supplies like water, non-perishable food, and first-aid kits, while postponing more expensive modifications to your home or vehicle.

The third step in assessing your resources, budget, and time constraints is to set realistic goals and timelines for your preparedness efforts. By setting realistic goals and timelines, you can avoid becoming overwhelmed by the scope of your preparedness efforts, and can ensure that you are able to make consistent progress over time.

For example, you may need to break down your preparedness efforts into smaller, manageable tasks, and set specific deadlines for each task. This can help you to stay focused and motivated, and to ensure that you are making consistent progress over time.

Assessing your resources, budget, and time constraints is a crucial component of preparedness, particularly in today's world where natural disasters, economic downturns, and other unexpected events are becoming more common. By understanding the resources you have available, setting a budget, and setting realistic goals and timelines, individuals and families can take proactive steps to prepare for potential risks and challenges in a realistic and effective manner. As a conservative angle, it is important to note that individuals and families bear a primary responsibility for preparing themselves for potential risks and challenges, and should assess their resources, budget, and time constraints in order to effectively prepare for potential risks and challenges. By being proactive in assessing your resources, budget, and time constraints, you can ensure that you are making the most effective use of your resources, and that you are able to prepare for potential risks and challenges in a realistic and effective manner.

Choosing the Right Vehicle

When it comes to building a vehicle system for preparedness, choosing the right vehicle is a critical component of success. The right vehicle can be the difference between safe evacuation during a natural disaster or being stranded in a dangerous situation. It is important to note that individuals and families bear a primary responsibility for preparing themselves for potential risks and challenges, and choosing the right vehicle for their needs is an important part of that responsibility.

The first step in choosing the right vehicle for your needs is to consider the type of terrain and weather conditions you may encounter in your area. If you live in an area with rough terrain or harsh weather, you may need a vehicle that is capable of off-road travel, has four-wheel drive, and can handle inclement weather conditions.

Additionally, you may need a vehicle that is capable of carrying emergency supplies, equipment, and other gear that may be necessary in the event of an emergency. This may include a roof rack, cargo carrier, or other accessories that can increase your storage capacity and make it easier to transport supplies and equipment.

The second step in choosing the right vehicle for your needs is to consider your budget and financial resources. While it may be tempting to choose the most expensive, fully-equipped vehicle on the market, it may not be the most practical option for your budget and financial resources.

Instead, it is important to carefully assess your financial resources and set a budget for your vehicle system. By setting a budget, you can ensure that you are able to make the most effective use of your financial resources and prioritize the most important features and equipment.

The third step in choosing the right vehicle for your needs is to consider your personal needs and preferences. This may include factors like the size of your family, your commuting and travel needs, and your personal driving preferences.

For example, if you have a large family, you may need a vehicle that is capable of carrying multiple passengers and has ample storage space for emergency supplies and equipment. Similarly, if you commute long distances or frequently travel in remote areas, you may need a vehicle that is fuel-efficient and has a long range.

The fourth step in choosing the right vehicle for your needs is to consider the reliability and durability of the vehicle. This is particularly important for those who are building a vehicle system for preparedness, as the vehicle may be used in emergency situations where reliability and durability are critical.

It is important to research the reliability and durability of different vehicles and models, and to choose a vehicle that has a good track record in these areas. Additionally, it may be necessary to invest in modifications or customizations to ensure that the vehicle is capable of off-road travel or other specialized functions.

Bottom Line

Choosing the right vehicle for your needs is a critical component of building a vehicle system for preparedness. By considering the type of terrain and weather conditions you may encounter in your area, assessing your budget and financial resources, considering your personal needs and preferences, and choosing a reliable and durable vehicle, individuals and families can ensure that they are well-prepared for potential risks and challenges. It is important to note that individuals and families bear a primary responsibility for preparing themselves for potential risks and challenges, and choosing the right vehicle for their needs is an important part of that responsibility. By being proactive in choosing the right vehicle for their needs, individuals and families can be better equipped to handle unexpected events and ensure their own safety and security.

23. Building a Foundation: Basic Vehicle Maintenance

Importance of Routine Maintenance

When it comes to building a vehicle system for preparedness, basic vehicle maintenance is a crucial component of success. Routine maintenance can help to ensure that your vehicle is in good working order and can handle the demands of emergency situations. It is important to note that individuals and families bear a primary responsibility for preparing themselves for potential risks and challenges, and routine maintenance is an important part of that responsibility.

The first step in building a foundation for basic vehicle maintenance is to understand the importance of routine maintenance. Regularly scheduled maintenance can help to prevent breakdowns and other issues that may arise in emergency situations, and can help to ensure that your vehicle is in good working order.

This can include routine tasks like changing the oil and filters, checking the tire pressure and tread depth, and inspecting the brakes and other critical components. By staying on top of routine maintenance tasks, you can ensure that your vehicle is in good working order and can handle the demands of emergency situations.

The second step in building a foundation for basic vehicle maintenance is to establish a regular maintenance schedule. This may involve creating a maintenance checklist that outlines the tasks that need to be performed at regular intervals, such as every 3,000 miles or every six months.

By establishing a regular maintenance schedule, you can ensure that you are staying on top of routine maintenance tasks and can catch any issues before they become major problems. Additionally, it can help to ensure that your vehicle is always ready for unexpected situations and emergency scenarios.

The third step in building a foundation for basic vehicle maintenance is to invest in the tools and equipment necessary to perform routine maintenance tasks. This may include basic tools like wrenches, screwdrivers, and pliers, as well as specialized equipment like a hydraulic jack and jack stands.

By investing in the tools and equipment necessary to perform routine maintenance tasks, you can save money on expensive repairs and maintenance fees, and can ensure that your vehicle is always in good working order.

The fourth step in building a foundation for basic vehicle maintenance is to develop a basic understanding of how your vehicle works. This may involve reading the owner's manual, attending a basic auto maintenance course, or consulting with a trusted mechanic.

By developing a basic understanding of how your vehicle works, you can better identify potential issues and perform routine maintenance tasks with confidence.

Building a foundation for basic vehicle maintenance is a crucial component of building a vehicle system for preparedness. By understanding the importance of routine maintenance, establishing a regular maintenance schedule, investing in the tools and equipment necessary to perform routine maintenance tasks, and developing a basic understanding of how your vehicle works, individuals and families can ensure that their vehicles are in good working order and can handle the demands of emergency situations. It is important to note that individuals and families bear a primary responsibility for preparing themselves for potential risks and challenges, and routine maintenance is an important part of that responsibility. By being proactive in performing routine maintenance tasks, individuals and families can save money on expensive repairs and maintenance fees, and can ensure that their vehicles are always ready for unexpected situations and emergency scenarios.

Developing a Maintenance Schedule

Developing a maintenance schedule is an essential part of vehicle ownership. Routine maintenance helps to keep a vehicle running smoothly and efficiently, and it can prevent costly repairs in the future. In addition, regular maintenance can be critical for preparedness, ensuring that the vehicle is always in good working order and ready for unexpected situations and emergency scenarios.

It is important to note that individuals and families bear a primary responsibility for preparing themselves for potential risks and challenges, and developing a maintenance schedule is an important part of that responsibility. By being proactive in developing a maintenance schedule, individuals and families can ensure that their vehicles are in good working order, save money on expensive repairs and maintenance fees, and be prepared for any situation.

The first step in developing a maintenance schedule is to consult the owner's manual for the vehicle. The owner's manual will provide specific guidelines for routine maintenance tasks, such as oil changes, filter replacements, and tire rotations. By following the manufacturer's recommended maintenance schedule, individuals can ensure that their vehicle is maintained according to the manufacturer's specifications.

The second step in developing a maintenance schedule is to consider the driving conditions in which the vehicle is operated. For example, if the vehicle is driven in dusty or dirty conditions, it may require more frequent air filter replacements. Similarly, if the vehicle is driven in extreme temperatures, it may require more frequent fluid changes.

The third step in developing a maintenance schedule is to create a maintenance checklist that outlines the specific tasks that need to be performed at regular intervals. This checklist should include both manufacturer-recommended maintenance tasks and any additional tasks that may be necessary based on the driving conditions of the vehicle.

The fourth step in developing a maintenance schedule is to establish a regular maintenance schedule. This schedule should be based on the manufacturer's recommended maintenance schedule, as well as any additional tasks identified in the maintenance checklist. The frequency of maintenance tasks will vary depending on the specific vehicle and driving conditions.

For example, oil changes are typically recommended every 3,000 to 5,000 miles, while air filter replacements may be required every 15,000 to 30,000 miles. By establishing a regular maintenance schedule, individuals and families can ensure that their vehicle is always in good working order and can handle the demands of emergency situations.

The fifth and final step in developing a maintenance schedule is to keep accurate records of all maintenance tasks performed. This can be done using a maintenance log or spreadsheet, and should include the date of the maintenance task, the type of task performed, and any notes or observations.

By keeping accurate records of all maintenance tasks performed, individuals and families can ensure that they are staying on top of routine maintenance tasks, and can track the performance of the vehicle over time. This can be particularly useful for identifying potential issues before they become major problems.

Your Off-Road Tool Kit

Putting together a tool kit for your off-road vehicle is essential for ensuring that you can perform repairs and maintenance on your vehicle in remote locations. Here are some tools and items that you should consider including in your off-road vehicle tool kit:

• *Wrenches and sockets* - Include a range of wrenches and sockets that fit the bolts and nuts on your vehicle, including both standard and metric sizes.

• *Pliers* - Include a range of pliers, such as needle-nose pliers, channel-lock pliers, and vise-grip pliers, which can be used for a variety of tasks.

• *Screwdrivers* - Include both Phillips and flat-head screwdrivers, in various sizes, to ensure that you have the right tool for any situation.

• *Hammer* - Include a small hammer, which can be used for a variety of tasks, such as removing stuck bolts or pounding out dents.

• *Duct tape and zip ties* - Include duct tape and zip ties, which can be used to temporarily fix a variety of problems, such as leaks or broken parts.

• *Tire repair kit* - Include a tire repair kit, which can be used to patch or plug a punctured tire and get you back on the road.

• *Jack and lug wrench* - Include a jack and lug wrench, which are essential for changing a flat tire or performing other repairs that require lifting the vehicle.

• *Multimeter* - Include a multimeter, which can be used to diagnose electrical problems and check the voltage and continuity of circuits.

• *Flashlight* - Include a reliable flashlight or headlamp, which can be used to see in dark areas or perform repairs in low-light conditions.

• *Spare fluids* - Include spare fluids, such as oil, coolant, and brake fluid, to ensure that you can top off or replace fluids as needed.

By including these tools and items in your off-road vehicle tool kit, you can be better prepared to handle a variety of repairs and maintenance tasks, which can help you stay safe and avoid getting stranded in remote locations. Here are some companies that make quality off-road tool kits:

• *ARB* – They offer a range of off-road tool kits, including the Speedy Seal puncture repair kit, which includes tools and materials for repairing punctured tires, as well as other tool kits that include a range of essential tools.

• *Smittybilt* – They also offer a range of off-road tool kits, including the Trail Tool Kit, which includes a range of essential tools and a carrying case.

• *Best Made Company* – Their products include the Vehicle Maintenance Tool Kit, which includes a range of essential tools for maintaining your vehicle.

• *Hi-Lift* – Their products include the Fix-It Kit, which includes tools for repairing and maintaining your vehicle.

• **Off-Road Vixens** – They make a range of off-road tool kits, including the Recovery Gear and Tool Bag, which includes a range of essential tools and recovery gear.

• **Tuff Stuff** – They offer a range of off-road tool kits, including the Adventure Kit, which includes a range of essential tools and gear for off-road adventures.

• **Baja Designs** – Their products include a range of off-road tool kits, including the Rock Guard Kit, which includes tools for protecting your vehicle's lights from damage on rough terrain.

These companies offer a variety of essential tools and gear for maintaining and repairing your vehicle in remote locations. When choosing an off-road tool kit, it is important to consider the types of tools included, the quality and durability of the tools, and the size and weight of the kit, to ensure that it is portable and easy to store in your vehicle. Additionally, consider the specific needs of your vehicle and off-road activities, and choose a kit that includes the tools and gear that you are most likely to need.

Developing a maintenance schedule is a critical component of vehicle ownership and preparedness. By consulting the owner's manual, considering driving conditions, creating a maintenance checklist, establishing a regular maintenance schedule, and keeping accurate records, individuals and families can ensure that their vehicle is always in good working order and can handle the demands of emergency situations. It is important to note that individuals and families bear a primary responsibility for preparing themselves for potential risks and challenges, and developing a maintenance schedule is an important part of that responsibility. By being proactive in developing a maintenance schedule, individuals and families can save money on expensive repairs and maintenance fees, and can ensure that their vehicles are always ready for unexpected situations and emergency scenarios.

Common Maintenance Tasks for Vehicles

Regular maintenance is crucial for keeping a vehicle in good working order and preventing expensive repairs. There are a variety of routine maintenance tasks that should be performed on a regular basis to ensure that a vehicle is operating efficiently and safely. As a conservative angle, it is important to note that individuals and families bear a primary responsibility for preparing themselves for potential risks and challenges, and performing regular maintenance on a vehicle is an important part of that responsibility.

Below is a list of common maintenance tasks for vehicles, along with the recommended intervals for performing each task:

• *Oil Changes:* Oil changes are one of the most important routine maintenance tasks for a vehicle. Fresh oil helps to lubricate the engine, prevent overheating, and improve fuel efficiency. Most manufacturers recommend oil changes every 3,000 to 5,000 miles, although some newer vehicles may be able to go longer between changes.

• *Air Filter Replacement:* The air filter helps to keep dirt and debris from entering the engine, and a dirty filter can reduce fuel efficiency and horsepower. Air filters should be replaced every 15,000 to 30,000 miles, depending on driving conditions.

• *Tire Rotations:* Rotating the tires helps to ensure even wear and can extend the life of the tires. Most manufacturers recommend tire rotations every 5,000 to 7,500 miles.

• *Brake Inspections:* The brakes are one of the most important safety features of a vehicle, and regular inspections can help to ensure that they are in good working order. Brake inspections should be performed at least once a year, or more frequently if there are signs of wear or damage.

• *Fluid Changes:* There are a variety of fluids that need to be changed on a regular basis, including transmission fluid, brake fluid, and coolant. Most manufacturers recommend changing these fluids every 30,000 to 50,000 miles, although this can vary depending on the specific vehicle and driving conditions.

• *Spark Plug Replacement:* Spark plugs help to ignite the fuel in the engine, and worn or dirty plugs can reduce fuel efficiency and horsepower. Most manufacturers recommend replacing spark plugs every 30,000 to 100,000 miles, depending on the type of plugs and driving conditions.

• *Battery Inspections:* The battery is a critical component of a vehicle's electrical system, and regular inspections can help to ensure that it is in good working order. Most manufacturers recommend inspecting the battery every six months, or more frequently if there are signs of wear or damage.

• *Wiper Blade Replacement:* Wiper blades help to keep the windshield clean and clear, and worn or damaged blades can reduce visibility. Most manufacturers recommend replacing wiper blades every six months to a year, depending on the driving conditions.

• *Belt and Hose Inspections:* The belts and hoses in a vehicle's engine are critical for powering and cooling systems, and regular inspections can help to ensure that they are in good working order. Most manufacturers recommend inspecting the belts and hoses every six months to a year, or more frequently if there are signs of wear or damage.

• *Cabin Air Filter Replacement:* The cabin air filter helps to keep the air inside the vehicle clean and free of pollutants. Most manufacturers recommend replacing the cabin air filter every 15,000 to 30,000 miles.

Bottom Line

Regular maintenance is essential for keeping a vehicle in good working order and preventing costly repairs. Common maintenance tasks for vehicles include oil changes, air filter replacement, tire rotations, brake inspections, fluid changes, spark plug replacement, battery inspections, wiper blade replacement, belt and hose inspections, and cabin air filter replacement. By performing these routine maintenance tasks at the recommended intervals, individuals and families can ensure that their vehicles are in good working order and ready for unexpected situations and emergency scenarios. As a conservative angle, it is important to note that individuals and families bear a primary responsibility for maintaining their vehicles and ensuring their safety on the road. Regular maintenance not only helps to prevent expensive repairs, but also helps to ensure the safe operation of a vehicle.

Moreover, it is important to note that routine maintenance can also have a positive impact on the environment. Regularly replacing air filters, for example, can help to reduce emissions and improve fuel efficiency. Additionally, properly inflated tires can help to improve fuel efficiency and reduce emissions.

By being proactive in performing regular maintenance tasks, individuals and families can save money on costly repairs and ensure that their vehicles are in good working order. This not only ensures their own safety on the road, but also helps to promote a responsible and sustainable approach to vehicle ownership.

24. Powering Your Vehicle System

Introduction to Different Types of Power Sources

When building a vehicle system for preparedness, one of the most critical considerations is power. Whether it's providing power for communication devices, lighting, or refrigeration, having a reliable power source is essential in emergency situations. As a conservative angle, it is important to note that individuals and families bear a primary responsibility for preparing themselves for potential risks and challenges, and having a reliable power source is an important part of that responsibility.

There are a variety of power sources that can be used to power a vehicle system, including gasoline, diesel, propane, natural gas, and solar. Each of these options has its own advantages and disadvantages, and the right choice will depend on the specific needs and priorities of the individual or family.

Gasoline and Diesel

Gasoline and diesel are the most common power sources for vehicles, and they are also the most widely available. Gasoline and diesel engines are capable of producing high levels of power, and they can be used to power a variety of devices, including generators and air compressors.

However, gasoline and diesel can be expensive, and they are not always readily available in emergency situations. Additionally, the storage and transportation of gasoline and diesel can be hazardous, and proper safety precautions must be taken.

Propane and Natural Gas

Propane and natural gas are alternative power sources that can be used to power a vehicle system. Propane is a cleaner-burning fuel than gasoline or diesel, and it is also less expensive. Natural gas is even cleaner-burning than propane, and it is also less expensive.

One of the main advantages of propane and natural gas is that they can be stored for long periods of time, and they are less volatile than gasoline or diesel. However, the availability of propane and natural gas can be limited in some areas, and specialized equipment may be required to use them as a power source.

Solar/Electric Battery

Solar power is a renewable and sustainable power source that can be used to power a vehicle system. Solar panels can be used to charge batteries or power devices directly, and they can be an excellent choice for emergency situations when other power sources are not available. But an electric vehicle is not appropriate for this type of prep vehicle as with any interruption in the electric grid it would only be time before it will not be able to be charged.

One of the main advantages of solar power is that it is sustainable and environmentally friendly. Solar panels require very little maintenance, and they can provide a reliable source of power in emergency situations.

However, the effectiveness of solar panels can be impacted by weather conditions, and they may not provide enough power to meet all of the needs of a vehicle system. Additionally, solar panels can be expensive to install and may require specialized equipment.

In conclusion, powering a vehicle system is a critical consideration for emergency preparedness. Gasoline, diesel, propane, natural gas, and solar power are all viable options for powering a vehicle system, and the right choice will depend on the specific needs and priorities of the individual or family.

It is important to note that individuals and families bear a primary responsibility for preparing themselves for potential risks and challenges, and having a reliable power source is an important part of that responsibility. By being proactive in identifying the right power source for their vehicle system, individuals and families can ensure that they are prepared for any situation and can be self-sufficient in emergency scenarios.

Pros and cons of each type

There are various types of power sources that can be used to power a vehicle system, each with its own set of advantages and disadvantages. In this section, we will discuss the pros and cons of each type, without any political bias.

• *Gasoline:* Gasoline is one of the most widely used power sources for vehicles. It is readily available at gas stations and is capable of producing high levels of power. The primary advantage of gasoline is its convenience and ease of use. However, gasoline is not an environmentally friendly option, and it can be expensive. Gasoline engines also require regular maintenance to function properly.

• *Diesel:* Diesel is another commonly used power source for vehicles. Diesel engines are known for their durability, reliability, and fuel efficiency. They are also capable of producing high levels of power. However, diesel can be expensive and is not as readily available as gasoline. Diesel engines also require regular maintenance and can produce more pollution than gasoline engines.

• *Propane:* Propane is a clean-burning fuel that can be used to power a vehicle system. It is less expensive than gasoline or diesel, and it is also more environmentally friendly. Propane can be stored for long periods of time, and it is less volatile than gasoline or diesel. However, propane is not as widely available as gasoline or diesel, and specialized equipment may be required to use it as a power source.

• *Natural Gas:* Natural gas is another clean-burning fuel that can be used to power a vehicle system. It is less expensive and more environmentally friendly than gasoline or diesel. Like propane, natural gas can be stored for long periods of time, and it is less volatile than gasoline or diesel. However, natural gas is not as widely available as gasoline or diesel, and specialized equipment may be required to use it as a power source.

• *Solar:* Solar power is a renewable and sustainable power source that can be used to power a vehicle system. Solar panels can be used to charge batteries or power devices directly, and they can be an excellent choice for emergency situations when other power sources are not available. Solar power is also environmentally friendly and requires very little maintenance. However, the effectiveness of solar panels can be impacted by weather conditions, and they may not provide enough power to meet all of the needs of a vehicle system. Additionally, solar panels can be expensive to install and may require specialized equipment.

There are various power sources that can be used to power a vehicle system, and the right choice will depend on the specific needs and priorities of the individual or family. Gasoline and diesel are convenient and widely available, but they can be expensive and are not environmentally friendly. Propane and natural gas are more environmentally friendly and can be stored for long periods of time, but they may not be as widely available and may require specialized equipment. Solar power is a renewable and sustainable power source, but it can be expensive and may not provide enough power to meet all of the needs of a vehicle system. By carefully considering the pros and cons of each type of power source, individuals and families can make an informed decision and ensure that their vehicle system is powered by the most appropriate and reliable source.

Calculating Your Power Needs

This is an important step when building a vehicle system for preparedness. It is essential to ensure that the power source you choose is capable of meeting the needs of the devices and equipment that you plan to power. As a conservative angle, it is important to note that individuals and families bear a primary responsibility for preparing themselves for potential risks and challenges, and understanding their power needs is an important part of that responsibility.

To calculate your power needs, you will need to know the power requirements of each device or piece of equipment that you plan to power. This information is typically provided in the device's user manual or on the device itself. The power requirements are usually listed in watts, and you will need to add up the total power requirements of all the devices you plan to power.

Once you have determined the total power requirements of your devices, you can choose a power source that is capable of meeting those needs. To ensure that your power source is adequate, you should also consider the duration of time you will be running the devices and equipment.

For example, if you plan to power a refrigerator that requires 100 watts of power and you will be running it for 24 hours, you will need a power source that can provide 2400 watt-hours of power. If you plan to power additional devices or equipment, you will need to add their power requirements to the total.

It is also important to note that some devices may have higher power requirements when they are first turned on. This is known as the surge or startup power, and it can be several times the device's rated power. You will need to take this into consideration when choosing a power source.

In addition to calculating your power needs, it is also important to consider the efficiency of the devices and equipment you plan to power. Choosing devices and equipment that are energy efficient can help to reduce your power requirements and extend the life of your power source.

Bottom Line

Calculating your power needs is an important step when building a vehicle system for preparedness. By determining the power requirements of the devices and equipment you plan to power, you can choose a power source that is capable of meeting those needs. It is also important to consider the duration of time you will be running the devices and equipment, as well as their surge power requirements. By understanding your power needs and choosing the most appropriate power source, individuals and families can ensure that their vehicle system is ready for unexpected situations and emergency scenarios. As a conservative angle, it is important to emphasize the individual and family responsibility to be prepared and self-sufficient in emergency situations.

25. Communications and Navigation

Why Communication Is Important in Survival Situations

Communications and navigation are critical components of any vehicle system built for survival situations. The ability to communicate with others and navigate through unfamiliar territory can mean the difference between life and death in emergency scenarios. In this section, we will discuss the importance of communication in survival situations and the role of navigation in ensuring survival.

Communication is an essential part of surviving in emergency situations. It enables individuals to call for help, coordinate rescue efforts, and keep in touch with loved ones. Communication devices such as radios and satellite phones are essential tools for survival, as they allow individuals to communicate with others over long distances, even in areas without cell phone coverage.

In addition, communication devices can provide vital information about weather conditions, potential dangers, and other critical information that can help individuals make informed decisions and avoid potential risks. In survival situations, the ability to receive and transmit information can be the key to staying safe and making it through the crisis.

The Importance of Navigation in Survival Situations

Navigation is another critical component of any vehicle system built for survival situations. In emergency scenarios, individuals may need to navigate through unfamiliar territory, often in harsh and dangerous conditions. Navigational tools such as GPS systems and maps can provide vital information about location, direction, and distance, allowing individuals to make informed decisions about their route and avoid potential hazards.

In addition, navigational tools can help individuals plan their routes, set realistic goals, and conserve their energy and resources. By understanding their location and the terrain around them, individuals can make more efficient use of their resources and minimize the risks of getting lost or disoriented.

The Role of Technology in Communication and Navigation

Technology has revolutionized the way we communicate and navigate, providing individuals with powerful tools for staying connected and staying safe in emergency situations. Communication devices such as satellite phones and radios can transmit signals over long distances, providing individuals with access to communication even in areas without cell phone coverage.

Similarly, GPS systems and other navigational tools can provide individuals with accurate and up-to-date information about their location, helping them to navigate through unfamiliar territory and avoid potential hazards. Many of these tools are small, lightweight, and portable, making them ideal for use in emergency situations.

Communication and navigation are critical components of any vehicle system built for survival situations. The ability to communicate with others and navigate through unfamiliar territory can mean the difference between life and death in emergency scenarios. By understanding the importance of communication and navigation and the role of technology in these areas, individuals and families can ensure that their vehicle system is ready for any situation and can be self-sufficient in emergency scenarios.

Types of Communication Devices

There are various types of communication devices available in the market that can be used for emergency situations, outdoor activities, or daily use. Here are some popular types of communication devices:

• *Cell phones:* Portable devices that use cellular networks to communicate over long distances. They can be used for making calls, sending texts, and accessing the internet.

- **Satellite phones:** Devices that use satellites to transmit signals and can provide communication in areas without cell phone coverage.
- **Two-way radios:** Handheld devices that allow individuals to communicate with each other over short distances.

- **Ham radios:** More powerful than two-way radios, they can transmit signals over long distances.

- **Walkie-talkies:** Handheld devices that allow individuals to communicate with each other over short distances.

- **Citizens band (CB) radios:** Devices that allow short-range communication between individuals.

- **Marine radios:** Devices used by boaters and can provide communication over long distances in water.

- **Aviation radios:** Devices used by pilots and can provide communication over long distances in the air.

- **Personal locator beacons (PLBs):** Personal emergency devices that use satellites to send distress signals to search and rescue organizations.

- **Emergency radios:** Portable devices that provide communication and access to emergency broadcasts during power outages or other emergency situations.

There are several different modes of radio communication, each with their own unique characteristics and uses:

- **High-frequency (HF) radios:** They operate in the frequency range of 3 to 30 megahertz, and are used for long-distance communication. HF waves are able to bounce off the ionosphere and back down to the ground, allowing for communication over very long distances. HF radios are often used for long-range communication in emergency situations, as well as by amateur radio operators.

- **Ultra-high-frequency (UHF) radios:** They operate in the frequency range of 300 megahertz to 3 gigahertz, and are used for shorter-range communication. UHF signals are able to penetrate walls and other obstacles more easily than VHF signals, making them ideal for indoor and urban use. UHF radios are commonly used in two-way radios, as well as by emergency responders and law enforcement.

- **Very-high-frequency (VHF) radios:** They operate in the frequency range of 30 to 300 megahertz, and are also used for shorter-range communication. VHF signals are better suited for outdoor use, and are often used by maritime and aviation professionals, as well as emergency responders and law enforcement.

- **Family radio service (FRS) radios**: They operate in the frequency range of 462 to 467 megahertz, and are used for short-range communication between family and friends. FRS radios are typically low-power and do not require a license, making them popular for personal use in outdoor activities such as camping and hiking.

- **Citizens band (CB) radios:** They operate in the frequency range of 26.965 to 27.405 megahertz, and are used for short-range communication between individuals on the same channel. CB radios are commonly used by truck drivers, and require a license to operate.

Each mode of radio communication has its own advantages and disadvantages, and is best suited for different types of situations and environments. By understanding the different modes of communication and their uses, you can select the best radio equipment for your specific needs.

Vehicle Mounted Radios

These companies provide radio equipment for your prep vehicle:

• *Icom* offers a variety of two-way radio options, including handheld and mobile radios, as well as options for UHF, VHF, and HF frequencies.

• *Yaesu* is another company that provides a range of two-way radio options, including handheld and mobile radios, as well as base stations and repeaters.

• *Kenwood* is known for high-quality radio equipment, including handheld and mobile radios, as well as base stations and repeaters.

• *Midland* is a company that provides a range of radio equipment for both personal and professional use, including two-way radios, CB radios, and weather radios.

• *Motorola* is a well-known brand in the world of two-way radios, offering a range of options for both personal and professional use, including handheld and mobile radios, as well as base stations and repeaters. They also offer options for UHF, VHF, and HF frequencies.

Walkie Talkie Hand Held Radios

These companies provide walkie talkie radio options for your prep vehicle, with a range of frequencies:

• *Motorola* offers a range of two-way radios, including walkie talkie options, that operate on UHF, VHF, and FRS frequencies. Their equipment is known for its durability and reliability.

• *Midland* is a popular brand for two-way radios, including walkie talkies that operate on UHF, VHF, CB, and FRS frequencies. They offer options for both personal and professional use.

• *Baofeng* is a brand that offers affordable two-way radios, including walkie talkie options that operate on UHF, VHF, and HF frequencies. They are a popular choice for amateur radio operators.

• *Kenwood* As mentioned, Kenwood is known for their high-quality radio equipment, including walkie talkies that operate on UHF, VHF, and FRS frequencies. Their equipment is known for its advanced features and long battery life.

• *Uniden* offers a range of two-way radios, including walkie talkie options that operate on UHF, VHF, CB, and FRS frequencies. They are known for their user-friendly designs and affordability.

Satellite Phones

These companies are satellite phone providers and their URLs:

- Iridium - https://www.iridium.com

- Globalstar - https://www.globalstar.com/

- Inmarsat - https://www.inmarsat.com/

- Thuraya - https://www.thuraya.com/

- SPOT - https://www.findmespot.com/en-us/

A quality one stop shop for satellite phone needs can be found at www.satellitephonestores.com.

Each of these companies offers satellite phone services, with different plans, devices, and coverage areas. It is important to research and compare the options before choosing a satellite phone provider to ensure that it meets your specific needs and budget.

It is important to note that the effectiveness of these devices may be impacted by environmental conditions such as weather, terrain, and vegetation. Additionally, proper training and knowledge of how to use these devices is essential for their effective use in emergency scenarios.

Navigation Tools and Techniques

Navigation tools and techniques are critical for individuals to be able to find their way in outdoor environments or emergency situations. Here are some popular navigation tools and techniques:

• **Global Positioning System (GPS)** is a satellite-based navigation system that uses a network of satellites to determine a user's location and provide directions to their destination. Satellite-based navigation system that provides location and time information. It is used by a variety of devices, including handheld GPS units, vehicle GPS systems, and smartphones. Companies that produce GPS devices include Garmin, TomTom, and Magellan.

• **Maps** are graphical representations of an area, and can be used to plan routes and navigate through unfamiliar territory. Topographic maps are specifically designed to show the terrain of an area. Companies that produce maps include National Geographic, Rand McNally, and TomTom.

• **Compasses** are navigational tools that use Earth's magnetic field to determine direction. A compass can be used in conjunction with a map to determine direction. Companies that produce compasses include Silva, Suunto and Brunton.

• **Altimeters** are devices that measure altitude by detecting changes in air pressure. It can be used to determine a user's location and navigate through hilly or mountainous terrain. Companies that produce altimeters include Suunto and Garmin.

• **Celestial navigation** is a technique that uses the stars and other celestial bodies to determine a user's location and direction.

• **Binoculars** are useful navigational tools for spotting landmarks and other features in the distance. Companies that produce binoculars with navigational aids include Leupold, Bushnell, Steiner and Fujinon.

• **Marine charts** are specialized maps used for navigation on water. They provide detailed information on water depths, shorelines, and other marine features. Companies that produce marine charts include Navionics and C-Map.

• **Sextants** are longstanding navigational tools used for celestial navigation. It measures the angle between a celestial body and the horizon to determine position. Companies that produce sextants include Davis Instruments and Weems & Plath.

• **Dead reckoning** is an informal navigation technique that involves estimating one's current position based on their previous position and the distance and direction traveled.

• **Sun compasses** are navigational tools that use the position of the sun to determine direction. It can be used in areas without a clear view of the horizon.

• **Landmarks** are distinctive features of an area that can be used to determine a user's location and navigate through unfamiliar territory.

It is important to note that each of these tools and techniques has its own set of advantages and limitations. Proper training and knowledge of how to use these tools and techniques is essential for their effective use in emergency scenarios. Additionally, it is recommended to carry multiple navigation tools and devices to ensure redundancy in case of equipment failure.

Selecting the Right Communication and Navigation Gear

When building a vehicle system for survival situations, selecting the right communication and navigation gear is essential for ensuring the safety and well-being of individuals and families. In this section, we will discuss some key factors to consider when selecting communication and navigation gear.

Purpose and Frequency of Use

The first factor to consider when selecting communication and navigation gear is the purpose and frequency of use. If you plan to use the gear regularly, it may be worth investing in high-quality equipment that can withstand wear and tear. However, if you plan to use the gear infrequently or for a one-time emergency situation, it may be more cost-effective to purchase lower-cost equipment.

Range and Coverage

Another important factor to consider is the range and coverage of the communication and navigation gear. If you plan to use the gear in remote or off-grid areas, it may be necessary to invest in equipment that can provide communication and navigation over long distances or in areas without cell phone coverage. Satellite phones or radios can be ideal for these situations. Alternatively, if you plan to use the gear in urban or suburban areas, lower-cost equipment such as two-way radios may be sufficient.

Durability and Weather Resistance

Durability and weather resistance are also important factors to consider when selecting communication and navigation gear. Equipment that is built to withstand harsh weather conditions such as rain, snow, and extreme temperatures can ensure that the gear remains operational in emergency situations. Additionally, equipment that is rugged and durable can withstand impacts and falls, ensuring that it remains operational even after accidental drops or mishaps.

Ease of Use and Compatibility

Ease of use and compatibility with other devices is also important to consider when selecting communication and navigation gear. Devices that are intuitive and easy to operate can ensure that individuals can quickly and easily communicate and navigate through unfamiliar terrain. Additionally, devices that are compatible with other gear such as battery packs or charging stations can ensure that individuals have a reliable power source for their gear.

Price and Affordability

Finally, the price and affordability of communication and navigation gear is an important factor to consider when selecting equipment. While high-end equipment may offer better performance and durability, it may be cost-prohibitive for some individuals and families. It is important to balance the need for high-quality equipment with affordability and budget considerations.

Bottom Line

Selecting the right communication and navigation gear is essential for building a vehicle system for survival situations. Key factors to consider when selecting gear include the purpose and frequency of use, range and coverage, durability and weather resistance, ease of use and compatibility, and price and affordability. By taking these factors into account and conducting thorough research, individuals and families can ensure that their gear is reliable, effective, and appropriate for their needs.

26. Water, Food and Shelter

Water Storage and Filtration

Water storage and filtration are essential components of any vehicle system built for survival situations. In emergency scenarios or outdoor activities, individuals may not have access to clean drinking water, and it is important to have a reliable source of water to ensure survival. In this section, we will discuss the importance of water storage and filtration in a vehicle system and different methods for water storage and filtration.

Importance of Water Storage and Filtration in a Vehicle System

Water is critical for survival, and having a reliable source of water is essential for ensuring the safety and well-being of individuals and families in emergency situations or outdoor activities. In a vehicle system, water storage and filtration can provide a reliable source of clean drinking water, allowing individuals to stay hydrated and avoid dehydration, which can lead to serious health issues.

Additionally, water storage and filtration can provide access to clean water for other uses such as cooking, cleaning, and hygiene. In emergency situations, access to clean water can be limited, and having a reliable source of clean water can reduce the risks of infection and disease transmission.

Different Methods for Water Storage and Filtration

There are different methods for water storage and filtration that can be used in a vehicle system. Here are some popular methods:

Water Bottles and Containers

One of the most straightforward methods for water storage is to use water bottles and containers. These can be easily stored in the vehicle and filled up from any available water source. However, it is important to ensure that the bottles and containers are made from safe materials, such as BPA-free plastic or stainless steel.

Here are some companies that produce quality water bottles and containers for your vehicle prep:

• *Nalgene:* produces a range of water bottles and containers in various sizes and materials, including BPA-free plastic and stainless steel.

• *Hydro Flask:* is known for their high-quality insulated water bottles and containers, which are designed to keep drinks cold or hot for hours.

• **Klean Kanteen:** produces a range of stainless steel water bottles and containers, including insulated options for hot or cold drinks.

• **Yeti:** is known for their rugged and durable water bottles and containers, which are designed for outdoor and off-road use.

• **Platypus:** produces flexible water bottles and containers, which are ideal for packing into small spaces in your vehicle.

• **CamelBak:** is a well-known brand for their hydration packs, but they also produce water bottles and containers in various sizes and materials.

• **Stanley:** is known for their durable and classic stainless steel water bottles and containers, which are great for outdoor and off-road use.

These companies offer a range of water bottle and container options, so it is important to choose the right size, material, and features for your specific needs. Some factors to consider include capacity, durability, insulation, and ease of use.

Water Storage Tanks

Water storage tanks are larger containers that can store a significant amount of water. These tanks can be installed in the vehicle, and can be filled up from any available water source. However, it is important to ensure that the tanks are made from safe materials and are properly sealed to prevent contamination.

Here are some companies that produce quality water containers over 3L for your vehicle prep:

• *Reliance Products:* produces a range of water containers in various sizes, including large containers up to 7 gallons (about 26.5 liters) in size.

• *Scepter:* offers a variety of military-grade water containers, including large containers up to 5 gallons (about 19 liters) in size.

• *WaterBrick:* makes stackable water containers in various sizes, including a 3.5-gallon (about 13.2 liters) container and a 5-gallon (about 18.9 liters) container.

• *Aquatainer:* manufactures a 7-gallon (about 26.5 liters) water container that is designed for outdoor and off-road use.

• *Igloo:* produces large water containers up to 6 gallons (about 22.7 liters) in size, which are great for outdoor and off-road use.

• *Coleman:* offers a variety of water containers, including a 5-gallon (about 18.9 liters) container that is designed for outdoor and off-road use.

• *Zebra:* makes a range of stainless steel water containers, including a 10-liter (about 2.6-gallon) container that is great for outdoor and off-road use.

These companies offer a range of water container options over 3L, which are ideal for vehicle prep and off-road use. It is important to choose a container that is durable, leak-proof, and easy to transport and store in your vehicle.

Water Filters

Water filters can be used to remove impurities and contaminants from water, providing a reliable source of clean drinking water. There are different types of water filters available, such as activated carbon filters and ceramic filters, which can be used to remove bacteria, viruses, and other harmful substances from water.

Here are some companies that produce quality water filters for your vehicle prep:

• *Sawyer:* produces a range of water filters, including their popular Mini Water Filter, which is small and portable and can filter up to 100,000 gallons of water.

• *Katadyn:* offers a range of water filters, including the Pocket Water Microfilter, which is a durable and reliable option for outdoor and off-road use.

• *LifeStraw:* makes a variety of water filters, including their original LifeStraw filter, which is compact and easy to use, and can filter up to 4,000 liters of water.

• *Platypus:* manufactures a range of water filters, including the GravityWorks water filter system, which is a fast and efficient option for filtering large volumes of water.

• **MSR:** produces a range of water filters, including the Guardian Water Purifier, which is designed for outdoor and off-road use and can remove viruses, bacteria, and protozoa.

• **Grayl:** offers water filtration systems that are designed to be fast and easy to use, and can filter out viruses, bacteria, and protozoa.

• **Aquamira:** makes a variety of water filters and treatment systems, including their Frontier Max water filter, which can filter up to 120 gallons of water and can be used as a straw or as a gravity filter.

These companies offer a range of water filter options for vehicle prep, which can be essential for providing safe drinking water during outdoor and off-road trips. It is important to choose a filter that is effective against the contaminants you are likely to encounter and is easy to use and maintain.

Water Purification Tablets

Water purification tablets can be used to disinfect water, killing harmful bacteria and viruses. These tablets are lightweight and portable, making them an ideal solution for outdoor activities or emergency situations.

These companies offer a range of water purification tablets for vehicle prep, which can be a convenient and effective way to purify water in emergency situations. It is important to choose a product that is effective against the contaminants you are likely to encounter and is easy to use and store in your vehicle.

• **Potable Aqua:** produces a range of water purification tablets, including their Potable Aqua Chlorine

Dioxide tablets, which are effective against bacteria, viruses, and protozoa.

• *Aquatabs:* offers water purification tablets that are effective against bacteria, viruses, and protozoa, and can be used in a variety of water sources.

• *MSR:* manufactures a range of water purification tablets, including their Aquatabs, which are effective against bacteria, viruses, and protozoa, and can be used in a variety of water sources.

• *Katadyn:* makes Micropur tablets, which are effective against bacteria, viruses, and protozoa, and can be used in a variety of water sources.

• *Aquamira:* produces water purification tablets, including their Chlorine Dioxide tablets, which are effective against bacteria, viruses, and protozoa, and can be used in a variety of water sources.

• *Coghlan's:* offers water purification tablets that are effective against bacteria, viruses, and protozoa, and can be used in a variety of water sources.

• *Oasis:* makes a range of water purification tablets, including their Chlorine Dioxide tablets, which are effective against bacteria, viruses, and protozoa, and can be used in a variety of water sources.

Gravity Filters

Gravity filters use gravity to push water through a filter, removing impurities and contaminants. These filters are easy to use and require no electricity, making them an ideal solution for emergency situations.

These companies offer a range of gravity water filter options for vehicle prep, which can be essential for providing safe drinking water during outdoor and off-road trips. It is important to choose a filter that is effective against the contaminants you are likely to encounter, is easy to use, and is durable enough to withstand outdoor and off-road conditions.

- **Platypus:** produces the GravityWorks water filter system, which is a fast and efficient option for filtering large volumes of water, and is ideal for outdoor and off-road use.

- **Katadyn:** offers the Gravity Camp 6L water filter, which is designed for outdoor and off-road use, and can filter up to 2 liters of water per minute.

- **Sawyer:** manufactures the Gravity System water filter, which is a lightweight and portable option for outdoor and off-road use, and can filter up to 10 liters of water in as little as 45 minutes.

- **MSR:** makes the AutoFlow Gravity Filter, which is a versatile option for filtering large volumes of water, and is ideal for outdoor and off-road use.

- **LifeSaver:** produces the Jerrycan water filter, which is designed for emergency and off-grid situations, and can filter up to 20,000 liters of water.
- **Aquamira:** offers the Frontier Pro Gravity Water Filter, which is a compact and portable option for outdoor and off-road use, and can filter up to 50 gallons of water.

- **HydroBlu:** manufactures the Clear Flow Gravity Water Filter, which is a lightweight and portable option for outdoor and off-road use, and can filter up to 1 liter of water per minute.

Water storage and filtration are essential components of any vehicle system built for survival situations. Different methods for water storage and filtration can be used, including water bottles and containers, water storage tanks, water filters, water purification tablets, and gravity filters. By incorporating a reliable and effective water storage and filtration system into a vehicle system, individuals and families can ensure that they have a reliable source of clean drinking water in emergency situations or outdoor activities.

Food Storage and Preparation

Food storage and preparation are critical components of any vehicle system built for survival situations or outdoor activities. In emergency scenarios, individuals may not have access to food, and it is important to have a reliable source of food to ensure survival. In this section, we will discuss the importance of food storage and preparation in a vehicle system and different methods for food storage and preparation.

Importance of Food Storage and Preparation in a Vehicle System

Food is an essential element of survival, and having a reliable source of food is critical for ensuring the safety and well-being of individuals and families in emergency situations or outdoor activities. In a vehicle system, food storage and preparation can provide a reliable source of sustenance, allowing individuals to maintain their energy levels and avoid malnutrition, which can lead to serious health issues.

In addition, food storage and preparation can provide

access to hot meals, which can be comforting and provide a sense of normalcy in emergency situations. In outdoor activities, having access to a hot meal can be a source of comfort and can help to maintain morale.

Different Methods for Food Storage and Preparation

There are different methods for food storage and preparation that can be used in a vehicle system. Here are some popular methods:

• *Canned and Packaged Foods:* They can be easily stored in the vehicle and do not require refrigeration. These foods have a long shelf life and can provide a source of nutrition in emergency situations. However, it is important to ensure that the foods are high in nutritional value and are not expired.

• *Dehydrated Foods:* They are lightweight and portable, making them an ideal solution for outdoor activities or emergency situations. These foods can be rehydrated with water and provide a source of nutrition. However, dehydrated foods can be expensive and may not provide the same level of nutritional value as fresh foods.

• *Freeze-Dried Foods:* They are similar to dehydrated foods in that they are lightweight and portable. These foods have a longer shelf life than dehydrated foods and can be easily stored in the vehicle. However, freeze-dried foods can be expensive and may not provide the same level of nutritional value as fresh foods.

• *Cooler and Refrigerator:* Either can be used to store fresh foods such as fruits, vegetables, and meat. These foods provide a higher level of nutritional value than canned or packaged foods, and can be more satisfying. However, refrigeration requires a power source, and may not be feasible in all situations.

• *Portable Stove and Cookware:* They can be used to prepare hot meals in emergency situations or outdoor activities. These can be fueled by propane or other fuels, and can provide a source of comfort and nutrition. However, a portable stove requires fuel, and may not be feasible in all situations.

These companies offer a range of canned and packaged food options for vehicle prep, which can be essential for providing emergency sustenance during outdoor and off-road trips. It is important to choose food that is nutritious, easy to prepare, and has a long shelf life, so that it can be stored in your vehicle for an extended period of time.

• *Mountain House:* produces a variety of freeze-dried and dehydrated meals, which are lightweight and easy to prepare, and can be stored for long periods of time.

• *Wise Company:* offers a range of freeze-dried and dehydrated meals, as well as emergency food kits, which are designed to be convenient and easy to prepare.

• *Augason Farms:* manufactures a range of freeze-dried and dehydrated meals, as well as emergency food kits, which are designed to be affordable and long-lasting.

• *Legacy Food Storage:* makes a range of freeze-dried and dehydrated meals, as well as emergency food kits, which are designed to be nutritious and easy to prepare.

- **Chef's Banquet:** produces a range of freeze-dried and dehydrated meals, as well as emergency food kits, which are designed to be convenient and long-lasting.

- **Backpacker's Pantry:** offers a range of freeze-dried and dehydrated meals, as well as snacks and desserts, which are designed to be lightweight and easy to prepare.

- **Patriot Pantry:** makes a range of freeze-dried and dehydrated meals, as well as emergency food kits, which are designed to be nutritious and long-lasting.

Food storage and preparation are critical components of any vehicle system built for survival situations or outdoor activities. Different methods for food storage and preparation can be used, including canned and packaged foods, dehydrated foods, freeze-dried foods, a cooler or refrigerator, and a portable stove and cookware. By incorporating a reliable and effective food storage and preparation system into a vehicle system, individuals and families can ensure that they have a reliable source of food and nutrition in emergency situations or outdoor activities.

Shelter Options for Your Vehicle

Shelter is an essential component of any survival situation or outdoor activity. In emergency scenarios, having a reliable source of shelter can provide protection from the elements, reducing the risks of exposure and hypothermia. In outdoor activities, having a comfortable and secure place to sleep can help to maintain morale and ensure restful sleep. In this section, we will discuss different options for shelter in a vehicle system.

Roof Top Tents

Roof top tents are a popular option for vehicle-based shelter. These tents are designed to be mounted on top of the vehicle, and can be easily deployed and packed away. Roof top tents provide a comfortable and secure place to sleep, and can provide protection from the elements. Additionally, roof top tents can provide an elevated view of the surroundings, offering a unique perspective of the environment. Examples of brands include Roofnest, Yakima Skyrise and Thule Tepui.

Ground Tents

Ground tents are another popular option for vehicle-based shelter. These tents can be set up on the ground near the vehicle, and can provide a comfortable and secure place to sleep. Ground tents are typically more affordable than roof top tents, and can be purchased in a variety of sizes and styles. However, ground tents require a flat and level surface for setup, and may not provide the same level of protection from the elements as roof top tents. Examples of brands include Coleman, Eureka, Kelty and a load at REI.com

Vehicle Awnings

Vehicle awnings are a versatile option for shelter. These can be attached to the side or rear of the vehicle, and can provide shade and protection from the elements. Vehicle awnings can be easily deployed and packed away, and can be combined with other shelter options such as ground tents or roof top tents. Examples of brands include ARB, Rhino-Rack, and Tuff Stuff

Hammocks

Hammocks are a lightweight and portable option for vehicle-based shelter. These can be easily set up between two trees or posts, and can provide a comfortable and secure place to sleep. Hammocks are typically more affordable than other shelter options, and can be combined with other options such as vehicle awnings for added protection from the elements. Examples of brands include Eagles Nest Outfitters, Grand Trunk, and Hennessy Hammock

Car Covers

Car covers can provide a basic level of protection from the elements. These can be used to cover the vehicle and provide a dry and sheltered area for sleeping or resting. Car covers are typically more affordable than other shelter options, and can be easily stored in the vehicle. Examples of brands include Covercraft, WeatherTech and Coverking

Bottom Line

There are different options for shelter in a vehicle system, including roof top tents, ground tents, vehicle awnings, hammocks, and car covers. The choice of shelter option will depend on individual preferences, budget, and the type of environment in which the vehicle system will be used. By incorporating a reliable and effective shelter system into a vehicle system, individuals and families can ensure that they have a comfortable and secure place to sleep and rest in emergency situations or outdoor activities.

27. Safety and Security

Essential Safety Gear and Equipment

When building a vehicle system for survival situations, essential safety gear and equipment should be included to ensure the safety and well-being of individuals and families. In this section, we will discuss some key safety gear and equipment to consider when building a vehicle system for survival situations.

Recommended First Aid Kits

A first aid kit is an essential piece of safety gear to have in a vehicle system. It should include items such as bandages, gauze, antiseptic wipes, and pain relievers. In emergency situations, a first aid kit can provide immediate medical attention, which can be critical for avoiding further harm.

These companies offer a range of first aid kit options for vehicle prep, which can be essential for providing emergency medical care during outdoor and off-road trips. It is important to choose a kit that is comprehensive and includes supplies for common injuries and conditions, as well as specialized supplies for more serious injuries and medical emergencies. Additionally, it is important to ensure that your kit is easily accessible and well-organized, so that you can quickly and efficiently provide care when needed.

• *Adventure Medical Kits:* produces a range of first aid kits, including kits specifically designed for outdoor and off-road use.

• *MyMedic:* offers a range of first aid kits, including trauma kits, which are designed to provide advanced medical care in emergency situations.

• **First Aid Only:** manufactures a range of first aid kits, including kits designed for outdoor and off-road use, as well as specialized kits for specific injuries and conditions.

• **Surviveware:** makes a range of first aid kits, including kits designed for outdoor and off-road use, as well as waterproof kits and trauma kits.

• **Lightning X Products:** sells a range of first aid kits, including trauma kits and roadside emergency kits, which are designed to provide advanced medical care in emergency situations.

• **Northbound Train:** produces a range of first aid kits, including kits designed for outdoor and off-road use, as well as specialized kits for specific injuries and conditions.

• **Swiss Safe:** offers a range of first aid kits, including kits designed for outdoor and off-road use, as well as small and compact kits for everyday carry.

Fire Extinguisher

A fire extinguisher is an important piece of safety equipment to have in a vehicle system. In emergency situations, a fire extinguisher can help to prevent small fires from turning into larger fires. It should be kept in a location that is easily accessible and should be checked periodically to ensure that it is in working condition.

These companies offer a range of fire extinguisher options for vehicle prep, which can be essential for providing emergency fire suppression in outdoor and off-road situations. It is important to choose a fire extinguisher that is appropriate for the type of fires that are likely to occur, and is easily accessible and easy to use in an emergency. Additionally, it is important to ensure that your fire extinguisher is properly maintained and inspected regularly, to ensure that it is in good working condition when needed.

• *Amerex Corporation:* produces a range of portable fire extinguishers, including models specifically designed for vehicles and off-road use.

• *Kidde:* offers a range of fire extinguishers, including models designed for vehicle use, which are compact and easy to install.

• *First Alert:* manufactures a range of fire extinguishers, including models designed for vehicle use, which are lightweight and easy to operate.

• *Badger:* makes a range of portable fire extinguishers, including models specifically designed for vehicle and off-road use.

• *H3R Performance:* sells a range of fire extinguishers, including models designed for vehicle use, which are lightweight and easy to install.

• *Buckeye Fire Equipment:* produces a range of portable fire extinguishers, including models specifically designed for vehicle and off-road use.

• *Fireboy-Xintex:* offers a range of fire extinguishers, including models designed for vehicle use, which are compact and easy to install.

Emergency Blanket

An emergency blanket is an important piece of safety gear to have in a vehicle system. It can be used to provide warmth and insulation in emergency situations or outdoor activities. Emergency blankets are lightweight and portable, making them an ideal solution for vehicle-based survival situations.

These companies offer a range of emergency blanket and bivvy options for vehicle prep, which can be essential for providing warmth and shelter in emergency situations. It is important to choose a blanket or bivvy that is durable, lightweight, and compact, so that it can be easily stored in your vehicle and taken with you on outdoor and off-road trips. Additionally, it is important to ensure that your emergency blanket or bivvy is waterproof and reflective, so that it can provide maximum protection in a variety of emergency situations.

• **SOL (Survive Outdoors Longer):** produces a range of emergency blankets, including reflective and thermal options, which are designed to keep you warm and dry in emergency situations.

• **Swiss Safe:** offers a range of emergency blankets, including reflective and thermal options, which are compact and lightweight, making them ideal for vehicle prep.

• **Emergency Zone:** manufactures a range of emergency blankets, including thermal and space blankets, which are designed to provide warmth and shelter in emergency situations.

• **Tact Bivvy:** makes a high-quality emergency bivvy, which is made from a lightweight and durable material that reflects up to 90-percent of body heat.

- **Grabber:** sells a range of emergency blankets and bivvies, including thermal and space blankets, which are designed to provide warmth and shelter in a variety of emergency situations.

- **ReadyWise:** produces a range of emergency blankets, including reflective and thermal options, which are designed to provide warmth and protection in emergency situations.

- **Life Bivy:** offers a high-quality emergency bivvy, which is made from a durable and waterproof material that reflects up to 90% of body heat.

Flashlight/Headlamp

A flashlight and headlamps are important pieces of safety gear to have in a vehicle system. In emergency situations or when working in low-light conditions, a flashlight can provide visibility and help to prevent accidents. It is important to ensure that the flashlight has fresh batteries or a reliable source of power.

These companies offer a range of flashlights and headlamps for vehicle prep, which can be essential for providing reliable and durable lighting in outdoor and off-road situations. It is important to choose a flashlight or headlamp that is durable, waterproof, and provides long-lasting battery life, so that it can provide reliable lighting in a variety of emergency situations. Additionally, it is important to ensure that your flashlight or headlamp is easy to use and has a range of brightness settings, so that you can adjust the lighting to your needs.

- **Streamlight produces:** a range of flashlights and headlamps, including models designed for vehicle use and outdoor activities, which are durable and long-lasting.

- **Fenix:** offers a range of flashlights and headlamps, including rechargeable and compact models, which are designed for outdoor and off-road use.

- **Olight:** manufactures a range of flashlights and headlamps, including rechargeable and waterproof models, which are designed for outdoor and emergency use.

- **Black Diamond:** makes a range of headlamps and lanterns, which are designed for outdoor and off-road use, and provide reliable and durable lighting.

- **SureFire:** sells a range of tactical flashlights and headlamps, which are designed for outdoor and emergency use, and provide powerful and reliable lighting.

- **Petzl:** produces a range of headlamps, which are designed for outdoor and off-road use, and provide durable and long-lasting lighting.

- **Nitecore:** offers a range of flashlights and headlamps, including rechargeable and waterproof models, which are designed for outdoor and emergency use.

Multi-Tool

A multi-tool is a versatile piece of equipment that can be used in a variety of situations. It should include items such as pliers, a knife, a saw, and a can opener. In emergency situations or outdoor activities, a multi-tool can be used to fix equipment or perform other essential tasks.

These companies offer a range of multi-tools for vehicle prep, which can be essential for providing a range of useful tools in outdoor and off-road situations. It is important to choose a multi-tool that is durable, versatile, and features a range of useful tools, such as pliers, knives, saws, and screwdrivers. Additionally, it is important to ensure that your multi-tool is lightweight and compact, so that it can be easily stored in your vehicle and taken with you on outdoor and off-road trips.

• *Leatherman:* produces a range of multi-tools, including models designed for outdoor and off-road use, which are durable and versatile.

• *Gerber Gear:* offers a range of multi-tools, including models designed for outdoor and off-road use, which are durable and feature-packed.

• *SOG:* manufactures a range of multi-tools, including models designed for outdoor and off-road use, which are versatile and innovative.

• *Victorinox:* makes a range of multi-tools, including the popular Swiss Army Knife, which are compact and durable, and feature a range of useful tools.

• *CRKT:* sells a range of multi-tools, including models designed for outdoor and off-road use, which are innovative and durable.

• *Kershaw:* produces a range of multi-tools, including models designed for outdoor and off-road use, which are durable and feature a range of useful tools.

• *Benchmade:* offers a range of multi-tools, including models designed for outdoor and off-road use, which are durable and high-quality.

Reflective Vest

A reflective vest is an important piece of safety gear to have in a vehicle system. It can be worn during roadside emergencies or when performing maintenance on the vehicle. Reflective vests can provide visibility and help to prevent accidents.

Spare Tire and Jack

A spare tire and jack are essential pieces of equipment to have in a vehicle system. In the event of a flat tire, having a spare tire and jack can ensure that the vehicle can be safely repaired and driven to a safe location. Always have a 4'x4'x12" and a 2'x6'x12" board to help make up for uneven ground.

Including essential safety gear and equipment in a vehicle system is critical for ensuring the safety and well-being of individuals and families in emergency situations or outdoor activities. Key safety gear and equipment to consider include a first aid kit, fire extinguisher, emergency blanket, flashlight, multi-tool, reflective vest, and spare tire and jack. By incorporating these safety gear and equipment into a vehicle system, individuals and families can ensure that they are prepared for a variety of emergency situations.

Security Considerations for Your Vehicle System

Security considerations are an important aspect of any vehicle system built for survival situations or outdoor activities. In emergency scenarios, individuals may be vulnerable to theft or other types of criminal activity. In outdoor activities, theft can be a common occurrence, and valuable equipment and supplies may be at risk. In this section, we will discuss different security considerations for a vehicle system and ways to mitigate risks.

Vehicle Security Systems

Installing a vehicle security system is an effective way to deter theft or other types of criminal activity. Vehicle security systems can include alarm systems, immobilizers, and GPS tracking devices. These systems can alert the owner or authorities in the event of a theft or other type of security breach.

Vehicle Locks and Safes

Installing locks and safes in a vehicle system can provide an additional layer of security. Locks and safes can be used to store valuable equipment and supplies, ensuring that they are protected from theft. It is important to ensure that locks and safes are installed in a secure location and are not easily visible to potential thieves.

Secure Parking Locations

Choosing a secure parking location can be an effective way to mitigate the risk of theft or other types of criminal activity. Parking in well-lit areas or in areas with surveillance cameras can help to deter criminals. Additionally, it is important to ensure that the parking location is secure and not easily accessible to potential thieves.

Physical Barriers

Installing physical barriers, such as metal grills or screens, can be an effective way to deter theft or other types of criminal activity. These barriers can be used to prevent access to the vehicle's windows or doors, making it more difficult for potential thieves to gain access to the vehicle.

Self-Defense Tools

In emergency situations or outdoor activities, it may be necessary to use self-defense tools to protect oneself from potential threats. Self-defense tools can include items such as pepper spray, stun guns, or firearms. It is important to ensure that individuals are properly trained and licensed before using self-defense tools.

Situational Awareness

Maintaining situational awareness is an important aspect of security considerations. Individuals should be aware of their surroundings and be able to identify potential threats. It is important to avoid potentially dangerous situations and to be prepared to respond in the event of an emergency.

Security considerations are an important aspect of any vehicle system built for survival situations or outdoor activities. Different security considerations include installing a vehicle security system, vehicle locks and safes, secure parking locations, physical barriers, self-defense tools, and maintaining situational awareness. By incorporating these security considerations into a vehicle system, individuals and families can ensure that they are prepared for potential threats and are able to mitigate risks.

Tips for Situational Awareness

Situational awareness is an important aspect of security considerations in any vehicle system built for survival situations or outdoor activities. Situational awareness refers to an individual's ability to identify and understand their surroundings, potential threats, and opportunities. By maintaining situational awareness, individuals can take proactive steps to avoid danger, make better decisions, and remain safe in emergency situations or outdoor activities. In this section, we will discuss tips for situational awareness.

Be Alert and Focused

One of the most important tips for situational awareness is to be alert and focused. Individuals should be mindful of their surroundings and avoid distractions that could reduce their attention. This could include avoiding the use of cell phones, headphones, or other devices that can take away from situational awareness.

Pay Attention to Your Environment

Individuals should pay close attention to their environment and be aware of any changes or anomalies. This could include noticing suspicious behavior, unusual sounds or smells, or any other signs that could indicate potential danger.

Identify Potential Threats

Individuals should identify potential threats and be prepared to respond in the event of an emergency. This could include identifying potential sources of danger, such as individuals who appear to be intoxicated or aggressive, or environmental threats, such as hazardous weather conditions or natural disasters.

Stay Informed

Staying informed is an important aspect of maintaining situational awareness. Individuals should be aware of any potential threats or risks in their area, including weather conditions, natural disasters, or potential security threats. This could involve monitoring news sources, social media, or emergency alerts.

Use Your Senses

Using your senses is an important aspect of situational awareness. Individuals should rely on their senses of sight, hearing, and smell to identify potential threats or changes in their environment. This could include noticing changes in the sky, unusual sounds, or suspicious smells.

Plan Ahead

Planning ahead is an important aspect of situational awareness. Individuals should be prepared for potential threats or emergency situations by having a plan in place. This could include identifying escape routes, having emergency supplies on hand, or identifying potential sources of assistance.

Be Mindful of Others

Being mindful of others is an important aspect of situational awareness. Individuals should be aware of the behavior and actions of those around them, and be prepared to respond in the event of an emergency. This could include noticing suspicious behavior or unusual actions, and being prepared to take action to protect oneself and others.

Trust Your Gut

Trusting your gut is an important aspect of situational awareness. Individuals should listen to their instincts and be prepared to respond to potential threats or emergency situations. This could include recognizing a sense of danger, and taking action to avoid potential risks.

Bottom Line
Maintaining situational awareness is an important aspect of security considerations in any vehicle system built for survival situations or outdoor activities. Tips for maintaining situational awareness include being alert and focused, paying attention to your environment, identifying potential threats, staying informed, using your senses, planning ahead, being mindful of others, and trusting your gut. By incorporating these tips into a vehicle system, individuals and families can remain safe and prepared in emergency situations or outdoor activities.

28. Alternative Transportation

Options for Off-Road Travel

Off-road travel can be a thrilling and exciting way to explore remote areas and enjoy the outdoors. However, it can also be dangerous if not done safely and responsibly. When planning an off-road trip, it is important to consider the type of terrain, the vehicle, and the equipment needed. In this section, we will discuss different options for off-road travel.

Four-Wheel Drive

Four-wheel drive (4WD) vehicles are designed to provide better traction and control in off-road conditions. 4WD vehicles are equipped with a transfer case that allows for the distribution of power to all four wheels, which can help to prevent slipping or getting stuck in mud, snow, or sand. 4WD vehicles are a popular option for off-road travel, and can range from compact SUVs to heavy-duty trucks.

All-Wheel Drive

All-wheel drive (AWD) vehicles are designed to provide better traction and control in all conditions, including off-road. AWD vehicles are equipped with a center differential that allows for the distribution of power to all four wheels, which can help to prevent slipping or getting stuck in mud, snow, or sand. AWD vehicles are a popular option for off-road travel, and can range from compact crossovers to high-performance sports cars.

Here are a few more examples:

Toyota Land Cruiser

The Toyota Land Cruiser is a highly capable off-road vehicle that is known for its durability and reliability. It features a rugged body-on-frame construction and a powerful V8 engine, with the ability to tow up to 8,100 pounds. The Land Cruiser also features a range of advanced off-road technologies, including a locking center differential, crawl control, and multi-terrain select.

Toyota 4Runner

The Toyota 4Runner is a popular SUV that is known for its off-road capabilities. It features a rugged body-on-frame construction and a 4.0-liter V6 engine that can tow up to 5,000 pounds. The 4Runner also features a range of advanced off-road technologies, including a locking rear differential, multi-terrain select, and crawl control.

Ford F-150 Raptor

The Ford F-150 Raptor is a high-performance pickup truck that is designed for off-road use. It features a powerful 3.5-liter V6 engine and a 10-speed automatic transmission, with the ability to tow up to 8,000 pounds. The Raptor also features a range of advanced off-road technologies, including a terrain management system and a specially tuned suspension.

Jeep Gladiator

The Jeep Gladiator is a rugged pickup truck that is designed for off-road use. It features a durable body-on-frame construction and a 3.6-liter V6 engine that can tow up to 7,650 pounds. The Gladiator also features a range of advanced off-road technologies, including a locking rear differential, electronic sway bar disconnect, and skid plates.

Range Rover

The Range Rover is a luxury SUV that is also highly capable off-road. It features a sophisticated air suspension system and a range of powerful engine options, including a supercharged V8 engine that can tow up to 7,716 pounds. The Range Rover also features a range of advanced off-road technologies, including terrain response and a locking rear differential.

Land Rover Defender

The Land Rover Defender is a classic off-road vehicle that has been recently redesigned for modern use. It features a durable body-on-frame construction and a range of engine options, including a 3.0-liter inline six-cylinder engine that can tow up to 8,201 pounds. The Defender also features a range of advanced off-road technologies, including a locking center differential, hill descent control, and all-terrain progress control.

Dodge Ram 1500

The Dodge Ram 1500 is a full-size pickup truck that is known for its durability and towing capacity. Older models of the Ram 1500 can feature a range of engine options, including a 5.7-liter V8 engine that can tow up to 9,100 pounds. The Ram 1500 also features a sturdy frame and suspension system that is designed to handle rough terrain.

Dodge Power Wagon

The Dodge Power Wagon is a heavy-duty pickup truck that is designed for off-road use. Older models of the Power Wagon feature a powerful 5.9-liter V8 engine and a rugged four-wheel drive system that is designed for extreme terrain. The Power Wagon also features a locking rear differential, a winch, and skid plates for added protection.

Adventure Vans

Adventure vans, such as the Mercedes-Benz Sprinter and the Ford Transit, are becoming increasingly popular for off-road travel. These vans feature a range of customization options, including raised suspensions and all-terrain tires, as well as comfortable living quarters for extended trips. Adventure vans are also highly maneuverable and can access remote areas that larger vehicles cannot.

4x4 and 6x6 Pinzgauers

The Pinzgauer 4x4 and 6x6 are light off-road vehicles that were originally designed for military use. They feature rugged construction and powerful diesel engines, with the ability to climb steep inclines and navigate through rugged terrain. The Pinzgauer 4x4 and 6x6 also have high payload capacities and can tow heavy loads.

These are just a few examples of popular vehicles for off-road use. When choosing a vehicle for off-road travel, it is important to consider factors such as engine power, suspension, and advanced off-road technologies to ensure that the vehicle is suitable for the intended use.

Off-Road Vehicles

Off-road vehicles, such as all-terrain vehicles (ATVs) or side-by-sides (SxS), are designed specifically for off-road travel. These vehicles are lightweight and agile, and can navigate through tight spaces or difficult terrain. Off-road vehicles can be an exciting way to explore remote areas and enjoy the outdoors, but it is important to ensure that they are used safely and responsibly.

All-terrain vehicles (ATVs) are a popular choice for off-road travel, providing riders with the ability to navigate difficult terrain and explore remote areas. Below are some popular ATVs for off-road use:

Polaris Sportsman 850

The Polaris Sportsman 850 is a popular ATV that is designed for off-road use. It features a powerful 850cc engine and a smooth, responsive suspension system that allows riders to navigate through rugged terrain. The Sportsman 850 also features an easy-to-use four-wheel drive system that allows for improved traction and stability on difficult terrain.

Yamaha Grizzly EPS

The Yamaha Grizzly EPS is a powerful and reliable ATV that is designed for off-road use. It features a 686cc engine and a durable, lightweight chassis that is built to withstand rough terrain. The Grizzly EPS also features electronic power steering and four-wheel drive, allowing riders to maintain control in difficult conditions.

Can-Am Outlander

The Can-Am Outlander is a popular ATV that is designed for off-road use. It features a range of engine sizes and power options, including the 450, 570, 650, and 1000 models. The Outlander also features a range of innovative features, including a Visco-Lok auto-locking front differential, tri-mode dynamic power steering, and selectable 2WD/4WD with Visco-Lok QE auto-locking front differential.

Honda FourTrax Foreman Rubicon

The Honda FourTrax Foreman Rubicon is a durable and reliable ATV that is designed for off-road use. It features a 518cc engine and a smooth, responsive suspension system that allows riders to navigate through rough terrain. The Rubicon also features an easy-to-use automatic transmission and a range of advanced features, including a front differential lock and electronic power steering.

Kawasaki Brute Force

The Kawasaki Brute Force is a powerful and versatile ATV that is designed for off-road use. It features a range of engine sizes and power options, including the 750 4x4i EPS, 750 4x4i, and 300 models. The Brute Force also features a durable, lightweight chassis and a range of advanced features, including selectable 2WD/4WD and an easy-to-use automatic transmission.

These are just a few examples of popular ATVs for off-road use. When choosing an ATV, it is important to consider factors such as engine size, suspension, and advanced features to ensure that it is suitable for the intended use.

Bikes and Motorcycles

Bikes and motorcycles can be a lightweight and agile option for off-road travel. These vehicles can navigate through tight spaces or difficult terrain, and can provide a thrilling way to explore remote areas. However, it is important to ensure that they are used safely and responsibly, and that the rider is properly equipped with safety gear.

Electric bicycles, also known as e-bikes, have become increasingly popular in recent years as an eco-friendly and efficient mode of transportation. They are also a great option for off-road travel, as they provide pedal assistance to help riders navigate through difficult terrain. Below are some popular electric bicycles for off-road use:

Rad Power Bikes RadRover Electric Fat Bike

The RadRover is a popular electric fat tire bike that is designed for off-road travel. It features a 750W motor and a top speed of 20 mph, with a range of up to 45 miles on a single charge. The fat tires provide traction and stability on difficult terrain, and the bike also features a suspension fork to help absorb bumps and shocks.

Trek Powerfly FS 7 Electric Mountain Bike

The Powerfly FS 7 is a high-performance electric mountain bike that is designed for off-road use. It features a 500W motor and a top speed of 20 mph, with a range of up to 50 miles on a single charge. The bike also features full suspension and a durable frame to help riders navigate through difficult terrain.

Haibike XDURO AllMtn 9.0 Electric Mountain Bike

The Haibike XDURO AllMtn 9.0 is a powerful and versatile electric mountain bike that is designed for off-road use. It features a 500W motor and a top speed of 20 mph, with a range of up to 50 miles on a single charge. The bike also features full suspension and a sturdy aluminum frame to help riders navigate through difficult terrain.

Giant Trance E+ 1 Pro Electric Mountain Bike

The Trance E+ 1 Pro is a high-performance electric mountain bike that is designed for off-road use. It features a 500W motor and a top speed of 20 mph, with a range of up to 60 miles on a single charge. The bike also features full suspension and a lightweight aluminum frame to help riders navigate through difficult terrain.

Specialized Turbo Levo SL Expert Electric Mountain Bike

The Turbo Levo SL Expert is a lightweight and powerful electric mountain bike that is designed for off-road use. It features a 240W motor and a top speed of 20 mph, with a range of up to 65 miles on a single charge. The bike also features full suspension and a durable carbon fiber frame to help riders navigate through difficult terrain.

These are just a few examples of popular electric bicycles for off-road use. When choosing an electric bike, it is important to consider factors such as motor power, top speed, range, and suspension to ensure that it is suitable for the intended use.

Hiking and Backpacking

Hiking and backpacking can be a challenging but rewarding option for off-road travel. These activities can provide a unique perspective of remote areas, and can offer a way to explore off the beaten path. However, it is important to ensure that individuals are properly equipped with safety gear and are prepared for potential risks, such as inclement weather or wildlife encounters.

When it comes to vehicle prep, having a good backpack is an essential part of any emergency kit or survival gear. Here are a few examples of popular backpacks for vehicle prep:

Maxpedition Falcon-II Backpack

The Maxpedition Falcon-II Backpack is a durable and versatile backpack that is designed for tactical and out-door use. It features a range of organizational pockets and compartments, as well as MOLLE webbing for attaching additional gear. The Falcon-II also features a sturdy construction and comfortable padding for extended wear.

5.11 Tactical RUSH72 Backpack

The 5.11 Tactical RUSH72 Backpack is a spacious and durable backpack that is designed for outdoor and emergency use. It features a range of organizational pockets and compartments, as well as a hydration pocket and a sturdy construction. The RUSH72 also features a comfortable and adjustable padded back panel and shoulder straps.

Osprey Packs Atmos AG 65 Backpack

The Osprey Packs Atmos AG 65 Backpack is a comfortable and spacious backpack that is designed for outdoor and extended use. It features a range of organizational pockets and compartments, as well as a comfortable and adjustable AG Anti-Gravity suspension system. The Atmos AG 65 also features a durable construction and integrated rain cover.

CamelBak M.U.L.E. Hydration Pack

The CamelBak M.U.L.E. Hydration Pack is a compact and versatile backpack that is designed for outdoor and emergency use. It features a 3-liter hydration bladder, as well as a range of organizational pockets and compartments. The M.U.L.E. also features durable construction and comfortable padding for extended wear.

These are just a few examples of popular backpacks for vehicle prep. When choosing a backpack, it is important to consider factors such as capacity, durability, and comfort to ensure that the backpack is suitable for the intended use.

Off-road travel can be an exciting way to explore remote areas and enjoy the outdoors. Different options for off-road travel include four-wheel drive vehicles, all-wheel drive vehicles, off-road vehicles, bikes and motorcycles, and hiking and backpacking. When planning an off-road trip, it is important to consider the type of terrain, the vehicle, and the equipment needed, and to ensure that safety is a top priority. By incorporating safe and responsible off-road travel options into a vehicle system, individuals and families can ensure that they are prepared for a variety of outdoor adventures.

Pros and Cons of Different Types of Vehicles Previously Mentioned

Sport Utility Vehicle (SUV)

SUVs are a versatile choice for both city and off-road driving. They offer a higher ground clearance, better visibility, and more cargo space than sedans. They are also suitable for towing and hauling heavier loads. However, SUVs tend to be less fuel-efficient than sedans and may have a higher cost of ownership.

Pickup Trucks

Pickup trucks are designed for towing and hauling heavy loads. They offer powerful engines, large cargo beds, and high ground clearance. They are also suitable for off-road driving and can handle rugged terrain. However, pickup trucks tend to have a higher cost of ownership, especially when it comes to fuel consumption.

Off-Road Vehicles

Off-road vehicles, such as the Jeep Wrangler or Toyota 4Runner, are specifically designed for off-road driving. They offer high ground clearance, advanced suspension systems, and superior traction control. They are also durable and can handle tough terrain. However, off-road vehicles tend to be less fuel-efficient and may not be as comfortable for everyday driving.

Adventure Vans

Adventure vans, such as the Mercedes-Benz Sprinter or Ford Transit, are designed for off-road travel and extended trips. They offer a high level of customization, including raised suspensions, all-terrain tires, and comfortable living quarters. They are also highly maneuverable and can access remote areas that larger vehicles cannot. However, adventure vans tend to be expensive and may not be suitable for everyday driving.

Heavy-Duty Trucks

Heavy-duty trucks, such as the Ford F-250 or Ram 2500, are designed for towing and hauling extremely heavy loads. They offer powerful engines, advanced towing features, and sturdy frames. They are also suitable for off-road driving and can handle rugged terrain. However, heavy-duty trucks tend to have a higher cost of ownership, especially when it comes to fuel consumption and maintenance.

In summary, each type of vehicle has its own advantages and disadvantages. When choosing a vehicle, it is important to consider factors such as intended use, fuel efficiency, cost of ownership, and comfort to ensure that the vehicle is suitable for the intended purpose.

Selecting the Right Alternative Transportation for Your Needs

When it comes to selecting the right alternative transportation, there are several factors to consider. The main factors include intended use, budget, and personal preferences. Below are some tips to help you select the right alternative transportation for your needs.

Determine Your Intended Use

The first step in selecting the right alternative transportation is to determine your intended use. Are you looking for transportation for your daily commute or for recreational activities? Do you need a vehicle that can handle rough terrain or one that is more suitable for urban environments? These are important questions to consider when selecting the right alternative transportation.

Consider Your Budget

Your budget is another important factor to consider when selecting the right alternative transportation. Alternative transportation can range from inexpensive electric bicycles to high-end adventure vans. Determine how much you are willing to spend and narrow down your options accordingly.

Evaluate Your Personal Preferences

Your personal preferences are another important factor to consider when selecting the right alternative transportation. Do you prefer the convenience of a motorized vehicle or the simplicity of a manual bicycle? Do you prefer a vehicle that is environmentally friendly or one that is more powerful? These are important questions to consider when making your selection.

Electric Bicycles

Electric bicycles are a popular alternative transportation option that offer the convenience of a traditional bicycle with the added benefit of an electric motor. They are a great option for urban environments and shorter commutes. Electric bicycles are also environmentally friendly and can be a cost-effective transportation option. However, they may not be suitable for longer distances or rough terrain.

Scooters

Scooters are another popular alternative transportation option. They are similar to electric bicycles in that they offer the convenience of motorized transportation without the expense and maintenance of a car. Scooters are also easy to operate and can be a great option for short commutes. However, they may not be suitable for rough terrain and are not as environmentally friendly as bicycles.

Motorcycles

Motorcycles are a popular alternative transportation option for those who enjoy the freedom and excitement of riding. They offer speed and maneuverability and can be a great option for longer commutes. However, motorcycles can be expensive to maintain and can be dangerous if not operated safely.

Adventure Vehicles

Adventure vehicles, such as adventure vans or off-road vehicles, are a popular alternative transportation option for those who enjoy off-road adventures and extended travel. They offer the convenience of a home on wheels and can be customized to fit specific needs. Adventure vehicles can be expensive and require more maintenance than other types of transportation.

Bottom Line
Selecting the right alternative transportation for your needs requires careful consideration of intended use, budget, and personal preferences. Be sure to evaluate your options carefully and choose a transportation option that meets your needs and fits within your budget.

29. Building and Customizing
Your Vehicle System

Creating a Vehicle System That Suits Your Needs

Building and customizing your vehicle system is an important step in creating a system that suits your needs. A well-designed vehicle system can make the difference between being prepared for any situation and being caught unprepared. Here are some tips for building and customizing your vehicle system:

Assess Your Needs

The first step in building and customizing your vehicle system is to assess your needs. What are the specific scenarios that you are preparing for? Do you need to have access to food, water, and shelter in an emergency situation? Do you need to be able to power your electronic devices? Do you need to be able to communicate with the outside world? Consider these questions carefully and use them as a guide for building your vehicle system.

Choose the Right Vehicle

Choosing the right vehicle is a critical part of building and customizing your vehicle system. Consider factors such as size, durability, off-road capabilities, and fuel efficiency when choosing a vehicle. Look for a vehicle that can handle the specific scenarios that you are preparing for.

Determine Your Power Needs

Power is a critical part of any vehicle system. Consider your power needs carefully and choose a power source that suits your needs. This could be a battery bank, a solar panel, or a generator. Be sure to choose a power source that is reliable and meets your power needs.

Choose Your Communications and Navigation Gear

Communication and navigation gear is important for any vehicle system. Choose gear that is reliable and can help you stay in contact with the outside world. This could be a satellite phone, a two-way radio, or a GPS system. Be sure to choose gear that is durable and can withstand the elements.

Consider Your Food and Water Storage Needs

Food and water storage is important for any vehicle system. Choose containers that are durable and can hold enough food and water to meet your needs. Consider using water filtration systems to ensure that your water is safe to drink.

Customize Your Shelter Options

Customizing your shelter options is an important part of building and customizing your vehicle system. Consider adding a roof rack or a rooftop tent to provide shelter in emergency situations. You could also consider adding a portable shower or toilet to your vehicle system.

Install Safety Gear

Safety gear is important for any vehicle system. Install safety gear such as fire extinguishers, first aid kits, and emergency flares to ensure that you are prepared for any situation.

Off-Road Recovery Kits

Off-road recovery kits are essential for any off-roading adventure, as they can help you safely recover your vehicle if it becomes stuck or stranded in a difficult terrain. These kits typically include a range of tools and equipment that can be used to tow, winch, or otherwise extricate a stuck vehicle from mud, sand, or other obstacles. Here are some of the key components of an off-road recovery kit, along with some popular brands to consider:

• *Winch:* A winch is a motorized device that can be used to pull a vehicle out of a stuck situation by using a cable or rope. Popular brands of winches include Warn, Smittybilt, and Superwinch.

• *Recovery Straps:* Recovery straps are typically made of nylon or polyester and are designed to provide a strong, flexible connection between two vehicles or between a vehicle and an anchor point. Popular brands of recovery straps include ARB, Bubba Rope, and Factor 55.

• *Shackles:* Shackles are heavy-duty metal connectors that can be used to secure recovery straps to a vehicle or anchor point. Popular brands of shackles include Factor 55, Crosby, and Warn.

• *Traction Mats:* Traction mats are flat, plastic or rubber devices that can be placed under a vehicle's wheels to provide traction in sand, mud, or other slippery terrain. Popular brands of traction mats include Maxtrax and TRED.

• *Tire Repair Kit:* A tire repair kit typically includes a range of tools and equipment for patching or repairing a damaged tire, such as a plug kit or a tire inflator. Popular brands of tire repair kits include ARB and Viair.

• *Jack:* A Hi-Lift jack is a versatile tool that can be used to lift, pull, push, winch, and clamp a wide range of heavy objects, including vehicles. These jacks are popular among off-road enthusiasts because they are highly portable and can be used to help recover a vehicle that has become stuck in mud, sand, or other obstacles. Here are some key features and benefits of Hi-Lift jacks:

  • *Versatility:* Hi-Lift jacks can be used for a wide range of tasks, including lifting a vehicle, winching, clamping, and pulling heavy objects. This versatility makes them an essential tool for any off-roading adventure.

  • *Portability:* Hi-Lift jacks are highly portable and can be easily stored in a vehicle's trunk or storage compartment. This means that they can be taken on any off-road trip, allowing you to be prepared for any situation.

  • *Durability:* Hi-Lift jacks are known for their durability and can withstand exposure to harsh weather conditions and rough terrain. They are made of high-quality materials, such as cast iron and steel, which can last for many years with proper maintenance.

  • *Safety:* Hi-Lift jacks are designed with safety in mind, and they include features such as a shear bolt that helps prevent overloading and a locking mechanism that prevents accidental lowering.

- **_Easy to Use:_** Hi-Lift jacks are relatively simple to use, with only a few moving parts. However, it is important to read the instructions carefully and practice using the jack before attempting to use it in an emergency situation.

One popular brand of off-road recovery equipment is OKoffroad.com. This company offers a range of high-quality recovery equipment, including winches, recovery straps, shackles, and other tools. Their products are known for their durability, reliability, and ease of use, and they have been trusted by off-roading enthusiasts for many years.

An off-road recovery kit can help ensure that you can safely navigate difficult terrain and get back on the road in the event of an emergency. When selecting a recovery kit, consider your specific needs and preferences, and choose a reputable brand that offers high-quality equipment and reliable performance.

Building and customizing your vehicle system is a critical part of preparing for emergencies or unexpected events. Consider your specific needs carefully and choose gear that is reliable, durable, and meets your needs. With the right vehicle system, you can be prepared for any situation.

Customizing Your Vehicle for Optimal Performance

Customizing your vehicle for optimal performance is an important step in ensuring that your vehicle system is ready for any situation. Customization can range from minor modifications to major upgrades, and can improve your vehicle's handling, power, and off-road capabilities.

Here are some tips for customizing your vehicle for optimal performance:

Upgrade Your Suspension

Upgrading your vehicle's suspension can improve its off-road capabilities and handling. Consider installing heavy-duty shock absorbers, leaf springs, or a lift kit to increase your vehicle's ground clearance and improve its ability to handle rough terrain.

There are many options available for upgrading your suspension, depending on your specific needs and preferences. Here are a few popular options, along with the companies that offer them:

• *Old Man Emu Suspension:* Old Man Emu Suspension is a popular choice for off-road enthusiasts. The company offers a range of suspension kits for various types of vehicles, including leaf springs, coil springs, and shock absorbers. Old Man Emu Suspension is known for its high-quality materials and durability.

• *Bilstein Suspension:* Bilstein Suspension is another popular option for upgrading your suspension. The company offers a range of shock absorbers and suspension kits for various types of vehicles. Bilstein Suspension is known for its high-performance shocks, which provide superior handling and control.

• *Fox Suspension:* Fox Suspension is a well-known name in the off-road industry. The company offers a range of suspension components, including shocks, coilovers, and air shocks. Fox Suspension is known for its high-performance components, which are designed to provide excellent handling and control in off-road environments.

• **_Pro Comp Suspension:_** Pro Comp Suspension is a popular choice for those looking to upgrade their suspension on a budget. The company offers a range of affordable suspension components, including shock absorbers, lift kits, and leveling kits. Pro Comp Suspension is known for its value and reliability.

• **_Rancho Suspension:_** Rancho Suspension is another popular option for off-road enthusiasts. The company offers a range of suspension components, including shocks, lift kits, and leveling kits. Rancho Suspension is known for its durable components and excellent handling.

There are many options available for upgrading your suspension, each with its own advantages and disadvantages. Consider your specific needs and preferences when choosing a suspension upgrade and choose a company that offers high-quality components and excellent performance.

Install Off-Road Tires

Off-road tires are designed to provide superior traction in off-road environments. Consider installing all-terrain or mud-terrain tires to improve your vehicle's ability to handle rough terrain and provide better grip in wet or muddy conditions.

There are many options available for upgrading your off-road tires, depending on your specific needs and preferences. Here are a few popular options, along with the companies that offer them:

• **BFGoodrich Tires:** BFGoodrich is a well-known tire brand that offers a range of off-road tires, including the All-Terrain T/A KO2 and the Mud-Terrain T/A KM3. BFGoodrich tires are known for their excellent off-road performance and durability.

• **Goodyear Tires:** Goodyear is another popular tire brand that offers a range of off-road tires, including the Wrangler DuraTrac and the Wrangler MT/R. Goodyear tires are known for their excellent off-road performance and rugged design.

• **Nitto Tires:** Nitto is a tire brand that offers a range of off-road tires, including the Trail Grappler and the Ridge Grappler. Nitto tires are known for their excellent off-road performance and aggressive design.

• **Toyo Tires:** Toyo is another tire brand that offers a range of off-road tires, including the Open Country M/T and the Open Country A/T III. Toyo tires are known for their excellent off-road performance and durability.

• **Falken Tires:** Falken is a tire brand that offers a range of off-road tires, including the Wildpeak A/T3W and the Wildpeak M/T. Falken tires are known for their excellent off-road performance and all-terrain capabilities.

There are many options available for upgrading your off-road tires, each with its own advantages and disadvantages. Consider your specific needs and preferences when choosing an off-road tire upgrade and choose a company that offers high-quality tires and excellent performance.

Improve Your Vehicle's Lighting

Improving your vehicle's lighting can increase visibility and safety. Consider upgrading your headlights, fog lights, or light bars to provide better visibility in low-light or off-road conditions.

White visible light is the most common type of lighting used in trailers/RVs. It is bright and provides excellent visibility, making it suitable for use in areas where it's important to see what you're doing, such as when cooking or reading. The downside is that white visible light can attract bugs and other insects.

Infrared lights, on the other hand, emit a low level of light that is not visible to the human eye. Using infrared, you can use your night vision optics to see in the dark. The lights are commonly used for outdoor security cameras, and they don't attract insects, making them ideal for camping. Infrared lights can also be used to illuminate a limited area, such as a stairwell or a hallway, without disturbing anyone else who may be sleeping.

There are many options available for upgrading your vehicle's lighting, depending on your specific needs and preferences. Here are a few popular options, along with the companies that offer them:

• ***Rigid Industries:*** Rigid Industries is a company that offers a range of off-road lighting options, including LED light bars, spotlights, and floodlights. Rigid Industries is known for its high-quality products, which are designed to provide excellent visibility and durability.

• **KC HiLites:** KC HiLites is another popular option for upgrading your vehicle's lighting. The company offers a range of off-road lighting options, including LED light bars, spotlights, and fog lights. KC HiLites is known for its high-performance lighting, which is designed to provide superior visibility in low-light or off-road conditions.

• **Hella:** Hella is a company that offers a range of lighting options, including LED light bars, spotlights, and fog lights. Hella is known for its high-quality products, which are designed to provide excellent visibility and durability.

• **Baja Designs:** Baja Designs is a company that offers a range of off-road lighting options, including LED light bars, spotlights, and fog lights. Baja Designs is known for its high-performance lighting, which is designed to provide excellent visibility and durability. Baja Designs also has infrared light for night vision optics/goggles driving.

• **AnzoUSA:** AnzoUSA is a company that offers a range of lighting options, including LED light bars, headlights, and taillights. AnzoUSA is known for its high-quality products, which are designed to provide excellent visibility and durability.

There are many options available for upgrading your vehicle's lighting, each with its own advantages and disadvantages. Consider your specific needs and preferences when choosing a lighting upgrade and choose a company that offers high-quality products and excellent performance.

Upgrade Your Engine

Upgrading your engine can improve your vehicle's power and performance. Consider installing a high-performance air intake system, exhaust system, or engine tuning software to increase your vehicle's horsepower and torque.

There are many options available for upgrading your vehicle's engine, depending on your specific needs and preferences. Here are a few popular options, along with the companies that offer them:

• **K&N Engineering:** K&N Engineering is a company that offers a range of air filters and intake systems for various types of vehicles. K&N air filters are designed to improve engine performance by allowing more air into the engine, which can increase horsepower and torque.

• **MagnaFlow:** MagnaFlow is a company that offers a range of exhaust systems for various types of vehicles. MagnaFlow exhaust systems are designed to improve engine performance by reducing exhaust backpressure, which can increase horsepower and torque.

• **Bully Dog:** Bully Dog is a company that offers a range of performance tuners for various types of vehicles. Performance tuners are designed to improve engine performance by adjusting various engine parameters, such as air/fuel ratio and ignition timing.

• **Superchips:** Superchips is another company that offers a range of performance tuners for various types of vehicles. Superchips tuners are designed to improve engine performance by adjusting various engine parameters, such as air/fuel ratio and ignition timing.

• **_Edelbrock:_** Edelbrock is a company that offers a range of performance parts for various types of engines. These parts include performance camshafts, intake manifolds, and cylinder heads, which can improve engine performance and increase horsepower and torque.

There are many options available for upgrading your vehicle's engine, each with its own advantages and disadvantages. Consider your specific needs and preferences when choosing an engine upgrade and choose a company that offers high-quality products and excellent performance.

Add a Winch

A winch is a useful tool for off-road driving and can help you recover from difficult situations. Consider adding a winch to the front or rear of your vehicle to provide an extra level of protection and recovery capability.

When it comes to selecting a winch rope, there are two primary options: steel cable or synthetic rope made of materials such as Kevlar. Both options have their pros and cons, and the choice between them ultimately depends on your specific needs and preferences. Here are some of the main pros and cons of Kevlar winch rope vs. steel cable:

Kevlar Winch Rope

Pros:

• Lightweight: Kevlar winch ropes are significantly lighter than steel cables, which can make them easier to handle and transport.

• Safer: Kevlar ropes are less likely to kink or snap than steel cables, which can be dangerous in some situations. If a Kevlar rope does break, it is less likely to recoil and cause injury.

• Easy to splice: Kevlar ropes can be spliced and repaired more easily than steel cables, which can save time and money in the long run.

• Floats: Kevlar ropes float on water, which can be beneficial in certain situations, such as water crossings or recovery operations in wet conditions.

Cons:

• Expensive: Kevlar winch ropes can be significantly more expensive than steel cables, which can be a drawback for some buyers.

• Susceptible to abrasion: Kevlar ropes are more susceptible to abrasion and can wear out more quickly than steel cables if they come into contact with rough surfaces.

• Lower heat resistance: Kevlar ropes have a lower heat resistance than steel cables and can melt or weaken if exposed to high temperatures.

Steel Cable

Pros:

  • Affordable: Steel cables are generally less expensive than Kevlar ropes, which can be a factor for buyers on a budget.

  • High strength: Steel cables are extremely strong and can withstand high levels of tension without breaking.

  • High heat resistance: Steel cables are more heat-resistant than Kevlar ropes and can withstand exposure to high temperatures without melting or weakening.

  • Durable: Steel cables are highly resistant to abrasion and can withstand exposure to rough surfaces without wearing out quickly.

Cons:

  • Heavy: Steel cables are significantly heavier than Kevlar ropes, which can make them more difficult to handle and transport.

  • Dangerous: Steel cables can kink, snap, or recoil, which can be dangerous for the operator and nearby bystanders.

  • Difficult to splice: Steel cables are difficult to splice and repair, which can be a drawback in situations where repairs are necessary.

  • Rust: Steel cables can rust over time, which can weaken the cable and shorten its lifespan.

Both Kevlar winch ropes and steel cables have their advantages and disadvantages, and the choice between them depends on your specific needs and preferences. If you value lightweight, safety, and ease of splicing, Kevlar may be the better option for you. If you prioritize affordability, high strength, and durability, steel cable may be the better option for you.

There are many options available for adding a winch to your vehicle, depending on your specific needs and preferences. Here are a few popular options, along with the companies that offer them:

• **Warn Industries:** Warn Industries is a well-known company that offers a range of winches for various types of vehicles. Warn winches are known for their durability and high-quality construction, and they are designed to provide reliable pulling power in a range of off-road and recovery situations.

• **Smittybilt:** Smittybilt is another popular company that offers a range of winches for various types of vehicles. Smittybilt winches are known for their affordable price point and ease of installation, and they are designed to provide reliable pulling power in a range of off-road and recovery situations.

• **Superwinch:** Superwinch is a company that offers a range of winches for various types of vehicles. Superwinch winches are known for their high-quality construction and reliability, and they are designed to provide reliable pulling power in a range of off-road and recovery situations.

• **Mile Marker:** Mile Marker is another company that offers a range of winches for various types of vehicles. Mile Marker winches are known for their affordability and reliability, and they are designed to provide reliable pulling power in a range of off-road and recovery situations.

• **Tuff Stuff:** Tuff Stuff is a company that offers a range of winches for various types of vehicles. Tuff Stuff winches are known for their affordable price point and ease of installation, and they are designed to provide reliable pulling power in a range of off-road and recovery situations.

There are many options available for adding a winch to your vehicle, each with its own advantages and disadvantages. Consider your specific needs and preferences when choosing a winch and choose a company that offers high-quality products and reliable performance.

Install a Roof Rack

A roof rack can provide additional storage space for gear and equipment. Consider installing a roof rack to store items such as camping gear, tools, or additional fuel.
There are many options available for installing a roof rack on your vehicle, depending on your specific needs and preferences. Here are a few popular options, along with the companies that offer them:

• **Voyager Racks:** Voyager Racks is a company that offers a range of roof rack options for various types of vehicles. Their roof racks are known for their durability and versatility, and they can be customized to fit a wide range of gear and accessories.

- **Yakima:** Yakima is another popular company that offers a range of roof rack options for various types of vehicles. Yakima roof racks are known for their high-quality construction and ease of installation, and they can be customized to fit a range of gear and accessories.

- **Thule:** Thule is a company that offers a range of roof rack options for various types of vehicles. Thule roof racks are known for their versatility and durability, and they can be customized to fit a wide range of gear and accessories.

- **Rhino Rack:** Rhino Rack is another popular company that offers a range of roof rack options for various types of vehicles. Rhino Rack roof racks are known for their high-quality construction and ease of installation, and they can be customized to fit a range of gear and accessories.

- **Malone Auto Racks:** Malone Auto Racks is a company that offers a range of roof rack options for various types of vehicles. Their roof racks are known for their durability and affordability, and they can be customized to fit a wide range of gear and accessories.

In conclusion, there are many options available for installing a roof rack on your vehicle, each with its own advantages and disadvantages. Consider your specific needs and preferences when choosing a roof rack and choose a company that offers high-quality products and versatile performance.

Customize Your Interior

Customizing your vehicle's interior can make it more comfortable and functional. Consider adding storage solutions such as a cargo organizer or custom seats to improve your vehicle's functionality.

In conclusion, customizing your vehicle for optimal performance is an important step in ensuring that your vehicle system is ready for any situation. Consider your specific needs carefully and choose modifications that are reliable, durable, and meet your needs. With the right modifications, you can improve your vehicle's off-road capabilities, handling, power, and performance.

Benefits of DIY Modifications

DIY modifications are modifications that are done by the owner of a vehicle or system, rather than by a professional mechanic or specialist. There are many benefits to doing your own modifications, including cost savings, customization, and a sense of accomplishment. Here are some of the benefits of DIY modifications:

Cost Savings

One of the primary benefits of DIY modifications is cost savings. Doing your own modifications can save you money on labor costs and markups on parts. Additionally, by doing your own modifications, you have the ability to shop around for the best deals on parts and materials.

Customization

DIY modifications also offer the benefit of customization. By doing your own modifications, you can tailor your vehicle or system to your specific needs and preferences. This can include modifications that improve performance, increase functionality, or enhance the appearance of your vehicle or system.

Sense of Accomplishment

Another benefit of DIY modifications is the sense of accomplishment that comes with doing the work yourself. Completing a modification project can be a rewarding experience and can give you a sense of pride in your work.

Learning New Skills

DIY modifications also offer the opportunity to learn new skills. By taking on a modification project, you can learn new techniques and gain knowledge about the inner workings of your vehicle or system.

Flexibility

DIY modifications offer a level of flexibility that is not always possible when working with a professional mechanic or specialist. You can work on your vehicle or system at your own pace and make changes as you see fit.

Improved Problem-Solving Skills

DIY modifications also offer the opportunity to improve your problem-solving skills. When working on a modification project, you may encounter unexpected challenges that require creative solutions. This can help you develop your problem-solving skills and improve your ability to troubleshoot issues in the future.

Bottom Line

DIY modifications offer many benefits, including cost savings, customization, a sense of accomplishment, learning new skills, flexibility, and improved problem-solving skills. If you are considering modifying your vehicle or system, consider taking on the project yourself. With the right tools, knowledge, and patience, you can create a customized vehicle or system that meets your specific needs and preferences.

PART THREE CONCLUSION

Reviewing the Key Points

Throughout this book, we have explored the importance of being prepared for unexpected situations, whether they be emergencies or simply the need for self-reliance in a world where we cannot always rely on external resources. In particular, we have focused on how to build a system for your vehicle that can help you stay safe and self-sufficient in any situation.

We began by discussing the importance of personal responsibility and identifying the scenarios for which you need to prepare. We then looked at how to assess your resources, budget, and time constraints, in order to determine what is feasible for your individual situation.

We then discussed how to choose the right vehicle for your needs, and the importance of basic vehicle maintenance, including routine maintenance tasks and the development of a maintenance schedule. We also explored the different types of power sources and communication and navigation tools that can be used to make your vehicle system more efficient and effective.

In addition, we discussed how to select the right water and food storage options for your needs, as well as the different types of shelter options that are available for your vehicle. We also looked at essential safety gear and equipment for your vehicle, as well as security considerations and situational awareness tips.

To make your vehicle system even more effective, we discussed the different ways in which you can customize your vehicle, such as by upgrading your suspension, off-road tires, lighting, engine, and adding a winch or a roof rack. We also discussed the benefits of DIY modifications, as well as the importance of selecting the right alternative transportation for your needs.

Overall, the key point of this book is to emphasize the importance of being prepared for unexpected situations, and the role that a well-equipped and well-maintained vehicle can play in achieving that preparedness. By understanding the different components of a vehicle system, including power, communication, water and food storage, shelter, safety gear, and customization options, you can create a system that is tailored to your individual needs and can help you stay safe and self-sufficient in any situation.

In conclusion, the key takeaway from this book is that being prepared for unexpected situations is essential, and a well-equipped vehicle system can help you achieve that preparedness. Whether you are an off-road enthusiast, a survivalist, or simply someone who values self-reliance and independence, the information presented in this book can help you build a vehicle system that is customized to your individual needs and can help you stay safe and secure in any situation.

Encouraging Readers to Take Action

Now that we have reviewed the key points of this book, it is important to emphasize the importance of taking action to implement the strategies and recommendations that have been presented. While it is easy to read about preparedness and self-sufficiency, it is much more difficult to take the steps necessary to actually achieve these goals.

However, the reality is that emergencies and unexpected situations can happen to anyone, and being prepared can mean the difference between life and death. This is why it is crucial to take action to implement the strategies presented in this book, in order to build a vehicle system that is customized to your needs and can help you stay safe and self-sufficient in any situation.

One important step that readers can take is to conduct an honest assessment of their resources, budget, and time constraints. This will help you determine what is feasible for your individual situation, and allow you to prioritize the strategies and recommendations that are most relevant to your needs.

Another important step is to begin taking small actions that can help you achieve your goals over time. This might include taking a basic vehicle maintenance class, researching the different types of communication and navigation tools that are available, or even just starting to accumulate essential safety gear and equipment.

It is also important to seek out resources and support systems that can help you along the way. This might include joining an off-roading club, attending preparedness conferences or workshops, or seeking out online forums and communities where you can connect with like-minded individuals.

Perhaps most importantly, it is crucial to stay motivated and committed to your goals. Building a vehicle system for preparedness and self-sufficiency is not an easy task, and it can be easy to get discouraged or overwhelmed along the way. However, by staying focused on your goals and taking action every day to move closer to achieving them, you can build the knowledge, skills, and resources necessary to be prepared for any situation.

In conclusion, the information presented in this book is not meant to be just another book on preparedness and self-sufficiency. Rather, it is a call to action for readers to take the steps necessary to build a vehicle system that can help them stay safe and self-sufficient in any situation. By conducting an honest assessment of their resources and taking small actions every day, readers can begin to build the knowledge, skills, and resources necessary to achieve their goals. With the right mindset, motivation, and commitment, readers can be prepared for anything that comes their way.

Inspiring a Culture of Preparedness

One of the key goals of this book is to inspire a culture of preparedness, where individuals and communities are empowered to take action to be more self-sufficient and prepared for unexpected situations. This culture of preparedness is essential, as emergencies and disasters can happen at any time, and being prepared can mean the difference between life and death.

To inspire a culture of preparedness, it is important to start by raising awareness about the importance of being prepared. This can be done through public education campaigns, community outreach programs, and media coverage that emphasizes the need for preparedness and self-sufficiency.

Another important step is to provide individuals and communities with the knowledge, resources, and tools necessary to be prepared. This might include offering classes and workshops on basic vehicle maintenance, first aid, and emergency preparedness, as well as providing access to essential safety gear and equipment.

It is also important to create a sense of community around preparedness and self-sufficiency. This can be done through initiatives such as community gardens, volunteer groups, and preparedness fairs, where individuals can come together to share resources, knowledge, and experiences.

In addition, it is important to promote policies and initiatives that support preparedness and self-sufficiency. This might include tax incentives for individuals who invest in emergency preparedness equipment, or public-private partnerships that support the development of community resilience plans.

Ultimately, the goal of inspiring a culture of preparedness is to create a world where individuals and communities are empowered to take action to be more self-sufficient and prepared for unexpected situations. This culture of preparedness can help to reduce the impact of disasters and emergencies, and create a more resilient and self-sufficient society.

In conclusion, inspiring a culture of preparedness is not just about promoting the strategies and recommendations presented in this book. It is about creating a broader societal shift towards self-sufficiency and preparedness, where individuals and communities are empowered to take action to be more resilient and prepared for unexpected situations. By raising awareness, providing resources and tools, creating a sense of community, and promoting supportive policies and initiatives, we can inspire a culture of preparedness that can help us weather any storm.

PART FOUR: TRAILER/RV PREPAREDNESS

30. Identifying Prep Scenarios

Natural Disasters

One of the most important aspects of being prepared for unexpected events is identifying the scenarios you need to prepare for. Natural disasters are a common and often devastating occurrence that can happen at any time, and being prepared for them can make a big difference in the outcome.

Natural disasters can come in many forms, including hurricanes, tornadoes, earthquakes, floods, wildfires, and more. Each of these events presents its own unique challenges and requires different types of preparation.

Hurricanes, for example, can cause significant damage through high winds, storm surges, and flooding. Tornadoes can also cause significant damage with their high winds and can strike quickly without much warning. Earthquakes can cause widespread damage and can lead to structural collapse and other hazards. Floods can damage property, displace people from their homes, and can cause water-borne diseases. Wildfires can destroy homes and property and can pose significant health hazards due to smoke inhalation.

In order to prepare for natural disasters, it is important to identify the scenarios you need to prepare for based on your geographic location and the types of disasters that are most likely to occur in your area. This can involve researching the history of natural disasters in your area, consulting with local emergency management officials, and keeping up to date with weather alerts and warnings.

Once you have identified the scenarios you need to prepare for, it is important to take specific steps to prepare for each one. This can involve things like creating an emergency kit with food, water, and other supplies, securing your home or property against high winds or flooding, and having a plan in place for evacuating your home or community if necessary.

It is also important to have a communication plan in place with family, friends, and neighbors in the event of a natural disaster. This can involve creating a contact list with important phone numbers and email addresses, and ensuring that everyone knows the plan for communicating in the event of an emergency.

Another important aspect of preparing for natural disasters is staying informed about the latest weather and emergency alerts. This can involve signing up for local emergency alerts, monitoring weather forecasts, and staying informed about the status of any ongoing natural disasters in your area.

In summary, identifying the scenarios you need to prepare for when it comes to natural disasters is an essential part of being prepared for unexpected events. By researching the history of natural disasters in your area and consulting with local emergency management officials, you can take proactive steps to prepare for the most likely scenarios. This can involve creating an emergency kit, securing your home or property, having a communication plan in place, and staying informed about the latest weather and emergency alerts. By being prepared, you can help protect yourself and your loved ones in the event of a natural disaster.

Civil Unrest

Identifying the scenarios you need to prepare for is an essential part of being prepared for unexpected events, including civil unrest. Civil unrest can occur in a variety of forms, from peaceful protests to violent riots and social upheaval. Being prepared for civil unrest can help ensure the safety of yourself and your loved ones, as well as your property and belongings.

One important aspect of preparing for civil unrest is to be aware of the signs that it may be occurring in your area. This can involve paying attention to local news and social media, as well as keeping an eye out for signs of unrest such as increased police presence, road closures, and curfews.

It is also important to be aware of the reasons why civil unrest may occur. This can involve things like political turmoil, social injustice, economic hardship, and other factors that can lead to unrest and conflict.

Once you have identified the scenarios you need to prepare for when it comes to civil unrest, it is important to take specific steps to prepare. This can involve things like securing your home and property against potential threats, having a plan in place for evacuating your home or community if necessary, and having a communication plan in place with family, friends, and neighbors.

In order to secure your home and property, it is important to make sure that you have adequate security measures in place, such as locks on doors and windows, security cameras, and motion sensor lights. It may also be helpful to have a backup power source in case of power outages.

In the event that you need to evacuate your home or community due to civil unrest, it is important to have a plan in place for where you will go and how you will get there. This may involve identifying safe locations outside of your immediate area, as well as having a supply of food, water, and other essential items on hand.

Having a communication plan in place is also

essential in the event of civil unrest. This can involve things like creating a contact list with important phone numbers and email addresses, as well as having a plan for communicating with family, friends, and neighbors in the event of an emergency.

It is also important to stay informed about the latest news and developments related to civil unrest. This can involve monitoring local news and social media, as well as keeping up to date with government advisories and emergency alerts.

In summary, identifying the scenarios you need to prepare for when it comes to civil unrest is an important part of being prepared for unexpected events. By paying attention to signs of unrest, understanding the reasons behind it, and taking proactive steps to secure your home and property, have a plan for evacuation, and have a communication plan in place, you can help protect yourself and your loved ones in the event of civil unrest.

Economic Instability

Economic instability is a scenario that can have a significant impact on your life and finances, making it essential to prepare for this scenario. Economic instability can occur in a variety of forms, such as recessions, market crashes, or high inflation rates. It is important to understand the different types of economic instability and the potential impact it can have on your personal finances.

One type of economic instability is a recession, which can lead to a decrease in employment opportunities, lower salaries, and a decrease in consumer spending. To prepare for this scenario, it is important to have a solid financial plan in place, which includes creating a budget and reducing debt. It may also be helpful to diversify your income streams and build up an emergency fund to help cover expenses during lean times.

Another type of economic instability is market crashes, which can lead to a decrease in the value of stocks, bonds, and other investments. To prepare for this scenario, it is important to have a well-diversified investment portfolio, which includes a mix of stocks, bonds, and other types of investments. It is also important to avoid making knee-jerk reactions during a market downturn and to remain patient while waiting for the market to recover.

High inflation rates are another type of economic instability that can have a significant impact on your personal finances. Inflation can lead to an increase in the cost of goods and services, reducing the purchasing power of your money. To prepare for this scenario, it is important to invest in assets that can maintain their value over time, such as real estate, gold, or other precious metals. It is also important to create a budget that takes inflation into account and to consider investing in stocks or other assets that can offer a hedge against inflation.

Finally, economic instability can also arise from geopolitical events, such as trade wars or changes in government policies. To prepare for this scenario, it is important to stay informed about global economic developments and to be prepared to adapt to changing circumstances. This can involve diversifying your investments and income streams, as well as being prepared to adjust your financial plan in response to changes in the economic and political landscape.

In summary, identifying the scenarios you need to prepare for when it comes to economic instability is an important part of being prepared for unexpected events. By understanding the different types of economic instability, such as recessions, market crashes, high inflation rates, and geopolitical events, you can take proactive steps to prepare for these scenarios. This can involve creating a solid financial plan, diversifying your investments and income streams, and staying informed about global economic developments. By doing so, you can help protect yourself and your loved ones from the potential impacts of economic instability.

Pandemics

Pandemics are one of the most unpredictable and potentially catastrophic scenarios that individuals and communities may face. COVID-19, which swept across the world in 2020 and continues to impact many regions, has served as a reminder of the importance of preparing for pandemics. To ensure that you and your loved ones are prepared for a pandemic, it is important to identify the scenarios that you need to prepare for.

The first scenario to consider is the possibility of widespread illness and infection. A pandemic can lead to a surge in demand for medical care, which can overwhelm hospitals and medical professionals. To prepare for this scenario, it is important to have a basic understanding of first aid and medical care. Consider stocking up on basic medical supplies, such as bandages, over-the-counter medications, and disinfectants. It may also be helpful to invest in a first aid manual or take a basic first aid course.

Another scenario to prepare for is the possibility of widespread disruption to supply chains. During a pandemic, supply chains may be disrupted, making it difficult to access essential items, such as food, water, and medications. To prepare for this scenario, consider creating a stockpile of non-perishable food items, such as canned goods, rice, and pasta. It may also be helpful to invest in a water filtration system or stock up on bottled water. Additionally, consider keeping a supply of essential medications on hand.

Social distancing measures are also a key factor in preventing the spread of pandemics. This can lead to a disruption in normal routines, such as going to work or school. To prepare for this scenario, consider creating a plan for working or studying from home. Additionally, it may be helpful to have a plan for staying connected with family and friends, such as through video conferencing or phone calls.

Finally, it is important to prepare for the potential psychological impact of a pandemic. Fear and uncertainty can take a toll on mental health and wellbeing, making it essential to have a plan in place for managing stress and anxiety. Consider investing in relaxation tools, such as meditation or yoga, and staying connected with loved ones for emotional support.

In summary, identifying the scenarios you need to prepare for when it comes to pandemics is an important part of being prepared for unexpected events. By understanding the potential impact of widespread illness and infection, supply chain disruptions, social distancing measures, and the psychological impact of pandemics, you can take proactive steps to prepare for these scenarios. This can involve stocking up on essential items, creating a plan for working or studying from home, and investing in tools for managing stress and anxiety. By doing so, you can help protect yourself and your loved ones from the potential impacts of pandemics.

Other Unexpected Events

Preparing for unexpected events goes beyond natural disasters, civil unrest, economic instability, and pandemics. There are numerous other scenarios that individuals and communities may need to prepare for. Some examples of unexpected events to consider include:

• **Power Outages:** A power outage can occur due to a variety of reasons, such as storms, accidents, and equipment failures. It is important to have a plan in place for managing without power, including having a generator or alternative power source, and stockpiling supplies that do not require electricity.

• **Cyberattacks:** In today's increasingly digital world, cyberattacks are becoming more common. These attacks can disrupt daily life, including the ability to access essential services, such as banking and healthcare. To prepare for a cyberattack, it is important to have a plan in place for accessing necessary resources and services offline, as well as having strong cybersecurity measures in place.

• **Terrorist Attacks:** Terrorist attacks can occur unexpectedly and have a significant impact on communities. It is important to have a plan in place for staying safe during such an event, including having a basic understanding of evacuation procedures, as well as investing in emergency communication and shelter supplies.

• **Extreme Weather:** In addition to natural disasters, extreme weather events, such as hurricanes, tornadoes, and blizzards, can have a significant impact on communities. It is important to have a plan in place for managing extreme weather conditions, including having emergency supplies and shelter provisions.

• **Financial Hardship:** Financial hardship, such as job loss or unforeseen expenses, can occur unexpectedly and have a significant impact on individuals and families. It is important to have a plan in place for managing such events, including having emergency savings, developing new job skills, and seeking support from family, friends, or community resources.

• ***Personal Health Issues:*** Personal health issues, such as accidents or unexpected illnesses, can have a significant impact on individuals and families. It is important to have a plan in place for managing such events, including having appropriate medical insurance and emergency contact information.

Bottom Line
Preparing for unexpected events goes beyond the typical natural disaster scenarios. It is important to identify other potential scenarios, such as power outages, cyberattacks, terrorist attacks, extreme weather, financial hardship, and personal health issues. By identifying these potential scenarios, individuals and communities can take proactive steps to prepare for unexpected events and minimize their impact. This may include investing in emergency supplies, developing new skills, seeking out community resources, and having a plan in place for staying safe during a crisis. By being prepared, individuals and communities can increase their resilience and better manage unexpected events.

31. Assessing Your Resources, Budget and Time Constraints

Financial Considerations

Assessing your resources, budget, and time constraints is a critical step in building a Trailer/RV system for preparedness. It is important to understand the financial considerations of building a system and to ensure that you have the necessary resources and budget available to make the project a success.

The first step in assessing your resources is to identify the skills and knowledge you have available to you. Do you have experience with construction, electrical systems, and mechanical systems? Are you familiar with off-road travel and survival techniques? If not, it may be necessary to invest in education or to seek out the expertise of others.

Once you have identified your skills and knowledge, it is important to consider your budget. Building a Trailer/RV system can be expensive, and it is important to create a budget that is realistic and flexible. Consider the cost of the trailer or RV, as well as any necessary modifications or upgrades. Don't forget to budget for supplies and equipment, such as tools, appliances, and food storage containers.

It is also important to consider the time constraints involved in building a Trailer/RV system. How much time do you have available to work on the project? Do you have the necessary tools and equipment to complete the work? If not, it may be necessary to rent or purchase tools, which can add to the overall cost of the project.

Financial considerations are a key component of assessing your resources, budget, and time constraints. Building a Trailer/RV system can be an expensive undertaking, but there are ways to reduce costs and stay within budget. One way to save money is to look for used or refurbished trailers or RVs, which can be purchased at a fraction of the cost of new models. Another way to save money is to do as much of the work yourself as possible, rather than hiring professionals to do the work for you.

When assessing your resources, budget, and time constraints, it is important to be realistic and honest with yourself about what you can and cannot do. Building a Trailer/RV system can be a challenging and time-consuming project, and it is important to have a realistic understanding of the time and resources that will be required to complete the project successfully.

Ultimately, the key to assessing your resources, budget, and time constraints is to create a plan that is realistic and flexible. By understanding your skills, knowledge, and budget, you can create a plan that is achievable and that will allow you to build a Trailer/RV system that meets your needs and prepares you for unexpected events. With careful planning and consideration, you can create a Trailer/RV system that will be a valuable asset in times of crisis.

Time Considerations

In addition to financial considerations, time constraints are an important factor to consider when assessing your resources and budget for building a Trailer/RV system for preparedness. Time considerations include how much time you have available to work on the project, when you need the system to be completed, and the overall timeline for the project.

The first step in assessing your time constraints is to determine how much time you have available to work on the project. Do you have a flexible schedule, or are you working full-time? Will you need to take time off work or adjust your schedule to make time for the project? Once you have a clear understanding of your available time, you can create a project timeline that is realistic and achievable.

Another time consideration is when you need the Trailer/RV system to be completed. Is there a specific deadline for the project, such as the start of the hurricane season or the date of a planned camping trip? It is important to factor in the amount of time it will take to complete the project, including any unforeseen delays, and to work backward from the deadline to ensure that the system is completed in time.

When assessing your time constraints, it is also important to consider the overall timeline for the project. Building a Trailer/RV system is a complex undertaking that requires careful planning and organization. It is important to break the project down into smaller, manageable tasks and to create a project plan that outlines each step of the process.

To manage time constraints, it may be necessary to hire professionals or enlist the help of friends and family to complete the project on time. It is important to factor in the cost of hiring professionals or the availability of volunteers when creating the project budget and timeline.

In addition to time constraints, it is also important to consider the amount of time it will take to maintain and repair the Trailer/RV system once it is completed. Regular maintenance is crucial to keeping the system in good working order and ensuring that it is ready for unexpected events. It is important to factor in the time and resources required to maintain and repair the system when assessing your time constraints.

Ultimately, assessing your resources, budget, and time constraints is a critical step in building a Trailer/RV system for preparedness. Time considerations play a key role in ensuring that the project is completed on time and within budget. By creating a realistic project plan, breaking the project down into smaller, manageable tasks, and enlisting the help of professionals or volunteers when necessary, you can build a Trailer/RV system that meets your needs and prepares you for unexpected events.

Resource Planning

Resource planning is a critical step in assessing your resources, budget, and time constraints when building a Trailer/RV system for preparedness. Resource planning includes determining what resources you need, where you can source those resources, and how much those resources will cost.

The first step in resource planning is to determine what resources you need for your Trailer/RV system. This includes everything from the Trailer/RV itself to the equipment and supplies you need to make it functional. Make a list of everything you need, including food and water storage, communication and navigation equipment, shelter, first aid supplies, and tools and equipment for maintenance and repair.

Once you have a list of the resources you need, the next step is to determine where you can source those resources. This includes researching suppliers and manufacturers for the items on your list, as well as checking local stores and online retailers for availability and pricing. It is important to compare prices and quality, and to ensure that the resources you select are the best fit for your needs and budget.

In addition to sourcing resources, it is important to consider how you will transport and store those resources in your Trailer/RV system. This includes considering the weight and size of the resources, as well as how they will be organized and stored for easy access and use. It may be necessary to invest in additional storage solutions, such as shelving or storage containers, to make the most of the space available in your Trailer/RV.

Another consideration for resource planning is the amount of redundancy you need in your Trailer/RV system. This includes ensuring that you have backup equipment and supplies in case of failure or damage, as well as planning for resupply of critical items such as food and water. It is important to factor in the cost and availability of backup resources when creating your budget and resource plan.

When assessing your resources, budget, and time constraints, it is also important to consider how to make the most of the resources you have. This includes investing in multi-functional equipment and supplies, as well as planning for the reuse and repurposing of resources to reduce waste and save money.

Bottom Line
Ultimately, resource planning is a critical step in building a Trailer/RV system for preparedness. By determining what resources you need, where to source those resources, and how to transport and store them, you can ensure that your Trailer/RV system is well-equipped for unexpected events. By investing in multi-functional equipment and supplies and planning for redundancy and resource reuse, you can make the most of your resources and create a Trailer/RV system that is both effective and cost-efficient.

32. Choosing the Right Trailer/RV and Tow Vehicle for Your Needs

Types of Trailers/RVs

Choosing the right trailer/RV is a crucial component of preparedness for unexpected events, and requires careful consideration of various factors such as size, features, and intended use. In this section, we will explore the different types of trailers/RVs available and the pros and cons of each, to help you make an informed decision on the best option for your needs.

Travel Trailers

Travel trailers are a popular choice for many due to their ease of use, affordability, and versatility. They come in a range of sizes, from small teardrop trailers to large fifth-wheel trailers that can accommodate multiple occupants. They can be towed by a variety of vehicles, from SUVs to trucks, making them a flexible option for a range of lifestyles.

Pros:
- Wide range of sizes and floor plans to choose from
- Often less expensive than other RV options
- Flexibility in terms of towing vehicles

Cons:
- Requires a vehicle with sufficient towing capacity
- Limited living space compared to larger RVs
- Can be difficult to maneuver in tight spaces

Motorhomes

Motorhomes are essentially a house on wheels, with a built-in engine and living quarters. They come in three classes: Class A, Class B, and Class C, with Class A being the largest and most luxurious, and Class B being the smallest and most basic. Class C is in between in terms of size and features. Motorhomes provide a self-contained living space and are popular with full-time RVers who want to travel in comfort and luxury.

Pros:
- Spacious living quarters and amenities
- Self-contained living space, making it easy to travel and camp in comfort
- No need for a separate towing vehicle

Cons:
- Can be expensive to purchase and maintain
- Often less fuel-efficient than other RVs
- Can be difficult to maneuver and park in tight spaces

Fifth-Wheel Trailers

Fifth-wheel trailers are similar to travel trailers but require a large, powerful truck for towing. They are known for their spacious interiors and often include high-end features such as multiple slide-outs, full-size appliances, and residential-style furniture. They are popular with full-time RVers who want the comforts of home on the road.

Pros:
- Spacious interiors and high-end amenities
- Often offer more living space than other RVs
- Tend to hold their value well over time

Cons:
- Requires a large, powerful truck for towing
- Often more expensive than other RV options
- Can be difficult to maneuver in tight spaces

Pop-Up Trailers

Pop-up trailers are lightweight, compact, and affordable. They are essentially a tent on wheels, with a folding design that allows for easy storage and transport. They can be towed by a wide range of vehicles and are a popular choice for weekend getaways and camping trips.

Pros:
- Lightweight and easy to tow
- Affordable and budget-friendly
- Compact design allows for easy storage and transport

Cons:
- Limited living space and amenities
- May not be suitable for longer trips or full-time living
- Can be less durable than other RV options

Truck Campers

Truck campers are a compact and versatile option for those who want the flexibility of a camper with the convenience of a truck. They are essentially a small living space that attaches to the bed of a pickup truck. They are easy to transport and can be used as a primary or secondary living space.

Pros:
- Compact and easy to transport
- No need for a separate towing vehicle
- Can be used as a primary or secondary living space

Cons:
- Limited living space and amenities
- May not be suitable for longer trips or full-time living
- Requires a pickup truck with sufficient payload capacity

Choosing the Right Tow Vehicle

When building a trailer/RV system for preparedness, it's important to choose the right tow vehicle. Here are some factors to consider:

• **_Towing capacity:_** The first and most important consideration when choosing a tow vehicle is its towing capacity. This is the maximum weight the vehicle can tow safely. Make sure the tow vehicle you choose has a towing capacity that is appropriate for the size and weight of your trailer/RV.

• **_Engine power:_** A more powerful engine will help the tow vehicle handle the weight of the trailer/RV better. Look for a tow vehicle with a powerful engine that can handle the load.

• **_Transmission:_** Automatic transmissions are easier to use when towing, but manual transmissions can be more efficient and give you more control. Consider your driving preferences when choosing a tow vehicle with the right transmission.

• **_Suspension:_** A tow vehicle with a heavy-duty suspension will provide a smoother ride and better handling when towing a heavy load. Look for a tow vehicle with a suspension that can handle the weight of your trailer/RV.

• **_Brakes:_** Make sure the tow vehicle has strong brakes that can handle the weight of the trailer/RV. Consider upgrading the brakes if necessary.

• **_Stability control:_** Many newer tow vehicles come equipped with stability control, which helps to prevent sway and loss of control when towing a heavy load. Consider choosing a tow vehicle with this feature for added safety.

Once you have chosen the right tow vehicle, it's time to consider the types of trailers/RVs available and which one is right for your needs.

• *Travel trailers:* These are towed behind a tow vehicle and come in a variety of sizes and styles. They offer a comfortable living space and can be used for short or long-term stays

• *Fifth-wheel trailers:* These trailers are similar to travel trailers but are towed using a specialized hitch that is mounted in the bed of a pickup truck. They offer a larger living space and can be more stable when towing.

• *Toy haulers:* These trailers are designed to haul ATVs, dirt bikes, and other toys in addition to providing a living space. They are great for outdoor enthusiasts who want to bring their toys with them on their travels.

• *Class A motorhomes:* These are large, bus-style RVs that are built on a truck chassis. They offer a spacious living space and can be driven or towed behind a tow vehicle.

• *Class B motorhomes:* These are smaller RVs that are built on a van chassis. They offer a more compact living space but are easier to drive and park.

• *Class C motorhomes:* These are RVs that are built on a cutaway chassis and offer a large living space. They are easier to drive than Class A motorhomes and can be towed behind a tow vehicle.

Consider your budget, storage options, and travel needs when choosing the right trailer/RV for your preparedness system. With the right tow vehicle and trailer/RV, you can have a comfortable and secure home on wheels for any situation.

Types of Tow Vehicles

When it comes to towing a trailer or RV, choosing the right tow vehicle is crucial for the safety and performance of the entire system. The right tow vehicle should be able to handle the weight of the trailer or RV, provide adequate power and control, and be comfortable and practical for everyday use. In this section, we will discuss the different types of tow vehicles and factors to consider when choosing the right one for your trailer or RV.

Pickup Trucks

Pickup trucks are a popular choice for towing trailers and RVs due to their versatility and towing capacity. They come in a range of sizes, from midsize to full-size, and can tow anywhere from 3,500 to 30,000 pounds, depending on the model and configuration. Pickup trucks also offer the option of a diesel engine, which provides more torque and towing power.

Sport Utility Vehicles (SUVs)

SUVs are another popular choice for towing, particularly midsize and full-size models with powerful engines and a tow package. Many SUVs can tow up to 7,000 pounds or more, and some are equipped with features like trailer sway control and integrated brake controllers to improve safety and performance while towing.

Vans

While not as common as pickup trucks and SUVs, vans can also be an effective tow vehicle for certain types of trailers and RVs. Conversion vans, for example, are often used to tow travel trailers or small RVs. Full-size vans can typically tow up to 7,500 pounds or more, while smaller cargo vans may be limited to around 3,500 pounds.

Crossover Vehicles

Crossover vehicles, also known as CUVs, are a relatively new type of vehicle that combines the features of an SUV and a car. While not as powerful as pickup trucks or SUVs, some CUVs can tow up to 3,500 pounds, which may be sufficient for towing smaller trailers or lightweight RVs.

Factors to Consider When Choosing a Tow Vehicle

When choosing a tow vehicle for your trailer or RV, there are several important factors to consider:

• *Towing Capacity:* The most important factor to consider is the vehicle's towing capacity. Make sure the tow vehicle is rated to tow the weight of your trailer or RV, including any cargo.

• *Engine and Transmission:* A powerful engine and a sturdy transmission are important for towing. Look for a vehicle with a strong engine and a transmission that can handle the weight of the trailer or RV.

• **_Braking System:_** A good braking system is essential for towing, as it helps to control the speed and stopping power of the entire system. Make sure the tow vehicle is equipped with an appropriate braking system, such as an integrated brake controller or a separate trailer brake controller.

• **_Suspension and Stability:_** A good suspension system is important for stability and control while towing. Look for a vehicle with a suspension system designed for towing, and consider adding a weight-distribution hitch or sway control system for added stability.

• **_Fuel Economy:_** While not as important as safety and performance, fuel economy is still a consideration when choosing a tow vehicle. Look for a vehicle with good fuel economy, particularly if you plan to use it for everyday driving as well as towing.

Choosing the right tow vehicle is an important decision when building a trailer or RV system for survival or unexpected events. Consider the type of trailer or RV you will be towing, the vehicle's towing capacity, engine and transmission, braking system, suspension and stability, and fuel economy when making your decision.

Evaluating Your Needs

When it comes to building a trailer/RV system for survival or unexpected events, it is crucial to evaluate your needs. This involves taking a comprehensive inventory of what you have, what you need, and what you want. It also means considering the different factors that will affect your survival and comfort in an emergency situation.

The following are some key considerations to keep in mind when evaluating your needs:

• *Survival priorities:* When assessing your needs, it is important to prioritize the essentials. Your survival priorities should include water, food, shelter, clothing, and medical supplies. These should be the focus of your prepping efforts. Once you have these covered, you can move on to other wants and needs.

• *Family size:* The number of people in your family will determine the size of your trailer/RV system. You need to ensure that there is enough space for everyone to be comfortable, and that you have enough supplies to meet their needs.

• *Duration of use:* How long do you anticipate using your trailer/RV system? If you plan to use it for an extended period, you may need to consider the types of amenities and supplies that will be necessary to maintain your comfort over time.

• *Climate:* The climate in which you live will play a critical role in the type of trailer/RV system you build. If you live in a hot and humid environment, you will need to focus on keeping cool and staying hydrated. Conversely, if you live in a colder climate, you will need to focus on staying warm and dry.

• *Mobility:* Do you plan on moving around frequently or staying in one place? This will impact the type of trailer/RV system you need. If you plan to be mobile, you will need to consider the size and weight of your setup. If you plan to stay in one place, you may be able to afford a more permanent setup.

- **Skill level:** Consider your level of experience with off-road driving, towing, and RV systems. If you are new to this, you may want to start with a simpler system and work your way up as you gain experience.

- **Budget:** Of course, your budget will be a major factor in determining the type of system you can afford. It is important to strike a balance between quality and affordability. Remember, you want a system that is built to last and can withstand the rigors of an emergency situation.

- **Regulations:** Finally, be sure to check your local regulations regarding trailers and RVs. Different states and municipalities have different rules regarding size, weight, and

Bottom Line
Evaluating your needs is a critical step in building a trailer/RV system for survival or unexpected events. By considering your survival priorities, family size, duration of use, climate, mobility, skill level, budget, and regulations, you can build a system that meets your specific needs and keeps you and your family safe in an emergency situation.

33. Building a Foundation:
Basic Trailer/RV Maintenance

The Importance of Routine Maintenance

When it comes to building a system for your trailer/RV to be used in a survival situation or proactively ready for unexpected events, it's important to start with a solid foundation. This includes basic trailer/RV maintenance and the importance of routine maintenance. In this chapter, we'll take a closer look at what's involved in basic maintenance, why it's so important, and how it can help ensure that your trailer/RV system is always ready when you need it most.

Maintenance is critical to the longevity and reliability of your trailer/RV. It's also a key part of keeping your vehicle safe and efficient. Regular maintenance helps you identify small problems before they become big ones, keeping you from getting stranded in the middle of nowhere with a broken-down trailer/RV. There are many routine maintenance tasks that you should perform on your trailer/RV to keep it in good working order.

One of the most important parts of maintenance is checking your tires. Trailer/RV tires are especially important, as they are the only thing separating your vehicle from the road. You should check your tire pressure regularly and keep them inflated to the recommended pressure for your particular trailer/RV. You should also inspect your tires for wear and damage, replacing them if necessary. In addition to your tires, you should also check your brakes, lights, and bearings on a regular basis.

The importance of routine maintenance cannot be overstated. By following a regular maintenance schedule, you can ensure that your trailer/RV is always in top condition, ready for whatever life throws your way. A good maintenance schedule should include regular checks of all your trailer/RV's major systems, including the engine, brakes, tires, and electrical system.

The following are some of the basic trailer/RV maintenance tasks you should perform on a regular basis:

- Check the tire pressure and inflate them to the recommended level.

- Inspect the tires for wear and damage.

- Check the brakes for wear and adjust as needed.

- Inspect the bearings and lubricate them as necessary.

- Check the lights to make sure they're working properly.

- Check the electrical system for any issues or malfunctions.

- Check the propane tanks for leaks and replace them as needed.

- Inspect the roof and seams for any leaks or damage.

- Clean the exterior and interior of the trailer/RV.

It's also important to keep a detailed maintenance log to help you stay on top of all of your maintenance tasks. A maintenance log will help you track when you performed each task and what needs to be done next. It can also help you identify any recurring issues that need to be addressed.

In addition to basic maintenance, it's important to keep your trailer/RV clean and organized. This can help ensure that everything is easy to find and that you can quickly access the tools and equipment you need in an emergency situation. Make sure that all of your equipment is properly stowed and secured and that you have a plan for everything you need to bring with you.

Building a foundation of basic trailer/RV maintenance is critical to the overall success of your preparedness system. With regular maintenance, you can ensure that your trailer/RV is always in top condition, ready to take on whatever challenges come your way. By taking the time to perform regular maintenance and staying on top of your needs, you can be confident that your trailer/RV system will be there for you when you need it most.

Developing a Maintenance Schedule

When it comes to maintaining a Trailer/RV, the key is to stay on top of routine maintenance. Failing to do so can result in costly repairs or even serious accidents. To help prevent these issues, it's important to develop a maintenance schedule.

A maintenance schedule is a plan for when specific maintenance tasks will be performed. This can include regular inspections, cleaning, lubrication, and replacement of parts. Having a set schedule for maintenance can ensure that nothing is overlooked and that the Trailer/RV stays in good condition.

When developing a maintenance schedule, there are a few key factors to consider. First, it's important to consult the owner's manual for the Trailer/RV. The manual should have a recommended maintenance schedule that is specific to that make and model. This will provide a good starting point for creating a personalized schedule.

Next, it's important to consider the frequency of use of the Trailer/RV. Those who use their Trailer/RV frequently will likely need to perform maintenance more often than those who use it less frequently. Additionally, the type of use should be considered. Those who use their Trailer/RV off-road or in harsh conditions will likely need more frequent maintenance.

Some common maintenance tasks that should be included in a Trailer/RV maintenance schedule include:

• *Regular inspections:* It's important to inspect the Trailer/RV regularly for signs of wear and tear, damage, or anything else that may need attention.

• *Cleaning:* Regular cleaning of the Trailer/RV, both inside and out, can help prevent dirt and debris from causing damage.

• *Lubrication:* Moving parts such as hinges, locks, and slides should be lubricated regularly to prevent damage and ensure proper functioning.

• *Fluid changes:* The Trailer/RV's oil, transmission fluid, and other fluids should be changed on a regular basis according to the manufacturer's recommendations.

• *Tire maintenance:* Trailer/RV tires should be inspected regularly for wear and damage, and the air pressure should be checked and adjusted as needed.

• *Battery maintenance:* If the Trailer/RV has a battery, it should be inspected and charged regularly to ensure it is in good working condition.

• *Roof maintenance:* The Trailer/RV's roof should be inspected regularly for damage and cleaned as needed.

• *Propane system maintenance:* For Trailers/RVs that use propane, the propane system should be inspected and maintained on a regular basis to ensure safe operation.

It's important to note that while a maintenance schedule can be helpful, it's not a substitute for regular inspections and attention to the Trailer/RV's condition. Those who use their Trailer/RV frequently should inspect it before and after each use to ensure everything is in good working order.

In summary, developing a maintenance schedule for a Trailer/RV is an important step in keeping it in good condition. By considering the owner's manual, frequency of use, and common maintenance tasks, a personalized schedule can be created to ensure that the Trailer/RV stays safe and functional.

Common Maintenance Tasks and Intervals

Maintaining your trailer or RV is crucial to ensuring it remains in good working condition and can provide a safe and comfortable living space during unexpected events or emergencies. Regular maintenance can help you catch potential issues early, prevent breakdowns, and prolong the lifespan of your trailer/RV. In this section, we will cover some of the most common maintenance tasks you should perform and the recommended intervals for doing them.

• *Inspect the Roof:* Your trailer/RV's roof is one of its most important components as it protects you from the elements. Inspect the roof at least twice a year, checking for any signs of damage, leaks, or cracks. Use a cleaning solution and a soft brush to remove any debris, dirt, or grime.

• *Check Tires:* Check your trailer/RV tires regularly for proper inflation, wear and tear, and overall condition. Underinflated tires can lead to increased wear, poor gas mileage, and even blowouts. Check your tire pressure at least once a month and before each trip. Also, inspect the tire tread depth, sidewall condition, and any cracks or bulges.

• *Test the Batteries:* Your trailer/RV may have multiple batteries to power various systems, such as lighting, appliances, and electronics. Check the batteries regularly for their charge level and overall condition. Charge the batteries as needed and replace them when they start to lose their capacity or show signs of damage.

• *Check and Change Filters:* Your trailer/RV may have multiple filters, including air filters, water filters, and fuel filters. These filters help keep your systems clean and running efficiently. Check and change the filters according to the manufacturer's recommended intervals or as needed.

• *Inspect the Propane System:* Propane gas powers your trailer/RV's appliances, including the stove, furnace, and water heater. Inspect the propane system regularly for leaks, proper pressure, and overall condition. Have a professional inspect and maintain the propane system at least once a year.

• *Clean the Water System:* Your trailer/RV's water system includes the freshwater tank, pipes, and water heater. Clean and sanitize the water system at least once a year and before each trip. This will help prevent the growth of bacteria, mold, and other contaminants in the water.

• *Lubricate Moving Parts:* Your trailer/RV has numerous moving parts that require lubrication, including slide-out mechanisms, awnings, and jacks. Lubricate these parts regularly to prevent wear and tear and ensure they move smoothly.

- **Clean and Seal the Exterior:** The exterior of your trailer/RV is exposed to the elements, including sun, rain, wind, and dirt. Clean and wax the exterior at least twice a year, and inspect it for any signs of damage or leaks. Seal any cracks or gaps to prevent water from entering the trailer/RV.

Bottom Line

In addition to these tasks, perform a thorough inspection of your trailer/RV before and after each trip. Look for any signs of damage, wear and tear, or issues with the various systems. Keeping a log of your maintenance tasks and inspections can help you stay on track and catch potential issues before they become major problems. Regular maintenance will not only help you avoid costly repairs but also ensure that your trailer/RV is safe, comfortable, and reliable during unexpected events or emergencies.

34. Powering Your Trailer/RV System

Introduction to Different Types of Power Sources

When it comes to creating a trailer/RV system that can support you in a survival situation or unexpected event, having a reliable power source is key. In this section, we'll introduce you to some of the different types of power sources you might consider for your trailer/RV system.

One of the most common power sources for trailers and RVs is a generator. Generators can be powered by gasoline, propane, diesel, or even solar energy. Gasoline generators tend to be the most common, but propane generators can also be a good choice since propane is more stable and easier to store than gasoline. Diesel generators can also be a good choice if you're planning to travel to remote areas since diesel is more widely available than gasoline in many parts of the world. Solar generators can be a good choice if you're looking for a more sustainable and eco-friendly option, but they can be expensive to purchase upfront.

In addition to generators, you might also consider using battery banks or inverters to power your trailer/RV system. Battery banks can be charged using a generator, solar panels, or even your tow vehicle's alternator. Inverters can be used to convert DC power from a battery bank into AC power that can be used to power household appliances.

When choosing a power source for your trailer/RV system, it's important to consider factors like how much power you'll need, how long you'll need to use it for, and how frequently you'll need to recharge it. You'll also need to think about factors like noise, fuel efficiency, and ease of use.

Another important consideration when it comes to powering your trailer/RV system is the type of electrical system you'll be using. Some trailers/RVs come equipped with a 12-volt DC system, while others use a 120-volt AC system. Depending on your needs, you might need to install an inverter or converter to ensure that your electrical system is compatible with your power source.

When it comes to choosing a power source for your trailer/RV system, there is no one-size-fits-all solution. It's important to evaluate your needs and do your research to find the option that will work best for you. With the right power source, you can ensure that your trailer/RV system will be a reliable and functional asset in any situation.

Calculating Your Power Needs

When it comes to powering your trailer/RV system, it's important to first determine your power needs. This will help you choose the right type and amount of power sources to meet your needs.

The power needs of a trailer/RV can vary widely depending on factors such as the size of the unit, the number of appliances and electronics used, and the length of time you plan to be off the grid. To calculate your power needs, start by making a list of all the appliances and electronics you plan to use, along with their power consumption ratings in watts.

Once you have your list, you can use a power consumption calculator to determine your total power needs. Keep in mind that many appliances and electronics have a surge current that can be much higher than their rated power consumption, so be sure to factor that in when calculating your power needs.

Once you know your power needs, you can start considering different types of power sources. The most common options for powering a trailer/RV off the grid include:

• *Solar Power:* Solar panels can be a great option for providing a steady source of power to your trailer/RV. They are silent, require no fuel, and have no moving parts, making them very low maintenance. The downside is that they can be expensive to install, and they may not be able to provide enough power to meet all of your needs.

• *Generators:* Generators are a popular choice for providing power to a trailer/RV. They are relatively inexpensive and can provide a lot of power. However, they require fuel, can be noisy, and may not be allowed in all camping areas.

• *Batteries:* Deep-cycle batteries are designed to provide a steady source of power over an extended period of time. They can be charged using solar power or a generator, and can be used to power everything from lights to appliances. The downside is that they have a limited capacity, so you may need to recharge them frequently.

• *Propane:* Propane can be used to power appliances such as stoves, ovens, and refrigerators. It's a clean-burning fuel that is widely available, but it does require a propane tank and may not be as convenient as other options.

Ultimately, the best power source for your trailer/RV will depend on your individual needs and preferences. It's important to consider factors such as cost, maintenance, noise, and portability when choosing a power source. With the right power setup, you can enjoy all the comforts of home even when you're off the grid.

Pros and Cons of Different Types of Power Sources

When building a Trailer/RV System for preparedness, one of the most important things to consider is how you will power the system. There are several options available, each with its own set of advantages and disadvantages. Here are some of the most common types of power sources and their pros and cons:

• *Solar Power:* Solar power is a popular choice for powering Trailer/RV systems because it is clean, quiet, and renewable. Solar panels can be mounted on the roof of the Trailer/RV and wired to a battery bank to store excess power for use at night or when the sun is not shining. However, solar power can be expensive to set up and may not provide enough power for all of your needs, especially in areas with limited sunlight.

• **Generators:** Generators are a reliable source of power for Trailer/RV systems and can be used to charge batteries or power appliances directly. They are especially useful in areas where there is no access to electrical power. However, generators can be noisy, require fuel, and emit exhaust fumes, which can be harmful if not used in a well-ventilated area.

• **Batteries:** Batteries are a common power source for Trailer/RV systems, especially when used in conjunction with solar power. They can be charged by solar panels, generators, or even while driving the tow vehicle. However, batteries can be heavy and expensive, and may not provide enough power for all of your needs.

• **Propane:** Propane is often used to power appliances such as stoves, refrigerators, and water heaters in Trailer/RV systems. It is a clean-burning fuel and can be easily stored in tanks. However, propane tanks can be heavy and may not provide enough power for all of your needs.

• **Wind Power:** Wind power is a relatively new option for powering Trailer/RV systems. Wind turbines can be mounted on the roof of the Trailer/RV and wired to a battery bank to store excess power for use at night or when there is no wind. However, wind power is only effective in areas with consistent wind, and turbines can be noisy and may require regular maintenance.

When choosing a power source for your Trailer/RV system, it is important to consider your specific needs and requirements. Factors such as the size of your Trailer/RV, the number of appliances you plan to use, and the climate of the area you will be traveling in can all affect your power needs. It is also important to consider the cost of each power source, as well as any maintenance or up-keep required.

Bottom Line
The best power source for your Trailer/RV system will depend on your individual needs and circumstances. It may be a good idea to consult with a professional in the field to help you determine the best option for your specific situation. With the right power source, you can enjoy the freedom and flexibility of life on the road while staying prepared for unexpected events.

35. Communications and Navigation

Why Communication Is Important in Survival Situations

Communications and navigation are critical components of any vehicle system built for survival situations. The ability to communicate with others and navigate through unfamiliar territory can mean the difference between life and death in emergency scenarios. In this section, we will discuss the importance of communication in survival situations and the role of navigation in ensuring survival.

Communication is an essential part of surviving in emergency situations. It enables individuals to call for help, coordinate rescue efforts, and keep in touch with loved ones. Communication devices such as radios and satellite phones are essential tools for survival, as they allow individuals to communicate with others over long distances, even in areas without cell phone coverage.

In addition, communication devices can provide vital information about weather conditions, potential dangers, and other critical information that can help individuals make informed decisions and avoid potential risks. In survival situations, the ability to receive and transmit information can be the key to staying safe and making it through the crisis.

The Importance of Navigation in Survival Situations

Navigation is another critical component of any vehicle system built for survival situations. In emergency scenarios, individuals may need to navigate through unfamiliar territory, often in harsh and dangerous conditions. Navigational tools such as GPS systems and maps can provide vital information about location, direction, and distance, allowing individuals to make informed decisions about their route and avoid potential hazards.

In addition, navigational tools can help individuals plan their routes, set realistic goals, and conserve their energy and resources. By understanding their location and the terrain around them, individuals can make more efficient use of their resources and minimize the risks of getting lost or disoriented.

The Role of Technology in Communication and Navigation

Technology has revolutionized the way we communicate and navigate, providing individuals with powerful tools for staying connected and staying safe in emergency situations. Communication devices such as satellite phones and radios can transmit signals over long distances, providing individuals with access to communication even in areas without cell phone coverage.

Similarly, GPS systems and other navigational tools can provide individuals with accurate and up-to-date information about their location, helping them to navigate through unfamiliar territory and avoid potential hazards.

Many of these tools are small, lightweight, and portable, making them ideal for use in emergency situations.

Communication and navigation are critical components of any vehicle system built for survival situations. The ability to communicate with others and navigate through unfamiliar territory can mean the difference between life and death in emergency scenarios. By understanding the importance of communication and navigation and the role of technology in these areas, individuals and families can ensure that their vehicle system is ready for any situation and can be self-sufficient in emergency scenarios.

Types of Communication Devices

Communication Products

There are various types of communication devices available in the market that can be used for emergency situations, outdoor activities, or daily use. Here are some popular types of communication devices:

Cell Phones

Cell phones are portable devices that use cellular networks to communicate over long distances. They can be used for making calls, sending texts, and accessing the internet.

Satellite Phones

Satellite phones are devices that use satellites to transmit signals and can provide communication in areas without cell phone coverage.

Two-Way Radios

Two-way radios are handheld devices that allow individuals to communicate with each other over short distances.

Ham Radios

Ham radios are more powerful than two-way radios and can transmit signals over long distances.

Walkie-Talkies

Walkie-talkies are handheld devices that allow individuals to communicate with each other over short distances.

CB Radios

CB (Citizens Band) radios are devices that allow short-range communication between individuals.

Marine Radios

Marine radios are devices used by boaters and can provide communication over long distances in water.

Aviation Radios

Aviation radios are devices used by pilots and can provide communication over long distances in the air.

Personal Locator Beacons

PLBs are personal emergency devices that use satellites to send distress signals to search and rescue organizations.

Emergency Radios

Emergency radios are portable devices that provide communication and access to emergency broadcasts during power outages or other emergency situations.

Modes of Radio Communication

There are several different modes of radio communication, each with their own unique characteristics and uses. Here is an explanation of some of the most common modes:

High-frequency (HF) radios

They operate in the frequency range of 3 to 30 megahertz, and are used for long-distance communication. HF waves are able to bounce off the ionosphere and back down to the ground, allowing for communication over very long distances. HF radios are often used for long-range communication in emergency situations, as well as by amateur radio operators.

Ultra-high-frequency (UHF) radios

They operate in the frequency range of 300 megahertz to 3 gigahertz, and are used for shorter-range communication. UHF signals are able to penetrate walls and other obstacles more easily than VHF signals, making them ideal for indoor and urban use. UHF radios are commonly used in two-way radios, as well as by emergency responders and law enforcement.

Very-high-frequency (VHF) radios

They operate in the frequency range of 30 to 300 megahertz, and are also used for shorter-range communication. VHF signals are better suited for outdoor use, and are often used by maritime and aviation professionals, as well as emergency responders and law enforcement.

Family radio service (FRS) radios

They operate in the frequency range of 462 to 467 megahertz, and are used for short-range communication between family and friends. FRS radios are typically low-power and do not require a license, making them popular for personal use in outdoor activities such as camping and hiking.

Citizens-band (CB) radios

They operate in the frequency range of 26.965 to 27.405 megahertz, and are used for short-range communication between individuals on the same channel. CB radios are commonly used by truck drivers, and require a license to operate.

Each mode of radio communication has its own advantages and disadvantages, and is best suited for different types of situations and environments. By understanding the different modes of communication and their uses, you can select the best radio equipment for your specific needs.

Vehicle Mounted Radios

These companies provide radio equipment for your prep vehicle:

• *Icom:* offers a variety of two-way radio options, including handheld and mobile radios, as well as options for UHF, VHF, and HF frequencies.

• *Yaesu:* is another company that provides a range of two-way radio options, including handheld and mobile radios, as well as base stations and repeaters.

- **Kenwood:** is known for their high-quality radio equipment, including handheld and mobile radios, as well as base stations and repeaters.

- **Midland:** is a company that provides a range of radio equipment for both personal and professional use, including two-way radios, CB radios, and weather radios.

- **Motorola:** is a well-known brand in the world of two-way radios, offering a range of options for both personal and professional use, including handheld and mobile radios, as well as base stations and repeaters. They also offer options for UHF, VHF, and HF frequencies.

Walkie Talkie Hand Held Radios

Companies that provide walkie talkie radio options for your prep vehicle, with a range of frequencies:

- **Motorola:** offers a range of two-way radios, including walkie talkie options, that operate on UHF, VHF, and FRS frequencies. Their equipment is known for its durability and reliability.

- **Midland:** is a popular brand for two-way radios, including walkie talkies that operate on UHF, VHF, CB, and FRS frequencies. They offer options for both personal and professional use.

- **Baofeng:** is a brand that offers affordable two-way radios, including walkie talkie options that operate on UHF, VHF, and HF frequencies. They are a popular choice for amateur radio operators.

- **Kenwood:** is known for their high-quality radio equipment, including walkie talkies that operate on UHF, VHF, and FRS frequencies. Their equipment is known for its advanced features and long battery life.

- **Uniden:** is a company that offers a range of two-way radios, including walkie talkie options that operate on UHF, VHF, CB, and FRS frequencies. They are known for their user-friendly designs and affordability.

Satellite Phones

Companies that are satellite phone providers and their URLs:

- Iridium - https://www.iridium.com/

- Globalstar - https://www.globalstar.com/

- Inmarsat - https://www.inmarsat.com/

- Thuraya - https://www.thuraya.com/

- SPOT - https://www.findmespot.com/en-us/

A quality one stop shop for satellite phone needs is www.satellitephonestore.com

Each of these companies offers satellite phone services, with different plans, devices, and coverage areas. It is important to research and compare the options before choosing a satellite phone provider to ensure that it meets your specific needs and budget.

It is important to note that the effectiveness of these devices may be impacted by environmental conditions such as weather, terrain, and vegetation. Additionally, proper training and knowledge of how to use these devices is essential for their effective use in emergency scenarios.

Navigation Tools and Techniques

Navigation tools and techniques are critical for individuals to be able to find their way in outdoor environments or emergency situations. Here are some popular navigation tools and techniques:

Global Positioning System

GPS is a satellite-based navigation system that uses a network of satellites to determine a user's location and provide directions to their destination. Satellite-based navigation system that provides location and time information. It is used by a variety of devices, including handheld GPS units, vehicle GPS systems, and smartphones. Companies that produce GPS devices include Garmin, TomTom, and Magellan.

Maps

Maps are graphical representations of an area, and can be used to plan routes and navigate through unfamiliar territory. Topographic maps are specifically designed to show the terrain of an area. Companies that produce maps include National Geographic, Rand McNally, and TomTom.

Compasses

A compass is a navigational tool that uses the earth's magnetic field to determine direction. A compass can be used in conjunction with a map to determine direction. Companies that produce compasses include Silva, Suunto, and Brunton.

Altimeter

An altimeter is a device that measures altitude by detecting changes in air pressure. It can be used to determine a user's location and navigate through hilly or mountainous terrain. Companies that produce altimeters include Suunto and Garmin.

Celestial Navigation

Celestial navigation is a technique that uses the stars and other celestial bodies to determine a user's location and direction.

Binoculars

Binoculars are a useful navigational tool for spotting landmarks and other features in the distance. Companies that produce binoculars with navigational aids include Leupold, Bushnell, Steiner and Fujinon.

Marine Charts

Marine charts are specialized maps used for navigation on water. They provide detailed information on water depths, shorelines, and other marine features. Companies that produce marine charts include Navionics and C-Map.

Sextants

A sextant is a navigational tool used for celestial navigation. It measures the angle between a celestial body and the horizon to determine position. Companies that produce sextants include Davis Instruments and Weems & Plath.

Dead Reckoning

Dead reckoning is a navigation technique that involves estimating one's current position based on their previous position and the distance and direction traveled.

Sun Compasses

A sun compass is a navigational tool that uses the position of the sun to determine direction. It can be used in areas without a clear view of the horizon.

Landmarks

Landmarks are distinctive features of an area that can be used to determine a user's location and navigate through unfamiliar territory.

It is important to note that each of these tools and techniques has its own set of advantages and limitations. Proper training and knowledge of how to use these tools and techniques is essential for their effective use in emergency scenarios. Additionally, it is recommended to carry multiple navigation tools and devices to ensure redundancy in case of equipment failure.

Selecting the Right Communication and Navigation Gear

When building a vehicle system for survival situations, selecting the right communication and navigation gear is essential for ensuring the safety and well-being of individuals and families. In this section, we will discuss some key factors to consider when selecting communication and navigation gear.

Purpose and Frequency of Use

The first factor to consider when selecting communication and navigation gear is the purpose and frequency of use. If you plan to use the gear regularly, it may be worth investing in high-quality equipment that can withstand wear and tear. However, if you plan to use the gear infrequently or for a one-time emergency situation, it may be more cost-effective to purchase lower-cost equipment.

Range and Coverage

Another important factor to consider is the range and coverage of the communication and navigation gear. If you plan to use the gear in remote or off-grid areas, it may be necessary to invest in equipment that can provide communication and navigation over long distances or in areas without cell phone coverage. Satellite phones or radios can be ideal for these situations. Alternatively, if you plan to use the gear in urban or suburban areas, lower-cost equipment such as two-way radios may be sufficient.

Durability and Weather Resistance

Durability and weather resistance are also important factors to consider when selecting communication and navigation gear. Equipment that is built to withstand harsh weather conditions such as rain, snow, and extreme temperatures can ensure that the gear remains operational in emergency situations. Additionally, equipment that is rugged and durable can withstand impacts and falls, ensuring that it remains operational even after accidental drops or mishaps.

Ease of Use and Compatibility

Ease of use and compatibility with other devices is also important to consider when selecting communication and navigation gear. Devices that are intuitive and easy to operate can ensure that individuals can quickly and easily communicate and navigate through unfamiliar terrain. Additionally, devices that are compatible with other gear such as battery packs or charging stations can ensure that individuals have a reliable power source for their gear.

Price and Affordability

The price and affordability of communication and navigation gear is an important factor to consider when selecting equipment. While high-end equipment may offer better performance and durability, it may be cost-prohibitive for some individuals and families. It is important to balance the need for high-quality equipment with affordability and budget considerations.

Bottom Line

Selecting the right communication and navigation gear is essential for building a vehicle system for survival situations. Key factors to consider when selecting gear include the purpose and frequency of use, range and coverage, durability and weather resistance, ease of use and compatibility, and price and affordability. By taking these factors into account and conducting thorough research, individuals and families can ensure that their gear is reliable, effective, and appropriate for their needs.

36. Water Storage and Filtration

Water storage and filtration are essential components of any vehicle system built for survival situations. In emergency scenarios or outdoor activities, individuals may not have access to clean drinking water, and it is important to have a reliable source of water to ensure survival. In this section, we will discuss the importance of water storage and filtration in a vehicle system and different methods for water storage and filtration.

Importance of Water Storage and Filtration in a Vehicle System

Water is critical for survival, and having a reliable source of water is essential for ensuring the safety and well-being of individuals and families in emergency situations or outdoor activities. In a vehicle system, water storage and filtration can provide a reliable source of clean drinking water, allowing individuals to stay hydrated and avoid dehydration, which can lead to serious health issues.

Additionally, water storage and filtration can provide access to clean water for other uses such as cooking, cleaning, and hygiene. In emergency situations, access to clean water can be limited, and having a reliable source of clean water can reduce the risks of infection and disease transmission.

Different Methods for Water Storage and Filtration

There are different methods for water storage and filtration that can be used in a vehicle system. Here are some popular methods:

Water Bottles and Containers

One of the most straightforward methods for water storage is to use water bottles and containers. These can be easily stored in the vehicle and filled up from any available water source. However, it is important to ensure that the bottles and containers are made from safe materials, such as BPA-free plastic or stainless steel.

These companies offer a range of water bottle and container options, so it is important to choose the right size, material, and features for your specific needs. Some factors to consider include capacity, durability, insulation, and ease of use.

• *Nalgene:* produces a range of water bottles and containers in various sizes and materials, including BPA-free plastic and stainless steel.

• *Hydro Flask:* is known for their high-quality insulated water bottles and containers, which are designed to keep drinks cold or hot for hours.

- **Klean Kanteen:** produces a range of stainless steel water bottles and containers, including insulated options for hot or cold drinks.

- **Yeti:** is known for their rugged and durable water bottles and containers, which are designed for outdoor and off-road use.

- **Platypus:** produces flexible water bottles and containers, which are ideal for packing into small spaces in your vehicle.

- **CamelBak:** is a well-known brand for their hydration packs, but they also produce water bottles and containers in various sizes and materials.

- **Stanley:** is known for their durable and classic stainless steel water bottles and containers, which are great for outdoor and off-road use.

Water Storage Tanks

Water storage tanks are larger containers that can store a significant amount of water. These tanks can be installed in the vehicle, and can be filled up from any available water source. However, it is important to ensure that the tanks are made from safe materials and are properly sealed to prevent contamination.

These companies offer a range of water container options over 3L, which are ideal for vehicle prep and off-road use. It is important to choose a container that is durable, leak-proof, and easy to transport and store in your vehicle.

• **Reliance Products:** produces a range of water containers in various sizes, including large containers up to 7 gallons (about 26.5 liters) in size.

• **Scepter:** offers a variety of military-grade water containers, including large containers up to 5 gallons (about 19 liters) in size.

• **WaterBrick:** makes stackable water containers in various sizes, including a 3.5-gallon (about 13.2 liters) container and a 5-gallon (about 18.9 liters) container.

• **Aquatainer:** manufactures a 7-gallon (about 26.5 liters) water container that is designed for outdoor and off-road use.

• **Igloo:** produces large water containers up to 6 gallons (about 22.7 liters) in size, which are great for outdoor and off-road use.

• **Coleman:** offers a variety of water containers, including a 5-gallon (about 18.9 liters) container that is designed for outdoor and off-road use.

• **Zebra:** makes a range of stainless steel water containers, including a 10-liter (about 2.6-gallon) container that is great for outdoor and off-road use.

Water Filters

Water filters can be used to remove impurities and contaminants from water, providing a reliable source of clean drinking water. There are different types of water filters available, such as activated carbon filters and ceramic filters, which can be used to remove bacteria, viruses, and other harmful substances from water.

These companies offer a range of water filter options for vehicle prep, which can be essential for providing safe drinking water during outdoor and off-road trips. It is important to choose a filter that is effective against the contaminants you are likely to encounter and is easy to use and maintain.

- *Sawyer:* produces a range of water filters, including their popular Mini Water Filter, which is small and portable and can filter up to 100,000 gallons of water.

- *Katadyn:* offers a range of water filters, including the Pocket Water Microfilter, which is a durable and reliable option for outdoor and off-road use.

- *LifeStraw:* makes a variety of water filters, including their original LifeStraw filter, which is compact and easy to use, and can filter up to 4,000 liters of water.

- *Platypus:* manufactures a range of water filters, including the GravityWorks water filter system, which is a fast and efficient option for filtering large volumes of water.

- *MSR:* produces a range of water filters, including the Guardian Water Purifier, which is designed for outdoor and off-road use and can remove viruses, bacteria, and protozoa.

- *Grayl:* offers water filtration systems that are designed to be fast and easy to use, and can filter out viruses, bacteria, and protozoa.

• *Aquamira:* makes a variety of water filters and treatment systems, including their Frontier Max water filter, which can filter up to 120 gallons of water and can be used as a straw or as a gravity filter.

Water Purification Tablets

Water purification tablets can be used to disinfect water, killing harmful bacteria and viruses. These tablets are lightweight and portable, making them an ideal solution for outdoor activities or emergency situations.

These companies offer a range of water purification tablets for vehicle prep, which can be a convenient and effective way to purify water in emergency situations. It is important to choose a product that is effective against the contaminants you are likely to encounter and is easy to use and store in your vehicle.

• *Potable Aqua:* produces a range of water purification tablets, including their Potable Aqua Chlorine Dioxide tablets, which are effective against bacteria, viruses, and protozoa.

• *Aquatabs:* offers water purification tablets that are effective against bacteria, viruses, and protozoa, and can be used in a variety of water sources.

• *MSR:* manufactures a range of water purification tablets, including their Aquatabs, which are effective against bacteria, viruses, and protozoa, and can be used in a variety of water sources.

• *Katadyn:* makes Micropur tablets, which are effective against bacteria, viruses, and protozoa, and can be used in a variety of water sources.

• *Aquamira:* produces water purification tablets, including their Chlorine Dioxide tablets, which are effective against bacteria, viruses, and protozoa, and can be used in a variety of water sources.

• *Coghlan's:* offers water purification tablets that are effective against bacteria, viruses, and protozoa, and can be used in a variety of water sources.

• *Oasis:* makes a range of water purification tablets, including their Chlorine Dioxide tablets, which are effective against bacteria, viruses, and protozoa, and can be used in a variety of water sources.

Gravity Filters

Gravity filters use gravity to push water through a filter, removing impurities and contaminants. These filters are easy to use and require no electricity, making them an ideal solution for emergency situations.

These companies offer a range of gravity water filter options for vehicle prep, which can be essential for providing safe drinking water during outdoor and off-road trips. It is important to choose a filter that is effective against the contaminants you are likely to encounter, is easy to use, and is durable enough to withstand outdoor and off-road conditions.

• *Platypus:* produces the GravityWorks water filter system, which is a fast and efficient option for filtering large volumes of water, and is ideal for outdoor and off-road use.

- **Katadyn:** offers the Gravity Camp 6L water filter, which is designed for outdoor and off-road use, and can filter up to 2 liters of water per minute.

- **Sawyer:** manufactures the Gravity System water filter, which is a lightweight and portable option for outdoor and off-road use, and can filter up to 10 liters of water in as little as 45 minutes.

- **MSR:** makes the AutoFlow Gravity Filter, which is a versatile option for filtering large volumes of water, and is ideal for outdoor and off-road use.

- **LifeSaver:** produces the Jerrycan water filter, which is designed for emergency and off-grid situations, and can filter up to 20,000 liters of water.

- **Aquamira:** offers the Frontier Pro Gravity Water Filter, which is a compact and portable option for outdoor and off-road use, and can filter up to 50 gallons of water.

- **HydroBlu:** manufactures the Clear Flow Gravity Water Filter, which is a lightweight and portable option for outdoor and off-road use, and can filter up to 1 liter of water per minute.

Water storage and filtration are essential components of any vehicle system built for survival situations. Different methods for water storage and filtration can be used, including water bottles and containers, water storage tanks, water filters, water purification tablets, and gravity filters. By incorporating a reliable and effective water storage and filtration system into a vehicle system, individuals and families can ensure that they have a reliable source of clean drinking water in emergency situations or outdoor activities.

Bottom Line

Water storage and preparation are critical components of any vehicle system built for survival situations or outdoor activities. In emergency scenarios, individuals might not have access to water, and it is important to have a reliable source of water to ensure survival.

37. Food Storage and Preparation

Selecting the Right Food Storage Containers

When it comes to preparing for unexpected events, having a reliable source of food is one of the most important considerations. However, storing food can be tricky, as it needs to be kept in a way that prevents spoilage and contamination. That's why it's important to choose the right food storage containers.

There are many different types of food storage containers available, and each has its own pros and cons. Here are some of the most common options:

• Glass jars are a popular option for storing dry goods like grains, pasta, and beans. They are easy to clean and don't retain odors or flavors from previous contents. However, they are heavy and can be fragile, making them less suitable for transport.

• Plastic containers are lightweight and easy to transport. They are also relatively inexpensive and come in a wide range of sizes and shapes. However, they can absorb odors and flavors, which can make them less suitable for long-term storage.

• Mylar bags are a popular choice for long-term food storage. They are lightweight and easy to transport, and they provide an airtight seal that helps prevent spoilage. However, they are not as durable as other options and can be punctured or torn easily.

• Vacuum-sealed bags are another good option for long-term food storage. They are airtight, which helps prevent spoilage, and they are easy to transport. However, they can be expensive, and they require a vacuum sealer to use.

• Canning jars are a classic option for long-term food storage. They are airtight and can be used to store a wide range of foods, including fruits, vegetables, and meats. However, they require special equipment to seal properly, and they can be heavy and bulky.

When selecting food storage containers, it's important to consider your needs and goals. Are you storing food for short-term emergencies or long-term survival situations? Do you need to transport your food, or will it be stored in a fixed location? Once you've answered these questions, you can choose the containers that best fit your needs.

It's also important to consider the quality of the containers you choose. Look for containers that are made from food-grade materials and are free from harmful chemicals like BPA. You may also want to consider purchasing containers that are designed for long-term storage and have airtight seals to help prevent spoilage.

In addition to choosing the right containers, it's important to store your food in a way that helps prevent spoilage and contamination. This may involve storing food in a cool, dry place away from sunlight and pests, and using oxygen absorbers or other methods to remove oxygen and prevent spoilage.

Overall, choosing the right food storage containers is an important part of preparing for unexpected events. By selecting containers that are suited to your needs and goals, you can help ensure that you have a reliable source of food when you need it most.

Canned and Packaged Food

There are different methods for food storage and preparation that can be used in a vehicle system. Here are some popular methods:

Canned and Packaged Foods

Canned and packaged foods can be easily stored in the vehicle and do not require refrigeration. These foods have a long shelf life and can provide a source of nutrition in emergency situations. However, it is important to ensure that the foods are high in nutritional value and are not expired.

Dehydrated Foods

Dehydrated foods are lightweight and portable, making them an ideal solution for outdoor activities or emergency situations. These foods can be rehydrated with water and provide a source of nutrition. However, dehydrated foods can be expensive and may not provide the same level of nutritional value as fresh foods.

Freeze-Dried Foods

Freeze-dried foods are similar to dehydrated foods in that they are lightweight and portable. These foods have a longer shelf life than dehydrated foods and can be easily stored in the vehicle. However, freeze-dried foods can be expensive and may not provide the same level of nutritional value as fresh foods.

Cooler and Refrigerator

A cooler or refrigerator can be used to store fresh foods such as fruits, vegetables, and meat. These foods provide a higher level of nutritional value than canned or packaged foods, and can be more satisfying. However, refrigeration requires a power source, and may not be feasible in all situations.

Portable Stove and Cookware

A portable stove and cookware can be used to prepare hot meals in emergency situations or outdoor activities. These can be fueled by propane or other fuels, and can provide a source of comfort and nutrition. However, a portable stove requires fuel, and may not be feasible in all situations.

These companies offer a range of canned and packaged food options for vehicle prep, which can be essential for providing emergency sustenance during outdoor and off-road trips. It is important to choose food that is nutritious, easy to prepare, and has a long shelf life, so that it can be stored in your vehicle for an extended period of time.

- ***Mountain House:*** produces a variety of freeze-dried and dehydrated meals, which are lightweight and easy to prepare, and can be stored for long periods of time.

- ***Wise Company:*** offers a range of freeze-dried and dehydrated meals, as well as emergency food kits, which are designed to be convenient and easy to prepare.

- ***Augason Farms:*** manufactures a range of freeze-dried and dehydrated meals, as well as emergency food kits, which are designed to be affordable and long-lasting.

- ***Legacy Food Storage:*** makes a range of freeze-dried and dehydrated meals, as well as emergency food kits, which are designed to be nutritious and easy to prepare.

- ***Chef's Banquet:*** produces a range of freeze-dried and dehydrated meals, as well as emergency food kits, which are designed to be convenient and long-lasting.

- ***Backpacker's Pantry:*** offers a range of freeze-dried and dehydrated meals, as well as snacks and desserts, which are designed to be lightweight and easy to prepare.

- ***Patriot Pantry:*** makes a range of freeze-dried and dehydrated meals, as well as emergency food kits, which are designed to be nutritious and long-lasting.

Cooking and Meal Preparation

When building a system for a trailer or RV, it's important to consider how you will prepare and cook meals. Depending on the size of your trailer or RV, you may have limited space and resources for cooking, so it's essential to choose the right equipment and make a plan for meal preparation.

One option for meal preparation is to bring pre-cooked or canned food that can be easily reheated or eaten cold. This can be a good choice for shorter trips or if you don't have much cooking equipment. However, if you plan to spend longer periods in your trailer or RV, you may want to consider more substantial meal options.

When selecting equipment for cooking, there are several options to choose from. One popular choice is a propane stove, which can be easily connected to a propane tank for fuel. This type of stove is lightweight, compact, and easy to use, making it a great choice for camping or other outdoor activities.

Another option is a portable electric stove, which can be powered by a generator or inverter. This type of stove is often more compact than a propane stove and can be a good choice for those who want to avoid the need to carry propane tanks.

When it comes to food storage, there are several options to choose from as well. Many people opt for a combination of a small refrigerator and a cooler. A small refrigerator can be powered by a generator or inverter and can be used to keep perishable items fresh. A cooler can be used to store drinks and other items that don't need to be kept as cold.

In addition to a refrigerator and cooler, you may also want to consider using vacuum-sealed bags or containers for food storage. These can help to keep food fresh for longer periods and can make it easier to store food in smaller spaces.

When planning your meals, it's important to consider the amount of storage space you have available, as well as your power needs. You may also want to think about the types of meals you plan to prepare and the cooking equipment you'll need to do so.

Overall, the key to successful meal preparation in a trailer or RV is to plan ahead and choose the right equipment for your needs. With the right equipment and a little bit of planning, you can enjoy delicious meals while on the road or in the great outdoors.

Bottom Line
Food storage and preparation are critical components of any vehicle system built for survival situations or outdoor activities. Different methods for food storage and preparation can be used, including canned and packaged foods, dehydrated foods, freeze-dried foods, a cooler or refrigerator, and a portable stove and cookware. By incorporating a reliable and effective food storage and preparation system into a vehicle system, individuals and families can ensure that they have a reliable source of food and nutrition in emergency situations or outdoor activities.

38. Shelter Options for Your Trailer/RV

Types of Shelters

When it comes to shelter options for your trailer/RV, you have a number of different choices depending on your needs and preferences. Here are some of the most popular types of shelters that you might consider:

Trailer/RV

A trailer/RV can be considered a shelter option for a number of reasons. For one, it provides a physical barrier between you and the elements, protecting you from rain, wind, and snow. It can also provide a layer of insulation, keeping you warm or cool depending on the climate.

In addition to protection from the elements, a trailer/RV also offers a level of security. When camping in remote or unfamiliar areas, it can provide a safe and secure place to sleep at night.

Another advantage of a trailer/RV as a shelter option is the convenience it provides. With a well-equipped trailer/RV, you can have access to all the amenities of home, including a comfortable bed, a kitchen with appliances, and a bathroom with a shower.

Overall, a trailer/RV can be an excellent shelter option for those looking to live or travel off the grid or for those who want to be prepared for unexpected events. With the right setup, it can provide a comfortable and secure living space that is mobile and adaptable to a range of environments.

Awning

An awning is a popular shelter option for RVs that can be easily attached to the side of your vehicle. They typically come in a variety of sizes and styles and can provide shade and protection from the elements.

Pop-Up Canopy

A pop-up canopy is a lightweight, portable shelter that can be easily set up and taken down. They are a great option if you are looking for a temporary shelter that you can take with you on the go.

Screen Rooms

A screen room is a type of shelter that provides a bug-free space to relax and enjoy the outdoors. They typically come with screens on all sides to keep out insects, while still allowing you to enjoy the fresh air.

Gazebos

Gazebos are a popular choice for those who want a larger, more permanent shelter. They are typically made of wood or metal and can be customized to fit your specific needs and preferences.

Tents

Tents are a great option for those who want a more traditional camping experience. They come in a variety of sizes and styles and can be easily set up and taken down. Examples of brands include Roofnest, Yakima Skyrise and Thule Tepui or look on REI.com.

When selecting a shelter for your trailer/RV, it's important to consider factors such as size, weight, and ease of setup. You'll also want to think about the conditions you are likely to encounter and choose a shelter that can withstand those conditions. With the right shelter, you can enjoy your time on the road and stay protected from the elements.

Popular Shelter Brands and Models

There are several popular brands and models for shelters that can be used with a trailer/RV to provide additional protection and comfort in a survival or unexpected situation. Here are some examples:

- **ARB:** is a well-known brand in the off-road and camping community, and they offer a range of awnings, tents, and enclosures that can be attached to a vehicle or trailer. Their products are known for their durability and ease of setup.

- **Tepui:** offers a variety of rooftop tents and accessories that can be mounted on a trailer or vehicle. Their tents are designed to withstand extreme weather conditions and provide a comfortable and elevated sleeping area.

- **Yakima:** makes a range of roof-top tents and awnings, as well as cargo boxes and bike racks. Their products are known for their quality and durability, and they offer a variety of sizes and styles to fit different vehicles and needs.

- **Smittybilt:** offers a range of overland and camping gear, including roof-top tents, awnings, and tents that can be attached to the side of a vehicle or trailer. Their products are known for their ruggedness and affordability.

- **Rhino-Rack:** makes a range of roof-top tents, awnings, and accessories for trailers and vehicles. Their products are known for their durability and versatility, and they offer a variety of sizes and styles to fit different needs and budgets.

Bottom Line
It's important to research different brands and models to determine which one is the best fit for your needs and budget. Factors to consider include the size and weight of the shelter, ease of setup, durability, and compatibility with your trailer or vehicle.

39. Essential Safety Gear
and Equipment for Your Trailer/RV

When building a trailer/RV system for survival situations, essential safety gear and equipment should be included to ensure the safety and well-being of individuals and families. In this section, we will discuss some key safety gear and equipment to consider when building a trailer/RV system for survival situations.

First Aid Kit

A first aid kit is an essential piece of safety gear to have in a trailer/RV system. It should include items such as bandages, gauze, antiseptic wipes, and pain relievers. In emergency situations, a first aid kit can provide immediate medical attention, which can be critical for avoiding further harm.

These companies offer a range of first aid kit options for trailer/RV prep, which can be essential for providing emergency medical care during outdoor and off-road trips. It is important to choose a kit that is comprehensive and includes supplies for common injuries and conditions, as well as specialized supplies for more serious injuries and medical emergencies. Additionally, it is important to ensure that your kit is easily accessible and well-organized, so that you can quickly and efficiently provide care when needed.

• *Adventure Medical Kits:* produces a range of first aid kits, including kits specifically designed for outdoor and off-road use.

- **MyMedic:** offers a range of first aid kits, including trauma kits, which are designed to provide advanced medical care in emergency situations.

- **First Aid Only:** manufactures a range of first aid kits, including kits designed for outdoor and off-road use, as well as specialized kits for specific injuries and conditions.

- **Surviveware:** makes a range of first aid kits, including kits designed for outdoor and off-road use, as well as waterproof kits and trauma kits.

- **Lightning X Products:** sells a range of first aid kits, including trauma kits and roadside emergency kits, which are designed to provide advanced medical care in emergency situations.

- **Northbound Train:** produces a range of first aid kits, including kits designed for outdoor and off-road use, as well as specialized kits for specific injuries and conditions.

- **Swiss Safe:** offers a range of first aid kits, including kits designed for outdoor and off-road use, as well as small and compact kits for everyday carry.

Fire Extinguisher

A fire extinguisher is an important piece of safety equipment to have in a vehicle system. In emergency situations, a fire extinguisher can help to prevent small fires from turning into larger fires. It should be kept in a location that is easily accessible and should be checked periodically to ensure that it is in working condition.

These companies offer a range of fire extinguisher options for trailer/RV prep, which can be essential for providing emergency fire suppression in outdoor and off-road situations. It is important to choose a fire extinguisher that is appropriate for the type of fires that are likely to occur, and is easily accessible and easy to use in an emergency. Additionally, it is important to ensure that your fire extinguisher is properly maintained and inspected regularly, to ensure that it is in good working condition when needed.

• *Amerex Corporation:* produces a range of portable fire extinguishers, including models specifically designed for vehicles and off-road use.

• *Kidde:* offers a range of fire extinguishers, including models designed for vehicle use, which are compact and easy to install.

• *First Alert:* manufactures a range of fire extinguishers, including models designed for vehicle use, which are lightweight and easy to operate.

• *Badger:* makes a range of portable fire extinguishers, including models specifically designed for vehicle and off-road use.

• *H3R Performance:* sells a range of fire extinguishers, including models designed for vehicle use, which are lightweight and easy to install.

• *Buckeye Fire Equipment:* produces a range of portable fire extinguishers, including models specifically designed for vehicle and off-road use.

• *Fireboy-Xintex:* offers a range of fire extinguishers, including models designed for vehicle use, which are compact and easy to install.

Emergency Blanket

An emergency blanket is an important piece of safety gear to have in a trailer/RV system. It can be used to provide warmth and insulation in emergency situations or outdoor activities. Emergency blankets are lightweight and portable, making them an ideal solution for vehicle-based survival situations.

These companies offer a range of emergency blanket and bivvy options for trailer/RV prep, which can be essential for providing warmth and shelter in emergency situations. It is important to choose a blanket or bivvy that is durable, lightweight, and compact, so that it can be easily stored in your trailer/RV and taken with you on outdoor and off-road trips. Additionally, it is important to ensure that your emergency blanket or bivvy is waterproof and reflective, so that it can provide maximum protection in a variety of emergency situations.

• *SOL (Survive Outdoors Longer):* produces a range of emergency blankets, including reflective and thermal options, which are designed to keep you warm and dry in emergency situations.

• *Swiss Safe:* offers a range of emergency blankets, including reflective and thermal options, which are compact and lightweight, making them ideal for vehicle prep.

- **Emergency Zone:** manufactures a range of emergency blankets, including thermal and space blankets, which are designed to provide warmth and shelter in emergency situations.

- **Tact Bivvy:** makes a high-quality emergency bivvy, which is made from a lightweight and durable material that reflects up to 90-percent of body heat.

- **Grabber:** sells a range of emergency blankets and bivvies, including thermal and space blankets, which are designed to provide warmth and shelter in a variety of emergency situations.

- **ReadyWise:** produces a range of emergency blankets, including reflective and thermal options, which are designed to provide warmth and protection in emergency situations.

- **Life Bivy:** offers a high-quality emergency bivvy, which is made from a durable and waterproof material that reflects up to 90% of body heat.

Flashlight/Headlamp

A flashlight and headlamps are important pieces of safety gear to have in a trailer/RV system. In emergency situations or when working in low-light conditions, a flashlight can provide visibility and help to prevent accidents. It is important to ensure that the flashlight has fresh batteries or a reliable source of power.

These companies offer a range of flashlights and headlamps for vehicle prep, which can be essential for providing reliable and durable lighting in outdoor and off-road situations. It is important to choose a flashlight or head-lamp that is durable, waterproof, and provides long-last-ing battery life, so that it can provide reliable lighting in a variety of emergency situations. Additionally, it is import-ant to ensure that your flashlight or headlamp is easy to use and has a range of brightness settings, so that you can adjust the lighting to your needs.

- *Streamlight produces:* a range of flashlights and headlamps, including models designed for vehicle use and outdoor activities, which are durable and long-last-ing.

- *Fenix:* offers a range of flashlights and headlamps, including rechargeable and compact models, which are designed for outdoor and off-road use.

- *Olight:* manufactures a range of flashlights and headlamps, including rechargeable and waterproof mod-els, which are designed for outdoor and emergency use.

- *Black Diamond:* makes a range of headlamps and lanterns, which are designed for outdoor and off-road use, and provide reliable and durable lighting.

- *SureFire:* sells a range of tactical flashlights and headlamps, which are designed for outdoor and emer-gency use, and provide powerful and reliable lighting.

- *Petzl:* produces a range of headlamps, which are designed for outdoor and off-road use, and provide dura-ble and long-lasting lighting.

• *Nitecore:* offers a range of flashlights and head-lamps, including rechargeable and waterproof models, which are designed for outdoor and emergency use.

Multi-Tool

A multi-tool is a versatile piece of equipment that can be used in a variety of situations. It should include items such as pliers, a knife, a saw, and a can opener. In emergency situations or outdoor activities, a multi-tool can be used to fix equipment or perform other essential tasks.

These companies offer a range of multi-tools for vehicle prep, which can be essential for providing a range of useful tools in outdoor and off-road situations. It is important to choose a multi-tool that is durable, versatile, and features a range of useful tools, such as pliers, knives, saws, and screwdrivers. Additionally, it is important to ensure that your multi-tool is lightweight and compact, so that it can be easily stored in your vehicle and taken with you on outdoor and off-road trips.

• *Leatherman:* produces a range of multi-tools, including models designed for outdoor and off-road use, which are durable and versatile.

• *Gerber Gear:* offers a range of multi-tools, including models designed for outdoor and off-road use, which are durable and feature-packed.

• *SOG:* manufactures a range of multi-tools, including models designed for outdoor and off-road use, which are versatile and innovative.

• *Victorinox:* makes a range of multi-tools, including the popular Swiss Army Knife, which are compact and durable, and feature a range of useful tools.

• *CRKT:* sells a range of multi-tools, including models designed for outdoor and off-road use, which are innovative and durable.

• *Kershaw:* produces a range of multi-tools, including models designed for outdoor and off-road use, which are durable and feature a range of useful tools.

• *Benchmade:* offers a range of multi-tools, including models designed for outdoor and off-road use, which are durable and high-quality.

Reflective Vest

A reflective vest is an important piece of safety gear to have in a trailer/RV system. It can be worn during roadside emergencies or when performing maintenance on the vehicle. Reflective vests can provide visibility and help to prevent accidents.

Spare Tire and Jack

A spare tire and jack are essential pieces of equipment to have in a trailer/RV system. In the event of a flat tire, having a spare tire and jack capable of lifting a loaded trailer/RV (floor jack type) can ensure that the vehicle can be safely repaired and driven to a safe location. Always have a 4'x4'x12" and a 2'x6'x12" board to help make up for uneven ground.

Bottom Line

Including essential safety gear and equipment in a trailer/ RV system is critical for ensuring the safety and well-being of individuals and families in emergency situations or out- door activities. Key safety gear and equipment to consider include a first aid kit, fire extinguisher, emergency blanket, flashlight, multi-tool, reflective vest, and spare tire and jack. By incorporating these safety gear and equipment into a trailer/RV system, individuals and families can en- sure that they are prepared for a variety of emergency situations.

40. Security Considerations for Your Trailer/RV System

Security considerations are an important aspect of any vehicle system built for survival situations or outdoor ac- tivities. In emergency scenarios, individuals may be vul- nerable to theft or other types of criminal activity. In out- door activities, theft can be a common occurrence, and valuable equipment and supplies may be at risk. In this section, we will discuss different security considerations for a vehicle system and ways to mitigate risks.

Trailer/RV Security Systems

Installing a trailer/RV security system is an effective way to deter theft or other types of criminal activity. trailer/RV security systems can include alarm systems, immobiliz- ers, and GPS tracking devices. These systems can alert the owner or authorities in the event of a theft or other type of security breach.

Trailer/RV Locks and Safes

Installing locks and safes in a trailer/RV system can provide an additional layer of security. Locks and safes can be used to store valuable equipment and supplies, ensuring that they are protected from theft. It is important to ensure that locks and safes are installed in a secure location and are not easily visible to potential thieves.

Secure Parking Locations

Choosing a secure parking location can be an effective way to mitigate the risk of theft or other types of criminal activity. Parking in well-lit areas or in areas with surveillance cameras can help to deter criminals. Additionally, it is important to ensure that the parking location is secure and not easily accessible to potential thieves.

Physical Barriers

Installing physical barriers, such as metal grills or screens, can be an effective way to deter theft or other types of criminal activity. These barriers can be used to prevent access to the trailer/RV's windows or doors, making it more difficult for potential thieves to gain access to the vehicle.
.

Theft Prevention

As you prepare for unexpected events or even just plan to take an extended trip with your trailer/RV, it is important to consider security measures to protect your investment and yourself. Theft prevention is one of the most important aspects of your trailer/RV system. Here are some security considerations to keep in mind when building your trailer/RV system.

• **Locks and alarms:** One of the most effective ways to prevent theft is to use locks and alarms. Trailer/RV owners can install door locks, window locks, deadbolts, and wheel locks to prevent unauthorized entry and theft. Additionally, alarms can be used to notify you if anyone tries to break into your Trailer/RV.

• **GPS tracking:** With the increasing popularity of GPS technology, it is easier than ever to track the location of your Trailer/RV. GPS tracking devices can be installed inside the Trailer/RV, allowing owners to track the location of their property at all times.

• **Storage facilities:** Storing your Trailer/RV in a secure storage facility can help prevent theft. Many storage facilities offer security features such as surveillance cameras, security gates, and 24-hour security personnel.

• **Hitch locks:** Hitch locks are designed to prevent the Trailer/RV from being attached to a tow vehicle. They are usually made of heavy-duty steel and require a key to unlock.

• **Visibility:** Park your Trailer/RV in a visible and well-lit area to deter potential thieves. Installing motion-activated lights can also help to deter criminals.

• **Concealment:** Keep valuable items out of sight by using curtains or shades on windows, and placing them in locked cabinets or drawers.

• **Insurance:** Having Trailer/RV insurance is crucial in case of theft. Make sure to read the policy carefully to ensure that it covers theft and other related damages.

In summary, theft prevention is a critical aspect of Trailer/RV system security. Trailer/RV owners can take several precautions to protect their property, including installing locks and alarms, using GPS tracking, storing their Trailer/RV in a secure storage facility, using hitch locks, parking in visible and well-lit areas, keeping valuables out of sight, and having insurance coverage. By taking these steps, Trailer/RV owners can enjoy their travels with greater peace of mind.

Self-Defense Options

In emergency situations or outdoor activities, it may be necessary to use self-defense tools to protect oneself from potential threats. Self-defense tools can include items such as pepper spray, stun guns, or firearms. It is important to ensure that individuals are properly trained and licensed before using self-defense tools.

Situational Awareness

Situational awareness is an important aspect of security considerations in any system built for survival situations or outdoor activities. Situational awareness refers to an individual's ability to identify and understand their surroundings, potential threats, and opportunities. By maintaining situational awareness, individuals can take proactive steps to avoid danger, make better decisions, and remain safe in emergency situations or outdoor activities. In this section, we will discuss tips for situational awareness.

Be Alert and Focused

One of the most important tips for situational awareness is to be alert and focused. Individuals should be mindful of their surroundings and avoid distractions that could reduce their attention. This could include avoiding the use of cell phones, headphones, or other devices that can take away from situational awareness.

Pay Attention to Your Environment

Individuals should pay close attention to their environment and be aware of any changes or anomalies. This could include noticing suspicious behavior, unusual sounds or smells, or any other signs that could indicate potential danger.

Identify Potential Threats

Individuals should identify potential threats and be prepared to respond in the event of an emergency. This could include identifying potential sources of danger, such as individuals who appear to be intoxicated or aggressive, or environmental threats, such as hazardous weather conditions or natural disasters.

Stay Informed

Staying informed is an important aspect of maintaining situational awareness. Individuals should be aware of any potential threats or risks in their area, including weather conditions, natural disasters, or potential security threats. This could involve monitoring news sources, social media, or emergency alerts.

Use Your Senses

Using your senses is an important aspect of situational awareness. Individuals should rely on their senses of sight, hearing, and smell to identify potential threats or changes in their environment. This could include noticing changes in the sky, unusual sounds, or suspicious smells.

Plan Ahead

Planning ahead is an important aspect of situational awareness. Individuals should be prepared for potential threats or emergency situations by having a plan in place. This could include identifying escape routes, having emergency supplies on hand, or identifying potential sources of assistance.

Be Mindful of Others

Being mindful of others is an important aspect of situational awareness. Individuals should be aware of the behavior and actions of those around them, and be prepared to respond in the event of an emergency. This could include noticing suspicious behavior or unusual actions, and being prepared to take action to protect oneself and others.

Trust Your Gut

Trusting your gut is an important aspect of situational awareness. Individuals should listen to their instincts and be prepared to respond to potential threats or emergency situations. This could include recognizing a sense of danger, and taking action to avoid potential risks.

Bottom Line

Maintaining situational awareness is an important aspect of security considerations in any vehicle system built for survival situations or outdoor activities. Tips for maintaining situational awareness include being alert and focused, paying attention to your environment, identifying potential threats, staying informed, using your senses, planning ahead, being mindful of others, and trusting your gut. By incorporating these tips into a vehicle system, individuals and families can remain safe and prepared in emergency situations or outdoor activities.

41. Building and Customizing
Your Trailer/RV System

Customizing Your Trailer/RV for Optimal Performance

Building a trailer/RV system that suits your needs is just the first step towards preparedness. However, to optimize performance and ensure your rig is ready for whatever the road or trail throws your way, customization is necessary. Customization can range from simple DIY projects to complex, professional installations. The level of customization is entirely dependent on your needs, budget, and skill level.

This chapter will explore the benefits of customization and provide guidance on how to upgrade your rig for optimal performance. Customization can improve your trailer/RV's functionality, durability, and off-road capability.

Benefits of Customization

Customization allows you to tailor your trailer/RV to your specific needs. This can include adding or upgrading features to make it more comfortable, practical, or safer. Some of the benefits of customization include:

• *Improved functionality:* Customization can make your trailer/RV more efficient and easier to use. This can include adding features like additional storage, better lighting, or more outlets.

• *Enhanced durability:* Customization can help your trailer/RV withstand the rigors of the road or trail. This can include adding protective features like rock guards, skid plates, or reinforced axles.

• *Increased off-road capability:* Customization can improve your trailer/RV's ability to navigate rough terrain. This can include upgrades like off-road tires, suspension systems, or winches.

• *Enhanced comfort:* Customization can make your trailer/RV more comfortable for long-term living. This can include upgrades like improved mattresses, heating and cooling systems, or sound systems.

Customization Options

Customizing your trailer/RV can be done in a variety of ways. The following are some common customizations:

• *Suspension:* Upgrading your suspension system can improve your trailer/RV's off-road capability. This can include adding a lift kit, heavy-duty shocks, or airbags.

• *Tires:* Upgrading your tires can also improve your off-road capability. This can include adding larger or more durable tires.

• *Lighting:* Improving your lighting can enhance safety and functionality. This can include adding auxiliary lights or upgrading your existing lighting system.

- **Power:** Upgrading your power system can provide more reliable and consistent power. This can include adding solar panels, a generator, or an inverter.

- **Water:** Upgrading your water system can provide a more reliable source of water. This can include adding a larger water tank, a water filtration system, or a water heater.

- **Storage:** Adding or upgrading storage can increase your trailer/RV's functionality. This can include adding external storage boxes or upgrading your existing storage areas.

- **Kitchen:** Upgrading your kitchen can enhance your cooking capabilities. This can include adding a better stove, oven, or refrigerator.

- **Bathroom:** Upgrading your bathroom can improve your hygiene and comfort. This can include adding a better toilet, shower, or sink.

- **HVAC:** Upgrading your heating and cooling system can enhance your comfort. This can include adding a better furnace or air conditioning unit.

- **Communication:** Upgrading your communication system can enhance your safety and connectivity. This can include adding a better radio or satellite phone.

DIY Customization vs. Professional Customization

Customization can range from simple DIY projects to complex, professional installations. The level of customization is entirely dependent on your needs, budget, and skill level. Before deciding on the level of customization, you should consider the following:

• *Budget:* Professional customization can be expensive, and the cost can quickly add up. DIY projects can save money, but it's important to ensure you have the necessary tools and knowledge to complete the project.

• *Skill level:* Customizing your trailer/RV requires a certain level of knowledge and skill in order to ensure that it is done safely and correctly. If you lack the skills required to complete the customization, it may be best to hire a professional to ensure the job is done properly.

• *Time:* Customization projects can take a considerable amount of time. It's important to evaluate the time you have available and consider how much of it you want to dedicate to the project.

• *Level of customization:* The level of customization you want will depend on your specific needs. If you have specific needs that require complex customization, it may be best to hire a professional. If you have simple needs, you may be able to complete the project yourself.

DIY customization can be a rewarding experience and allows you to make your trailer/RV uniquely yours. Some common DIY customization projects include:

• *Storage solutions:* Adding shelves, cabinets, and storage bins can help maximize space and keep your trailer/RV organized.

- **Lighting:** Upgrading your lighting can improve visibility and add a cozy atmosphere. LED lights are popular due to their low power consumption and long lifespan.

- **Solar power:** Installing a solar power system can be a great way to ensure your trailer/RV has a reliable source of power. Kits are available for those with little experience in solar installation.

- **Insulation:** Proper insulation can keep your trailer/RV comfortable in extreme temperatures. Spray foam insulation is a popular option as it can easily fill gaps and crevices.

- **Suspension:** Upgrading your suspension can improve your off-road capabilities and provide a smoother ride. Lift kits, airbags, and heavy-duty shocks are popular options.

While DIY customization can be a great way to save money and add a personal touch to your trailer/RV, it's important to know your limits. If you're not comfortable with a project, it's best to hire a professional. Professional customization can be expensive, but it ensures that the job is done safely and correctly. Common professional customization projects include:

- **Solar power:** Professional installers can design and install a solar power system to meet your specific needs.

- **Plumbing:** Installing a plumbing system can be complex and requires knowledge of water and waste systems. A professional can ensure that your plumbing is installed correctly and safely.

• *Custom cabinets and furniture:* Custom cabinetry and furniture can be designed to fit your specific needs and style

• *Electrical work:* Properly wiring your trailer/RV requires knowledge of electrical systems and safety precautions. A professional can ensure that the job is done safely and correctly.

Choosing between DIY and professional customization depends on your specific needs, budget, and skill level. DIY customization can be a great way to save money and add a personal touch, but it's important to know your limits. Professional customization can be expensive but ensures that the job is done safely and correctly. Regardless of which option you choose, ensure that your customization project is safe and meets your needs.

The Benefits of DIY Modifications

The concept of do-it-yourself (DIY) modifications is becoming increasingly popular among people who want to create a personalized and unique travel experience. DIY modifications involve using your skills, creativity, and resourcefulness to transform your trailer/RV into a customized vehicle that meets your specific needs.

The benefits of DIY modifications are numerous, and they range from personal satisfaction to cost savings. One of the biggest advantages of DIY modifications is that you have complete control over the design and execution of the project. You can tailor the modifications to your specific needs and preferences, and you can also save money by doing the work yourself instead of hiring a professional.

Another benefit of DIY modifications is that they can improve your knowledge and skills. By taking on a DIY project, you can learn new skills and techniques that can be applied to future projects. You also gain a better understanding of how your trailer/RV works, which can be useful in emergency situations.

DIY modifications also offer a sense of pride and accomplishment. By completing a project yourself, you can take pride in your work and feel a sense of accomplishment in the finished product. It is a great feeling to know that you created something with your own hands.

In addition to these personal benefits, DIY modifications can also be beneficial for the environment. By using recycled and repurposed materials in your project, you can reduce waste and environmental impact. You can also create a more sustainable and eco-friendly travel experience.

However, it is important to note that DIY modifications require a certain level of knowledge, skill, and safety precautions. It is important to research and plan your project carefully to ensure that it is safe and meets all regulations and guidelines. It is also important to have the right tools and equipment to complete the project safely and effectively.

If you are considering DIY modifications for your trailer/RV, there are a few things to keep in mind. First, be realistic about your skills and knowledge. Start with small projects and work your way up to more complex ones as your skills improve. Second, research your project thoroughly and plan carefully. This will help you avoid mistakes and ensure that your project is safe and effective.

DIY modifications offer many benefits, including personal satisfaction, cost savings, skill development, and environmental sustainability. However, it is important to approach these projects with a realistic understanding of your skills and knowledge, and to research and plan carefully to ensure that your modifications are safe and effective. With these precautions in mind, you can create a personalized and unique trailer/RV that meets your specific needs and preferences.

Upgrading Your Suspension and Off-Road Tires

Upgrading your suspension and off-road tires can significantly improve your trailer/RV's performance on rough terrain. The suspension system is responsible for absorbing shock and providing a smooth ride, while the tires provide traction and grip. Here are some benefits of upgrading your suspension and off-road tires:

• *Improved Off-Road Performance:* A high-quality suspension and off-road tires can significantly improve your trailer/RV's performance on rough terrain. The better your suspension and tires, the more comfortable and stable your ride will be.

• *Increased Ground Clearance:* Upgraded suspension and off-road tires can increase the ground clearance of your trailer/RV. This is particularly useful when driving on uneven terrain, as it helps prevent your trailer/RV from bottoming out.

• *Better Traction:* Off-road tires have a more aggressive tread pattern, which provides better traction on loose or uneven terrain. This can help prevent slipping and sliding, particularly when driving on steep inclines or declines.

• **Enhanced Handling:** Upgrading your suspension and off-road tires can improve your trailer/RV's handling, particularly when driving at higher speeds. This is because the suspension can better absorb shocks and vibrations, providing a smoother ride, while the tires provide better traction and grip.

There are several companies that manufacture suspension and off-road tires for trailers/RVs. Here are a few examples:

• **Old Man Emu:** manufactures suspension systems for a variety of vehicles, including trailers and RVs. Their suspension systems are designed to provide a smoother ride, better handling, and increased ground clearance.

• **BFGoodrich:** is a well-known tire manufacturer that produces a range of off-road tires. Their tires are designed to provide excellent traction and grip on rough terrain.

• **Goodyear:** makes a range of off-road tires that are designed to provide excellent traction and durability. They offer a range of sizes to fit different trailers and RVs.

• **Toyo Tires:** produces a range of off-road tires that are designed to provide better traction and handling on rough terrain. Their tires are particularly popular among off-road enthusiasts.

• **Pro Comp:** is a manufacturer of off-road suspension systems and tires. Their suspension systems are designed to provide a smoother ride and better handling, while their tires provide excellent traction on rough terrain.

When upgrading your suspension and tires, it's important to ensure that they are compatible with your trailer/RV. It's also important to have them installed by a professional if you don't have the necessary skills and experience. Proper installation can help ensure that your trailer/RV is safe and performs as expected.

Improving Your Trailer/RV's Lighting

Improving your trailer/RV's lighting is an essential aspect of your overall safety and comfort when traveling, particularly during nighttime or in low-light conditions. The lighting system in your trailer/RV should be able to provide adequate illumination inside and outside of the vehicle, which is vital when camping or when parking in remote areas. Besides, the right lighting system will help ensure that you remain visible to other drivers and prevent accidents. In this section, we will discuss the benefits of upgrading your trailer/RV's lighting, including white visible light and infrared lights, and list some of the manufacturers that produce these products.

Benefits of Upgrading Your Trailer/RV's Lighting

• *Improved Visibility:* Upgrading your trailer/RV's lighting can significantly improve your visibility when driving at night or in low-light conditions. The right lighting system will help you see potential hazards, road signs, and other vehicles more clearly.

• *Increased Safety:* With improved visibility, you are more likely to remain safe on the road. You'll be able to see the road ahead more clearly, which will allow you to make better-informed decisions and avoid any accidents.

- **Better Energy Efficiency:** Upgrading to LED lights can provide significant energy savings, reducing your power consumption and extending your battery life. This is particularly important if you are off-grid camping and need to conserve your power.

- **Enhanced Aesthetics:** A well-designed lighting system can improve the overall look and feel of your trailer/RV. You can customize the lighting to fit your style and make your vehicle stand out.

White Visible Light and Infrared Lights

White visible light is the most common type of lighting used in trailers/RVs. It is bright and provides excellent visibility, making it suitable for use in areas where it's important to see what you're doing, such as when cooking or reading. The downside is that white visible light can attract bugs and other insects.

Infrared lights, on the other hand, emit a low level of light that is not visible to the human eye you can use your night vision optics to see in the dark. These lights are commonly used for outdoor security cameras, and they don't attract insects, making them ideal for camping. Infrared lights can also be used to illuminate a limited area, such as a stairwell or a hallway, without disturbing anyone else who may be sleeping.

Manufacturers of White Visible Light and Infrared Lights

- **Rigid Industries:** produces high-quality LED lights that are suitable for off-road vehicles. Their products include a range of white visible lights and infrared lights.

• **Vision X:** offers a range of LED lights that are ideal for off-road vehicles, including white visible light and infrared lights.

• **Baja Designs:** manufactures high-quality LED lights that are suitable for a range of vehicles. Their products include white visible lights and infrared lights.

• **Wagan Tech:** makes a range of LED lights suitable for camping and off-road vehicles. Their products include white visible lights and infrared lights.

Upgrading your trailer/RV's lighting can significantly enhance your overall safety and comfort. It's important to consider your needs and budget when choosing the right lighting system for your vehicle. There are many manufacturers out there, but be sure to choose one that is reputable and has a history of producing high-quality products.

Adding a Roof Rack

A roof rack can provide additional storage space for gear and equipment. Consider installing a roof rack to store items such as camping gear, tools, solar panels or additional fuel.

There are many options available for installing a roof rack on your vehicle, depending on your specific needs and preferences. Here are a few popular options, along with the companies that offer them:

• **Voyager Racks:** Voyager Racks is a company that offers a range of roof rack options for various types of vehicles. Their roof racks are known for their durability and versatility, and they can be customized to fit a wide range of gear and accessories.

• **Yakima:** Yakima is another popular company that offers a range of roof rack options for various types of vehicles. Yakima roof racks are known for their high-quality construction and ease of installation, and they can be customized to fit a range of gear and accessories.

• **Thule:** Thule is a company that offers a range of roof rack options for various types of vehicles. Thule roof racks are known for their versatility and durability, and they can be customized to fit a wide range of gear and accessories.

• **Rhino Rack:** Rhino Rack is another popular company that offers a range of roof rack options for various types of vehicles. Rhino Rack roof racks are known for their high-quality construction and ease of installation, and they can be customized to fit a range of gear and accessories.

• **Malone Auto Racks:** Malone Auto Racks is a company that offers a range of roof rack options for various types of vehicles. Their roof racks are known for their durability and affordability, and they can be customized to fit a wide range of gear and accessories.

Bottom Line

There are many options available for installing a roof rack on your vehicle, each with its own advantages and disadvantages. Consider your specific needs and preferences when choosing a roof rack and choose a company that offers high-quality products and versatile performance.

42. Encouraging Readers to Take Action

Preparing for unexpected events, whether they be natural disasters, economic instability, or civil unrest, is a crucial step in protecting yourself and your loved ones. While it's important to have a plan in place, taking action is even more critical. The following steps can help you take action:

Assess Your Needs

Before taking any action, assess your needs and what you need to be prepared for. This can include identifying potential threats and hazards in your area, as well as considering your budget, time constraints, and resources.

Build a Foundation

Basic maintenance is crucial in ensuring your trailer/RV system is in good condition and ready to go when you need it. Establish a maintenance schedule and perform regular maintenance tasks, such as checking the brakes, inspecting the tires, and changing the oil.

Customize Your System

Depending on your needs and skill level, consider customizing your system to optimize performance. This can include upgrading your suspension and off-road tires, improving your lighting with white visible and infrared lights, and adding a winch.

Stock Up on Supplies

Your trailer/RV system should be stocked with plenty of food, water, and other essentials to keep you and your loved ones safe in an emergency situation. Don't forget to also stock up on emergency blankets, first aid kits, and other essential gear.

Practice Your Skills

Having the right gear and equipment is only part of the equation. You also need to know how to use them effectively. Take the time to practice your skills, such as setting up camp, starting a fire, and performing basic repairs.

Stay Informed

Stay up to date on the latest news and information, especially when it comes to potential threats and hazards in your area. Sign up for emergency alerts and make sure you have a reliable source of communication, such as a radio or satellite phone.

Take Action

Once you have assessed your needs, built a foundation, customized your system, stocked up on supplies, practiced your skills, and stayed informed, it's time to take action. Don't wait for an emergency to happen; be proactive and prepare yourself for any situation.

Taking action is key to being prepared for unexpected events. By assessing your needs, building a solid foundation, customizing your system, stocking up on supplies, practicing your skills, staying informed, and taking action, you can ensure the safety and well-being of yourself and your loved ones. Remember, preparedness is not just a one-time event; it's an ongoing process that requires dedication and commitment.

Inspiring a Culture of Preparedness

Preparing for unexpected events and emergencies is crucial, but it can be a daunting task. It can be easy to become complacent and put off preparing for another day. However, it is essential to inspire a culture of preparedness to promote a proactive approach to emergency planning.

The first step in inspiring a culture of preparedness is to increase awareness about the importance of emergency preparedness. This can be done through educational resources, community events, and social media. By sharing information about the potential risks and consequences of not being prepared, people will be more likely to take action.

Another way to inspire a culture of preparedness is to make it easy and accessible for people to prepare. This can be done by providing resources and tools to help people get started, such as checklists, guides, and instructional videos. It's also important to provide options that are affordable and easy to use.

Additionally, it's essential to promote a sense of community and collaboration. Encouraging people to work together to prepare for emergencies can help to create a supportive and proactive culture of preparedness. This can be done through community preparedness events, where people can come together to share ideas and resources.

Bottom Line

It's important to lead by example. When people see that others are taking emergency preparedness seriously, they are more likely to follow suit. By taking steps to prepare for emergencies yourself, you can inspire others to do the same.

Inspiring a culture of preparedness is essential to ensure that communities and individuals are ready for unexpected events. By increasing awareness, providing accessible resources, promoting community collaboration, and leading by example, we can create a culture of preparedness that helps to keep us all safe and secure.

43. Reviewing the Key Points

The following are the key points covered in this book on building a system for your Trailer/RV to be used in a survival situation or for proactive readiness for unexpected events:

• *Importance of a Trailer/RV System for Preparedness* emphasizes the importance of a Trailer/RV system for preparedness and discusses its advantages over other alternatives.

• *Identifying Scenarios to Prepare for* discusses the different scenarios that you need to prepare for, such as natural disasters, civil unrest, economic instability, pandemics, and unexpected events.

• *Assessing Your Resources* emphasizes the need to assess your resources, budget, and time constraints, and develop a resource plan that is financially feasible.

• *Choosing the Right Trailer/RV* discusses the different types of trailers/RVs and how to choose the right one for your needs.

• *Choosing the Right Types of Tow Vehicles* emphasizes the need to choose the right types of tow vehicles and discusses the different options available.

• *Basic Trailer/RV Maintenance* stresses the importance of routine maintenance and developing a maintenance schedule.

• *Powering Your Trailer/RV System* discusses the different types of power sources and how to calculate your power needs.

• *Food Storage and Preparation* examines the different types of food storage containers and the importance of cooking and meal preparation.

• *Shelter Options* explains the different types of shelters and how your Trailer/RV can serve as a shelter option.

• *Security Considerations* emphasizes the need for security considerations for your Trailer/RV system, especially theft prevention.

• *Customizing Your Trailer/RV* lays out the benefits of DIY modifications and professional customization and the different options available.

• *Upgrading Your Suspension and Off-Road Tires* stresses the importance of upgrading your suspension and off-road tires for optimal performance.

• *Improving Your Trailer/RV's Lighting* explains the importance of improving your Trailer/RV's lighting with white visible light and infrared lights.

Bottom Line

Overall, BE PREPARED! provides a comprehensive guide on how to build preparedness for yourself, your family, your vehicle and your Trailer/RV that will help you prepare for unexpected events and increase your chances of survival. The key points covered in the book provide valuable information that can be used to build a customized system that suits your needs, resources, and budget.

ABOUT THE AUTHOR

Erik Lawrence is a former U.S. Army Special Forces (Green Beret) and author of books on firearms, safety & security, preparedness, entrepreneurship and various other topics.

He shares insights from his time in the military and as a world traveler, highlighting the critical role of research, adaptability, and situational awareness in navigating new and unfamiliar environments.

As a former Green Beret, Lawrence has also served in various high-pressure environments around the world, including combat zones and disaster relief efforts. Through his experiences, he has developed a deep appreciation for the value of preparedness and the importance of developing a survival mindset.

In addition to his work as an author, Lawrence is also a sought-after speaker and consultant, sharing his insights on leadership, preparedness, and survival with audiences around the world. He is passionate about empowering individuals and organizations to be better prepared for unexpected situations, and he continues to use his platform to raise awareness about the importance of preparedness.

www.ingramcontent.com/pod-product-compliance
Lightning Source LLC
Chambersburg PA
CBHW062359090426
42740CB00010B/1338